D0477974

CompTIA Cloud+™
Certification Study Guide

(Exam CV0-001)

Nate Stammer
Scott Wilson

Mc
Graw
Hill
Education

New York   Chicago   San Francisco
Athens   London   Madrid   Mexico City
Milan   New Delhi   Singapore   Sydney   Toronto

Cataloging-in-Publication Data is on file with the Library of Congress

McGraw-Hill Education books are available at special quantity discounts to use as premiums and sales promotions, or for use in corporate training programs. To contact a representative, visit the Contact Us pages at www.mhprofessional.com.

CompTIA Cloud+™ Certification Study Guide (Exam CV0-001)

45 6 7 8 9 10   DOC   20 19 18 17 16

ISBN: Book p/n 978-0-07-182818-5 and CD p/n 978-0-07-182883-3
of set 978-0-07-182886-4

MHID: Book p/n 0-07-182818-4 and CD p/n 0-07-182883-4
of set 0-07-182886-9

Sponsoring Editor
Meghan Manfre

Editorial Supervisor
Jody McKenzie

Project Editor
Howie Severson, Fortuitous
Publishing Services

Acquisitions Coordinator
Mary Demery

Technical Editor
Tim Pierson

Copy Editor
Jennifer McClain

Proofreader
Paul Tyler

Indexer
Jack Lewis

Production Supervisor
James Kussow

Composition
Cenveo® Publisher Services

Illustration
Cenveo Publisher Services

Art Director, Cover
Jeff Weeks

Cover Series Design
Peter Grame

ABOUT THE AUTHORS

Nate Stammer (Omaha, Nebraska) has worked in the IT industry for more than 15 years in various administrative roles, earning his first certification in Windows NT 4.0. For the past three years he has worked as a technical trainer specializing in various Microsoft technologies, including Windows Server and System Center. Nate is also co-owner of Courseware Experts, which develops and writes courseware, articles, and videos for a variety of large organizations. He holds various certifications from both Microsoft and CompTIA including CompTIA A+, CompTIA Cloud Essentials, CompTIA Cloud+, CompTIA Healthcare IT Technician, Microsoft Certified Trainer, MCSE, MCSA, MTA, MCITP, MCTS, and MCP.

Scott Wilson (Omaha, Nebraska) currently works as the director of technical operations at P&L Technology. He has 22 years of experience consulting, managing, and training IT organizations across multiple industries on how to better deliver value to their customers. He is also co-owner of Courseware Experts. Scott's certifications include CompTIA Cloud+, MCT, MCSE, MCSA, MCTS, MCITP, MCP, ITIL Certified Foundations 2011, Release Control and Validation, Operational Support and Analysis, and ITIL Certified Trainer.

About the Technical Editor

Tim Pierson, president, Data-Sentry, Inc., has been working with computers since 1981 and has always been fascinated by how they work. He has achieved over 29 certifications and is an SME on virtualization, the cloud, and security. Tim is a member of VMware's VMUG, OWASP, and BSides and has written a number of courses, including a virtualization and cloud security course as well as a top-level CAST course for the EC-Council, of which he is one of only ten master trainers in the world. Tim is most comfortable standing in front of a large security conference or classroom, and relishes the opportunity to provide clear and concise explanations for complex issues that are often unclear in today's enterprise. He is a frequent panelist on the Virtualization Security Roundtable podcast. In his free time, Tim enjoys working on various projects around his home in Dallas and spending time with his supportive family and longtime partner, Alex.

About LearnKey

LearnKey provides self-paced learning content and multimedia delivery solutions to enhance personal skills and business productivity. LearnKey claims the largest library of rich streaming-media training content that engages learners in dynamic, media-rich instruction, complete with video clips, audio, full motion graphics, and animated illustrations. LearnKey can be found on the web at www.LearnKey.com.

CompTIA Approved Quality Content

CompTIA®

It Pays to Get Certified

In a digital world, digital literacy is an essential survival skill. Certification proves you have the knowledge and skills to solve business problems in virtually any business environment. Certifications are highly valued credentials that qualify you for jobs, increased compensation, and promotion.

LEARN	CERTIFY			WORK
IT is Everywhere	**IT Knowledge and Skills Get Jobs**	**Job Retention**	**New Opportunities**	**High Pay-High Growth Jobs**
IT is mission critical to almost all organizations and its importance is increasing.	Certifications verify your knowledge and skills that qualifies you for:	Competence is noticed and valued in organizations.	Certifications qualify you for new opportunities in your current job or when you want to change careers.	Hiring managers demand the strongest skill set.
• 79% of U.S. businesses report IT is either important or very important to the success of their company	• Jobs in the high growth IT career field • Increased compensation • Challenging assignments and promotions • 60% report that being certified is an employer or job requirement	• Increased knowledge of new or complex technologies • Enhanced productivity • More insightful problem solving • Better project management and communication skills • 47% report being certified helped improve their problem solving skills	• 31% report certification improved their career advancement opportunities	• There is a widening IT skills gap with over 300,000 jobs open • 88% report being certified enhanced their resume

CompTIA Cloud+ Certification Advances Your Career

- The **CompTIA Cloud+ certification** designates an experienced IT professional as being equipped to provide secure technical solutions to meet business requirements in the cloud. CompTIA Cloud+:
  - certifies that the successful candidate has the knowledge and skills required to understand standard cloud terminologies and methodologies to implement, maintain, and support cloud technologies and infrastructure
  - enables understanding of relevant aspects of IT security and the use of industry best practices related to the application of virtualization
  - is a technical vendor neutral exam for a data center, storage, or systems administrator with 24-36 months of experience with cloud technologies and infrastructure
  - job roles include System Administrator, Network Administrator and Storage Administrator among many others
- The **market for cloud related jobs is growing** – with annual cloud market growth of almost 30% projected by research group IDC over the next several years.
- CompTIA Cloud+ is **a smart next step** after other CompTIA certifications in a growing market for cloud expertise.

Steps to Getting Certified and Staying Certified

1. **Review exam objectives.** Review the certification objectives to make sure you know what is covered in the exam: http://certification.comptia.org/examobjectives.aspx.
2. **Practice for the exam.** After you have studied for the certification exam, review and answer sample questions to get an idea of what type of questions might be on the exam: http://certification.comptia.org/samplequestions.aspx.
3. **Purchase an exam voucher.** You can purchase exam vouchers on the CompTIA Marketplace, www.comptiastore.com.

4. **Take the test!** Go to the Pearson VUE website, http://www.pearsonvue.com/comptia/, and schedule a time to take your exam.

5. **Stay Certified!** The CompTIA Cloud+ certification is valid for three years from the date of certification. There are a number of ways the certification can be renewed. For more information go to: http://certification.comptia.org/ce.

Content Seal of Quality

This courseware bears the seal of CompTIA Approved Quality Content. This seal signifies this content covers 100 percent of the exam objectives and implements important instructional design principles. CompTIA recommends multiple learning tools to help increase coverage of the learning objectives.

AUTHORIZED

CAQC Disclaimer

The logo of the CompTIA Approved Quality Content (CAQC) program and the status of this or other training material as "Approved" under the CompTIA Approved Quality Content program signifies that, in CompTIA's opinion, such training material covers the content of CompTIA's related certification exam.

The contents of this training material were created for the CompTIA Cloud+ exam covering CompTIA certification objectives that were current as of the date of publication.

CompTIA has not reviewed or approved the accuracy of the contents of this training material and specifically disclaims any warranties of merchantability or fitness for a particular purpose. CompTIA makes no guarantee concerning the success of persons using any such "Approved" or other training material in order to prepare for any CompTIA certification exam.

CONTENTS AT A GLANCE

CONTENTS

ACKNOWLEDGMENTS

We would like to thank our spouses, Megan and Cassie, for having the patience to allow us to complete this project. Without their love and support this project would have not been possible. Nate thanks his two sons, Gavin and Kaiden, for understanding that sometimes Dad has to work before he can go outside and have fun. Scott thanks his best friend and wife, Megan, for everything she does to manage their household in addition to her full-time job, and also thanks his parents, Dave and Karen Wilson, for their limitless encouragement. The support by our families throughout this project is the primary reason for its success.

We would also like to thank Meghan Manfre for giving us the opportunity to work with her and her amazing staff at McGraw-Hill Education throughout this entire process. We want to thank Mary Demery for working with us and being patient with us when we were a little behind on some of our deadlines. Mary's guidance was instrumental to the success of the book.

We wish to acknowledge as well all of the work that has been done by Howie Severson and his production team. Their comments and suggestions have been extremely helpful.

PREFACE

The objective of this study guide is to prepare you for the CompTIA Cloud+ (CV0-001) exam by familiarizing you with the technology and terminology tested on the exam. Because the primary focus of the book is to help you pass the test, we don't always cover every aspect of the related technology. Some aspects of the technology are covered only to the extent necessary to help you understand what you need to know to pass the exam, but we hope this book serves as a valuable professional resource long after the exam is over.

In This Book

This book is organized to serve as an in-depth review for the CompTIA Cloud+ exam for network administrators and cloud system engineers. Each chapter covers a major aspect of the exam, with an emphasis on the "why" as well as the "how to" of working with and implementing cloud technologies in a cloud computing environment.

On the CD-ROM

For more information on the CD-ROM, please see the "About the CD" appendix at the back of the book.

Exam Readiness Checklist

Following the introduction you will find an exam readiness checklist. This checklist has been constructed to allow you to cross-reference the official exam objectives with the objectives as they are presented and covered in this book. This checklist also helps you gauge your level of expertise with each objective at the outset of your studies. This will allow you to check your progress and ensure you spend the time you need on more difficult or unfamiliar sections. The objectives are listed as presented by the certifying body, with the corresponding section of the study guide that covers that objective and a chapter and page reference.

In the Chapters

We've created a set of chapter components that call your attention to important items, reinforce key points, and provide helpful exam-taking hints. Take a look at what you'll find in the chapters:

- Every chapter begins with **Certification Objectives**—what you need to know in order to pass the section on the exam dealing with the chapter topics. The Certification Objective headings identify the objectives within the chapter.

- **Exam Watch** notes call attention to information about, and potential pitfalls in, the exam.

e x a m

watch

Don't forget that resources are more than just people. Equipment, *facilities, and materials are resources, and these can affect the project duration, too.*

- **Exam at Work** notes provide real-world examples of cloud computing technologies in the workplace today.

- The **Key Terms** section highlights and defines the most important terms discussed in the chapter. A complete list of key terms and their definitions can be found in the glossary.

- The **Certification Summary** is a succinct review of the chapter and a restatement of salient points regarding the exam.

✓ - The **Two-Minute Drill** is a checklist of the main points of the chapter. It can be used for last-minute review.

Q&A - The **Self Test** offers questions similar to those found on the exam. The answers to these questions, as well as explanations of the answers, can be found at the end of each chapter. By taking the Self Test after completing each chapter, you'll reinforce what you've learned from that chapter while becoming familiar with the structure of the exam questions.

Some Pointers

Once you've finished reading this book, set aside some time to do a thorough review. You might want to return to the book several times and make use of all the methods it offers for reviewing the material:

1. *Reread all the Two-Minute Drills* or have someone quiz you. You also can use the drills as a way to do a quick cram before the exam. You may want to make flash cards out of 3x5 index cards with the Two-Minute Drill material.

2. *Reread all the Exam Watch notes and Exam at Work elements.* Remember that these notes are written by authors who have taken the exam and passed. They know what you should expect—and what you should be on the lookout for.

3. *Retake the Self Tests.* Taking the tests right after you've read the chapter is a good idea, because the questions help reinforce what you've just learned. However, it's an even better idea to go back later and answer all the questions in the book in a single sitting. Pretend that you're taking the live exam. When you go through the questions the first time, you should mark your answers on a separate piece of paper. That way, you can run through the questions as many times as you need to until you feel comfortable with the material.

Cloud computing is becoming more and more popular, and the skill sets required to support cloud computing environments are in high demand. Organizations are examining cloud computing and looking to implement cloud environments to reduce cost and increase IT capabilities.

Why Cloud Computing?

Cloud computing provides something that the IT industry has always needed: a way to increase capacity and add resources as necessary without having to invest in infrastructure. Cloud computing enables an organization to expand their business on demand as they grow.

Growing Need for Cloud Administrators

As more and more organizations adopt a cloud model, the need for cloud administrators increases. Whether the organization is implementing a private cloud, public cloud, or hybrid cloud, they are going to need someone to administer and maintain that cloud environment. Having the skills necessary to support a cloud environment will set you apart as an IT administrator.

Preparing for the CompTIA Cloud+ Exam

This book is designed to help you prepare for the CompTIA Cloud+ certification exam, CV0-001. After successfully passing this exam, you will have demonstrated that you have the knowledge required of IT practitioners working in a cloud environment and that you understand how to deliver a cloud infrastructure. Passing this exam is not an easy step on your way to being a cloud administrator; you will be required to learn new terminology and implementation concepts as they relate to a cloud computing environment.

How This Book Is Organized

This book is divided into chapters based on meeting the objectives of the CompTIA Cloud+ exam. While many individuals taking the exam have been in the IT industry for many years, the terminology used in a cloud computing environment and on the test may be new to them. Understanding this terminology is a key step to passing the CompTIA Cloud+ exam and becoming a cloud administrator. Throughout the book you will learn the different components that make up a cloud environment along with the best practices for implementing those components in the cloud. While some of these concepts will be familiar and something that you as an IT administrator have done for many years now, understanding how those components work in a cloud environment could be a challenge. This book is not meant to be a complete guide to cloud computing; it is designed to cover all of the objectives of the CompTIA Cloud+ exam.

Chapter 1: Cloud Computing Concepts, Models, and Terminology   This chapter focuses on the terminology as it pertains to a cloud environment. You will learn about the various cloud service models, along with cloud delivery models and key terms as they relate to cloud computing.

Chapter 2: Disk Storage Systems   Chapter 2 discusses how disk configurations and redundancy are implemented in the cloud. You will learn the different file types that are part of a cloud environment, along with how to use data tiering to maximize the organization's storage.

Chapter 3: Storage Networking   After becoming familiar with the disk storage systems involved in a cloud environment, the next thing to understand is how to implement and provision that disk storage system. In this chapter you will learn about the various storage technologies and how to implement them in the most efficient manner.

Chapter 4: Network Infrastructure   Network configuration is a primary component of cloud computing. In this chapter you will learn the different types of network configurations and how to optimize those networks. You will also be introduced to the different network ports and protocols that are part of cloud computing.

Chapter 5: Virtualization Components   Virtualization is the key component to cloud computing. This chapter explains the basic concepts of virtualization, including the virtualization host, hypervisor, and virtual machines.

Chapter 6: Virtualization and the Cloud   Chapter 6 expands on what you learned in Chapter 5 and explains the benefits of virtualization in a cloud environment. You will also learn how to migrate an organization's current environment to a virtual environment using the various tools that are available, including P2V and V2V.

Chapter 7: Network Management   Monitoring the cloud environment is just as important as configuring it. In this chapter you will learn how to monitor the cloud environment using a variety of different tools both locally and remotely.

Chapter 8: Performance Tuning   Optimizing performance and allocating resources is something that needs careful consideration and planning. You will learn how to configure virtualization host resources and virtual machine resources and how to optimize those configurations.

Chapter 9: Systems Management   This chapter explores the nontechnical aspects of implementing a cloud environment. You will learn how to implement the proper policies and procedures as they pertain to a cloud environment, along with best practices for systems management.

Chapter 10: Testing and Troubleshooting   Service and maintenance availability must be considered when choosing a cloud provider. This chapter explains the various testing techniques that are used in a cloud environment and the troubleshooting tolls that a cloud administrator should be familiar with.

Chapter 11: Security in the Cloud   This chapter explains a variety of security concepts as they pertain to a cloud environment. You will learn how to secure the network and the data that is part of the cloud environment.

Chapter 12: Business Continuity and Disaster Recovery   Disaster recovery and continuity are still primary concerns for an organization as they implement a cloud environment. This chapter describes the different options an organization has when building a disaster recovery plan and implementing high availability.

Glossary   The glossary has been put together to give you a place to go to quickly find key terms that are discussed throughout the book. We hope that it can become a reference to use both during your time studying for the test and after you successfully pass the CompTIA Cloud+ exam.

Certification Summary and Self Test Sections

One of the most important aspects of this study guide is the end-of-chapter Certification Summary and Self Test. In these sections you will find a high-level review of the chapter and all of the key subject matter that was discussed in the chapter as it pertains to the CompTIA Cloud+ exam.

The questions provided at the end of each chapter are to help you review what you have learned in that particular chapter. They serve as a guide to help you understand what was discussed and to help you determine if more studying is required on a particular subject. Obviously, answering all of the questions at the end of the chapters correctly does not guarantee that you will pass the CompTIA Cloud+ exam. Instead, they should be used as a guide to determine how comfortable you are with a given topic.

CD-ROM

Included with this book is a CD-ROM that contains even more practice questions with detailed explanations of the answers. Using this set of practice questions is another tool to help you prepare for the CompTIA Cloud+ exam.

Moving Forward

At this point, we hope that you are excited about cloud computing and all of the exciting new challenges that come with implementing a cloud computing environment. We wish you luck in your endeavors and want to be the first to welcome you to the field of cloud computing.

Exam CV0-001

Exam Readiness Checklist							
Official Objective	**Study Guide Coverage**	**Ch. No.**	**Pg. No.**	**Beginner**	**Intermediate**	**Expert**	
1.0 Cloud Concepts and Models							
1.1 Compare and contrast cloud services.	Cloud Service Models	1	2				
1.2 Compare and contrast cloud delivery models and services.	Cloud Delivery Models and Services	1	8				
1.3 Summarize cloud characteristics and terms.	Cloud Characteristics and Terms	1	14				
1. 4 Explain object storage concepts.	Object Storage Concepts	1	18				
2.0 Virtualization							
2.1 Explain the differences between hypervisor types.	Hypervisor	5	130				
2.2 Install, configure, and manage virtual machines and devices.	Virtual Resource Migrations	6	166				
2.3 Given a scenario, perform virtual resource migration.	Migration Considerations	6	173				
2.4 Explain the benefits of virtualization in a cloud environment.	Benefits of Virtualization in a Cloud Environment	6	162				
2.5 Compare and contrast virtual components used to construct a cloud environment.	Virtual Machine	5	140				
3.0 Infrastructure							
3.1 Compare and contrast various storage technologies.	Storage Technologies	3	68				
3.2 Explain storage configuration concepts.	Disk Types and Configurations	2	34				
	Tiering	2	40				
	Redundant Array of Independent Disks (RAID)	2	42				
3.3 Execute storage provisioning.	Storage Provisioning	3	74				

Exam Readiness Checklist

Official Objective	Study Guide Coverage	Ch. No.	Pg. No.	Beginner	Intermediate	Expert
3.4 Given a scenario, implement appropriate network configurations.	Routing and Switching	4	100			
3.5 Explain the importance of network optimization.	Network Optimization	4	93			
3.6 Given a scenario, troubleshoot basic network connectivity issues.	Troubleshooting and Tools	10	275			
3.7 Explain common network protocols, ports, and topologies.	Network Ports and Protocols	4	106			
3.8 Explain common hardware resources and features used to enable virtual environments.	Virtualization Host	5	134			
4.0 Network Management						
4.1 Given a scenario, implement and use proper resource monitoring techniques.	Resource Monitoring Techniques	7	192			
4.2 Given a scenario, appropriately allocate physical (host) resources using best practices.	Host Resource Allocation	8	216			
4.3 Given a scenario, appropriately allocate virtual (guest) resources using best practices.	Virtual Machine Resource Allocation	8	219			
4.4 Given a scenario, use appropriate tools for remote access.	Remote-Access Tools	7	197			
5.0 Security						
5.1 Explain network security concepts, tools, and best practices.	Network Security: Best Practices	11	294			
5.2 Explain storage security concepts, methods, and best practices.	Network Security: Best Practices	11	294			
5.3 Compare and contrast different encryption technologies and methods.	Data Security	11	300			
5.4 Identify access control methods.	Access Control Methods	11	306			
5.5 Implement guest and host hardening techniques.	Network Security: Best Practices	11	294			

Exam Readiness Checklist

Official Objective	Study Guide Coverage	Ch. No.	Pg. No.	Beginner	Intermediate	Expert
6.0 Systems Management						
6.1 Explain policies and procedures as they relate to a cloud environment.	Policies and Procedures	9	246			
6.2 Given a scenario, diagnose, remediate, and optimize physical host performance.	Optimizing Performance	8	223			
6.3 Explain common performance concepts as they relate to the host and the guest.	Optimizing Performance	8	223			
6.4 Implement appropriate testing techniques when deploying cloud services.	Testing Techniques	10	270			
7.0 Business Continuity in the Cloud						
7.1 Compare and contrast disaster recovery methods and concepts.	Disaster Recovery Methods	12	322			
7.2 Deploy solutions to meet availability requirements.	High Availability	12	329			

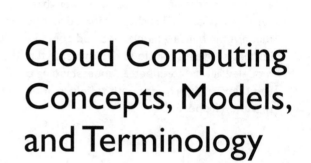

1
Cloud Computing Concepts, Models, and Terminology

M oving an organization's entire infrastructure to the cloud provides a number of benefits to that organization, including power savings, on-demand storage, ease of administration, ability to pay for only the resources they use, and a metered environment that can offer almost 100 percent uptime if included in the Service Level Agreement (SLA)—a costly undertaking when provided by the company itself. An SLA is a contract between a cloud provider and a cloud consumer that formally defines the cloud service and who is responsible for it. This chapter introduces you to the basic concepts, models, and terminology that are the building blocks of cloud computing. It lays a foundation for the rest of the book by building scenarios for cloud deployments that the subsequent chapters can be compared to and modeled against for a better understanding of what cloud computing is, how it can be deployed, and the value it provides both to information technology (IT) organizations and the customers that they support.

CERTIFICATION OBJECTIVE 1.01

Cloud Service Models

A cloud service model is a set of IT-related services offered by a cloud provider. The cloud provider is responsible for supplying cloud-based IT resources to a cloud consumer under a predefined and mutually agreed upon service agreement (SLA). The cloud provider is responsible for administrative maintenance and management of the cloud infrastructure, which allows the cloud consumer to focus their administrative effort on other aspects of the business. In essence, the cloud consumer is buying or leasing their IT infrastructure from the cloud provider.

The entity that legally owns the cloud service is known as the cloud service owner. Either the cloud provider or the cloud consumer can be the cloud service owner, depending on the terms of the SLA.

It is critical to understand who is responsible for the services hosted in the cloud. Before an organization migrates any piece of their business to the cloud, they need to understand who is "in control" of those resources. There are a variety of cloud service models that offer the cloud consumer a number of different options. You will need to understand each of the cloud service models and the service that they provide in order to implement a successful cloud deployment. In this section you will learn about each of the different cloud service models and when to implement them.

Infrastructure as a Service (IaaS)

Infrastructure as a Service (IaaS) is the model by which the cloud consumer outsources responsibility for their infrastructure to an external cloud provider. The cloud provider not only owns the equipment that provides the infrastructure resources but is also responsible for the ongoing operation and maintenance of those resources. In this model the cloud consumer is charged on a "pay-as-you-use" or "pay-as-you-grow" basis. IaaS can include the server storage, the infrastructure, and the connectivity domains. For example, the cloud consumer could deploy and run their own applications and operating systems, while the IaaS provider would handle the following:

- Storage resources, including replication, backup, and archiving
- Compute resources, which are the resources traditionally provided by servers or server farms, including processor, memory, disk, and networking
- Connectivity domains, including infrastructure management and security, such as network load balancing and firewalls

When an organization utilizes IaaS, they no longer have to buy, maintain, or upgrade server hardware, which can help them save resources, time, and money. Since IaaS allows an organization to pay only for the resources they use, the company no longer needs to outlay expenditures for hardware resources they are either not using or not using to maximum capacity. IaaS allows an organization to spin up additional resources quickly and efficiently without having to purchase physical hardware. For example, the IT department might need a development environment to test a new application; with IaaS this development environment could be spun up quickly and then removed when the new application has been fully tested. IaaS allows an organization to meet hardware capacity spikes without having to add resources to their data center. Figure 1-1 shows you a graphical representation of the services that are offered by an IaaS provider.

FIGURE 1-1

Infrastructure as a Service (IaaS) provider services.

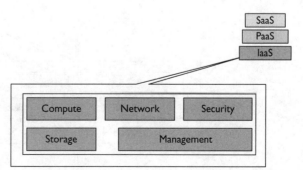

Platform as a Service (PaaS)

Platform as a Service (PaaS) enables customers to deploy applications without assuming the capital and resource costs that they would be obligated to pay if they had to purchase and maintain their own infrastructure. Instead, consumers either purchase or create applications or services that are available exclusively over the Internet. In addition to an infrastructure, these users also have access to both tools and programming languages that are required to create PaaS applications through their cloud provider via an API, or application programming interface. Because PaaS providers do not need to worry about configuring or maintaing an infrastructure for development, they are able to focus on what really matters to them: application development. This focus allows them to get design changes to market much faster than they would in a traditional environment, where they would need to split focus between their infrastructure and the code development itself. Figure 1-2 shows a graphical representation of the services offered by PaaS providers.

Software as a Service (SaaS)

Software as a Service (SaaS) is a cloud service model that allows a cloud consumer to take advantage of a software delivery model that provides on-demand applications over the Internet using a web browser. Like other cloud service models, SaaS is hosted at a cloud provider so the cloud consumer does not need to purchase the hardware required to deploy and operate the application. When an organization deploys SaaS, they no longer have to manage the installation or the infrastructure that supports the application hosted at the cloud providers. SaaS provides an efficient method for organizations to deploy line-of-business applications such as

FIGURE 1-2

Platform as a
Service (PaaS)
provider services.

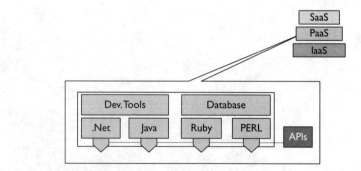

customer relationship management (CRM) and accounting. Figure 1-3 shows a graphical representation of the services offered by SaaS providers.

Database as a Service (DBaaS)

Database as a Service (DBaaS) is essentially a form of software specializing in the delivery of database operations. This service enables cloud providers to offer database functionality to multiple, discrete cloud consumers. DBaaS infrastructures support the following competencies:

- Self-service provisioning for the customer of database instances
- Monitoring of attributes and quality-of-service levels to ensure compliance with provider-defined service agreements
- Carefully measured usage of database services, enabling chargeback functionality for each individual cloud consumer

FIGURE 1-3

Software as a Service (SaaS) provider services.

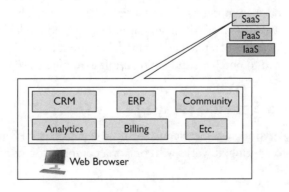

A DBaaS infrastructure may also support service elasticity, secure multitenancy, access using a wide range of devices, automated resource management, and capacity planning. These concepts will be discussed later in this chapter.

Communications as a Service (CaaS)

Communications as a Service (CaaS) is a cloud service model that enables an organization to use communications services in the cloud by using a cloud provider to access voice over IP (VoIP), instant messaging (IM), private branch exchange (PBX), and videoconferencing. CaaS allows an organization to deploy only the communication service that they need without the cost of the hardware or having to manage the communications infrastructure, allowing for significant cost savings for the organization.

Business Process as a Service (BPaaS)

Business Process as a Service (BPaaS) represents the penetration of the cloud model beyond the conventional technical IT service into the processes of the business itself. BPaaS is the combination of business process step execution monitoring with one of the primary cloud models: IaaS, Paas, or SaaS. Business process monitoring is the evaluation of a set of business activities to provide feedback on the progress of the defined steps within that process. The purpose of business process monitoring is to optimize the delivery of business services by analyzing which steps are completed efficiently and which steps fail on a regular basis, and to take appropriate actions for improving the process based on that analysis. The systems that handle this step execution monitoring are referred to as business process management systems (BPMS.)

When using BPaaS, the activities of these traditional business process management systems are uploaded to a cloud service that performs each of the steps in the process and then monitors the execution of each step. The advantage of BPaaS as opposed to a traditional BPMS is similar to other cloud model benefits; it gives its customers the flexibility of a pay-per-use model and reduces their cost of entry by eliminating the need to purchase and build an infrastructure to support it.

Anything as a Service (XaaS)

Anything as a Service (XaaS) is the delivery of IT as a service through hybrid cloud computing; it works with one or a combination of Software as a Service (SaaS),

Infrastructure as a Service (IaaS), Platform as a Service (PaaS), Communications as a Service (CaaS), Database as a Service (DBaaS), and/or Business Process as a Service (BPaaS). With XaaS the X is a variable that can be changed to represent a variety of different cloud services. XaaS is simply a term used to describe the distribution of different IT components within the cloud model.

Accountability and Responsibility by Service Model

Now that you understand all the different cloud service models, you need to become familiar with who is responsible for those services. Accountability in the cloud can be split between multiple parties, including cloud consumers, infrastructure providers, and cloud providers. Accountability in cloud computing is about creating a holistic approach to achieve security in the cloud and to address the lack of consumer trust. The very nature of cloud computing brings a new level of complexity to the issue of determining who is responsible for a service outage, and cloud providers are faced with the difficult task of achieving compliance across geographic boundaries. A service outage can be the result of a variety of issues, such as software vulnerabilities, power outages, hardware, network, application, and user error.

The three primary service models in cloud computing have differing security approaches for businesses. With SaaS the cloud provider is responsible for maintaining the agreed upon service levels between the cloud provider and the cloud consumer and for security, compliance, and liability expectations. When it comes to PaaS and IaaS, the cloud consumer is responsible for managing the same expectations, while the cloud provider takes some of the responsibility for securing the underlying infrastructure. Service outages can also be attributed to the end user device having misconfiguration or hardware failures. Table 1-1 provides a quick reference of the party responsible for maintaining the service levels of each cloud service model.

TABLE 1-1

Service Level Responsibility

Service Models	Cloud Provider Responsibility	Cloud Consumer Responsibility
Software as a Service (SaaS)	X	
Platform as a Service (PaaS)		X
Infrastructure as a Service (IaaS)		X

service
models and their
consumers.

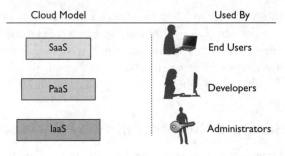

Cloud Model	Used By
SaaS	End Users
PaaS	Developers
IaaS	Administrators

When discussing accountability and responsibility in the cloud, it is important to classify risk according to the service model being utilized and the location of the data. For example, if a business is using a hybrid cloud, both the consumer and the cloud provider can be responsible for the same risks since part of the data is in the cloud and part is in the internal data center. It is important that the SLAs and any other agreements signed between the cloud consumer and cloud provider clearly state who is responsible for preventing and remedying outages and how those outages are classified, identified, and measured. Figure 1-4 shows who the typical cloud consumer is for each cloud model.

CERTIFICATION OBJECTIVE 1.02

Cloud Delivery Models and Services

You have just learned about the different service models available for implementing a cloud computing solution. In order to realize the value from these service models and for the customers to have access to them, a delivery model must be chosen. Implementing a cloud deployment model can vastly impact an organization. Implementation requires careful consideration and planning in order to be successful. If your role is the IT administrator, it is your responsibility to educate the organization on the benefits and challenges of implementing a cloud computing model. You need to evaluate the business needs and determine what benefits a cloud computing model would bring to your organization. Whichever cloud model you choose, whether it be private, public, or hybrid (described next), it needs to map well to the business processes you are trying to achieve.

Private Cloud

A private cloud is a cloud delivery model that is owned by a single organization and enables them to centrally access IT resources from a variety of locations, departments, and staff. A private cloud solution is implemented behind the corporate firewall and is maintained by the local IT department. A private cloud utilizes internal resources and is designed to offer the same benefits of a public cloud without relinquishing control, security, and recurring costs to a cloud provider. In a private cloud model the same organization is both the cloud consumer and the cloud provider.

The decision to implement a private cloud is usually driven by the need to maintain control of the environment because of regulatory or business reasons. For example, a bank might have data security issues that prevent them from using a public cloud service, so they might implement a private cloud to achieve the benefits of a cloud computing model.

A private cloud is a combination of virtualization, data center automation, chargeback metering, and identity-based security. Virtualization allows for easy scalability, flexible resource management, and maximum hardware utilization. A private cloud solution also involves having the ability to auto-provision physical host computers through orchestration software, which is discussed later in this chapter.

One of the downsides to a private cloud is that an organization does not get the return on investment it does with other cloud models. This is because the organization is still responsible for running and managing the resources instead of passing that responsibility to a cloud provider.

Public Cloud

Unlike a private cloud that is owned by the organization, a public cloud is a pool of computing services that are delivered over the Internet via a cloud provider. A cloud provider makes resources such as applications and storage available to organizations over the Internet. Public clouds generally use a pay-as-you-go model, which gives companies the benefit of paying only for the resources that they consume. Public clouds allow for easy and inexpensive setup because the hardware, application, and bandwidth costs are covered and maintained by the cloud provider and charged as part of the service agreement.

on the
Job

You may recognize SaaS offerings such as cloud storage and online office applications (e.g., Microsoft Office 365) as public cloud offerings. What you may not know is that IaaS and PaaS offerings, including cloud-based web hosting and development environments, can be part of a public cloud as well.

Public clouds are used when an organization is less likely to need the level of infrastructure and security offered by private clouds. Organizations requiring data security can still utilize public clouds to make their operations significantly more efficient with the storage of nonsensitive content, online document collaboration, and webmail.

A public cloud offers ultimate scalability because cloud resources are available on demand from the cloud provider's vast pool of resources. Organizations do not need to purchase and implement hardware to scale the environment; they just need to purchase more resources from the cloud provider. The availability of the public cloud via an Internet connection allows the services to be used wherever the client is located, making a public cloud location independent. Some examples of public cloud providers are HP Cloud Services, Microsoft Windows Azure, and Amazon Web Services.

Hybrid Cloud

A hybrid cloud is a cloud service that utilizes both private and public clouds to perform distinct functions within the same organization. An organization might have a need for both a local server running specific applications for security reasons and a public cloud hosting additional applications, files, and databases. These two environments would be configured for scalability and interoperability.

In a hybrid cloud model an organization continues to provide and manage some resources internally while other resources are provided externally by a cloud provider. A hybrid cloud allows an organization to take advantage of the scalability and cost-effectiveness of a public cloud without exposing mission-critical data to a public cloud provider.

A cloud model is defined as a hybrid cloud if an organization is using a public development platform that sends data to a private cloud. Another example of a hybrid cloud model is when an organization uses multiple SaaS applications and moves that application data between a private cloud or an internal data center.

A cloud is not considered a hybrid if an organization uses SaaS applications and does not move the data to a private cloud or internal data center. A cloud

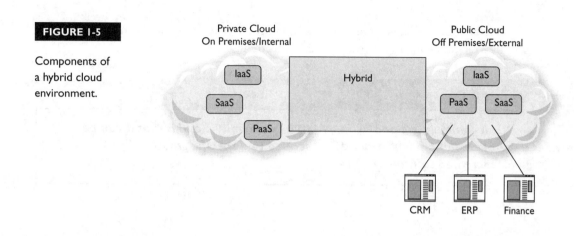

FIGURE 1-5

Components of a hybrid cloud environment.

environment is labeled as a hybrid cloud only if there is a combination of private and public clouds or if data is moved between the internal data center and the public cloud. You can see an example of a hybrid cloud environment in Figure 1-5.

e x a m

Ⓦatⅽh *Make sure you understand the different use case for each type of cloud: private, public, and hybrid. A hybrid cloud is a combination of both a private and a public cloud.*

Community Cloud

A community cloud is a cloud offering where the infrastructure is shared between several organizations from a specific group with common computing needs or objectives. Community clouds are built and operated specifically for a targeted group who have common cloud requirements and whose ultimate goal is to work together to achieve a specific business objective.

Community clouds are usually implemented for organizations working on joint projects that require a central cloud for managing and executing those projects. A finance community cloud, for example, could be set up to provide specific security requirements or optimized to provide low latency to execute financial transactions.

A community cloud can be either on premises or off premises and can be managed by a cloud provider or by the organizations themselves.

exam

⚐atch *A community cloud* *to a community cloud is that it can be*
provides a segregated approach to cloud *scoped to a specific group.*
computing for increased security. The key

EXAM AT WORK

Community Cloud in the Health Care Industry

IT shops that support the health care industry need to design solutions that satisfy regulatory compliance with the Health Insurance Portability and Accountability Act, or HIPAA. Community clouds provide IaaS, PaaS, and SaaS options that enable those IT departments to deliver technical service offerings that both fulfill their customer needs and pass regulatory inspection. To demonstrate the value of the community cloud to the health care industry, let's look at an example of how it could be implemented in a real-world IT scenario.

Deeter is an application developer who builds custom applications for a series of

family doctors' offices. All of these offices are tied into Midwest HealthNet, which is a community cloud solution that aggregates patient data across a number of health care providers, from hospitals to family practices, across the midwestern states. Their primary offering is an SaaS solution called "HealthNet Online" that is accessible only to members of the Midwest HealthNet network. Deeter uses PaaS to develop applications for his customers that present the data available in HealthNet Online in a format that is easier for them to work with and is customized for each of their practices. Since all of his development takes place in the community cloud, and HealthNet Online is also in the community cloud, the data is protected and remains in compliance with HIPAA regulations.

On-Premise Versus Off-Premise Hosting

On-premise hosting is the solution that IT professionals are most familiar with. On premise is the traditional way of managing a data center. In an on-premise environment the virtualized servers are hosted on-site at the organization's internal data center and the organization owns and maintains that server hardware. The benefit to on-premise hosting is that the organization has complete control over the daily management and maintenance of its servers. The downside to on-premise hosting is that the organization has to pay the costs of maintaining the internal data center, including power, security, maintenance, licenses, hardware, and other costs.

Off-premise hosting is sometimes referred to as cloud computing. With off-premise hosting the IT resources are hosted in the cloud and accessed online. Off premise can be used for server virtualization or applications to be hosted in the cloud. One of the benefits of off-premise hosting is that the cost is usually lower than on-premise hosting because the resources are hosted online instead of in the organization's data center. This allows the company to convert IT costs to the pay-as-you-grow model, keeping IT costs down. Off-premise hosting is sometimes perceived as less secure or as having a higher security risk since the organization loses control of their data because it is hosted in the cloud.

Orchestration Platforms

Automation of day-to-day administrative tasks is becoming more and more of a requirement for IT departments. Orchestration platforms provide an automated way to manage the cloud or computing environment. Automation makes it possible to achieve a dynamic data center by aligning business requests with applications, data, and infrastructure. A typical business model defines policies and service levels that an IT department must meet. Orchestration platforms help an IT department meet these requirements through automated workflows, provisions, and change management features. This allows for a dynamic and scalable infrastructure that is constantly changing based on the needs of the business. For example, with an orchestration platform a developer could request the creation of a virtual machine via a service portal, and the orchestration software would automatically create that virtual machine based on a predefined template. Orchestration software can also be used for centralized management of a resource pool, including billing, software metering, and chargeback or showback for resource utilization.

Orchestration platforms provide companies with automated tools to perform tasks that would normally take a team of administrators to complete. These platforms offer an automated approach to creating hardware and software, allowing them to work together to deliver a predefined service or application. Orchestration platforms make it possible for the cloud environment to easily scale and provision new applications and services on demand through workflows.

Some examples of orchestration platforms include HP Operations Orchestration, Flexiant Cloud Orchestrator, and Microsoft System Center Orchestrator. All of the orchestration platforms allow for the creation of workflows to automate day-to-day administrative tasks.

CERTIFICATION OBJECTIVE 1.03

Cloud Characteristics and Terms

When implementing a cloud computing model, an organization needs to understand the terminology of cloud computing and the characteristics of remote provision of a scalable and measured IT resource. The IT administrator as a cloud consumer needs to work with the cloud provider to assess these characteristics and measure the value offering of the chosen cloud platform.

Elasticity

Elasticity can be thought of as unlimited space that allows the organization to dynamically provision and de-provision processing, memory, and storage resources to meet the demands of their network. Elasticity allows an organization to shift and pool resources across dissimilar infrastructure, allowing data to be more synchronized and avoiding overprovisioning of hardware. It is one of the many benefits of cloud computing because it allows an IT department to be scalable without having to purchase and stand up hardware in their internal data center. The primary difference between elasticity and scalability is that scalability is the ability of a system to increase its workload on the current hardware resources, whereas elasticity is the ability to increase the workload on its current and additional hardware resources.

Demand-Driven Service

In an on-demand self-service environment, users have access to cloud services through an online portal. This gives them the ability to provision cloud resources on demand wherever and whenever they need to. On-demand, or "just-in-time," self-service allows cloud consumers to acquire computing resources automatically and on demand without human interaction from the cloud provider.

Pay-as-You-Grow

One of the advantages of the public cloud is the pay-as-you-grow philosophy. The pay-as-you-grow charging model allows an organization to pay for services by the hour or based on the compute resources they use. Therefore, pay-as-you-grow does not require a large up-front investment by the organization for infrastructure resources. It is important for a company to design and plan their cloud costs before deploying their first application in the cloud. Most cloud providers have a calculator to help organizations figure the costs they would incur by moving to the cloud. This gives companies a better understanding of the pay-as-you-grow model when it comes to cloud pricing and using the public cloud infrastructure.

Chargeback

IT chargeback is an accounting strategy that attempts to decentralize the costs of IT services and apply them directly to the teams or divisions that utilize those services. This system enables businesses to make better decisions about how their IT dollars are spent, as it can help determine the true cost of a particular service. Without a chargeback system, all IT costs are consolidated under the IT department umbrella, and the ability to determine the true profitability of the individual business services they support is limited or impossible. Chargeback allows an organization to charge the actual department or user of the IT resource instead of putting all of the expense under the IT umbrella. Most private clouds and internal IT departments use the term "showback" instead of chargeback to describe the amount of resources being consumed by a department.

Ubiquitous Access

With ubiquitous access a cloud provider's capabilities are available over the network and can be accessed through standard mechanisms by both thick and thin clients. This does not necessarily mean Internet access. Ubiquitous access does, however, allow a cloud service to be widely accessible via a web browser, from anywhere. A cloud consumer can get the same level of access whether at home, at work, or in a coffee shop.

Metering

Metering is the ability of a cloud platform to track the use of its IT resources and is geared primarily toward measuring usage by cloud consumers. A metering function allows the cloud provider to charge a cloud consumer only for the IT resources actually being used. Metering is closely tied to on-demand or demand-driven cloud usage.

Metering is not only used for billing purposes; it can also be used for general monitoring of IT resources and usage reporting for both the consumer and the provider. This makes metering a benefit for not only public clouds but private cloud models as well.

Multitenancy

Multitenancy is an architecture that provides a single instance of an application to serve multiple clients or tenants. Tenants are allowed to have their own view of the application and make customizations, while remaining unaware of other tenants who are using the same application.

Multitenant applications ensure that tenants do not have access to change the data and configuration of the application on their own. However, tenants are allowed to change the user interface to give the application their own look and feel.

Implementing a multitenant application is of course more complex than working with a single-tenant application. Multitenant applications must support the sharing of multiple resources by multiple users (e.g., databases, middleware, portals) while maintaining the security of the environment.

Cloud computing has broadened the definition of multitenancy because of the new service models that can take advantage of virtualization and remote access. An SaaS service provider can run an instance of its application on a cloud database and provide web access to multiple customers. Each tenant's data is isolated and remains invisible to other tenants.

Cloud Bursting

Cloud bursting is the concept of running an application on the organization's internal computing resources or private cloud and "bursting" that application into a public cloud on demand when they run out of resources on their internal private cloud. Cloud bursting is normally recommended for high-performance, noncritical applications that have nonsensitive data. It allows a company to deploy an application in an internal data center and "burst" to a public cloud to meet peak needs.

When an organization is looking to take advantage of cloud bursting, they need to consider security and regulatory compliance requirements. An example of when cloud bursting is a good option is in the retail world, where a company might experience a large increase in demand during the holiday season. The downside to this is that the retailers could be putting sensitive data into the public cloud and exposing their customers to risk. Figures 1-6 and 1-7 show an example of an application experiencing heavy use and subsequently "bursting" into the public cloud.

e x a m
ⓦatch

Cloud bursting is a short-term way to increase your available cloud resources on demand, but it does come *with the security risk of moving your data into a public cloud.*

FIGURE 1-6

Operating within the organization's internal computing resources (no public cloud needed).

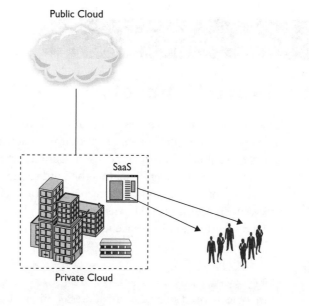

Public Cloud

SaaS

Private Cloud

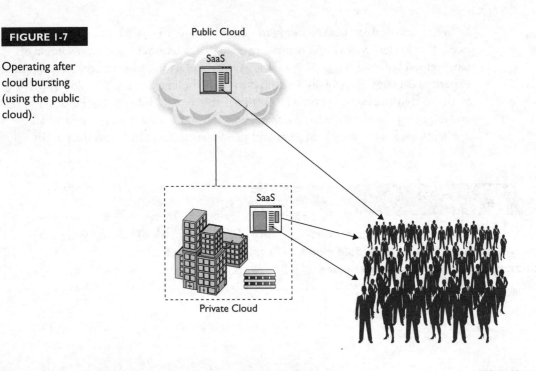

FIGURE 1-7

Operating after cloud bursting (using the public cloud).

CERTIFICATION OBJECTIVE 1.04

Object Storage Concepts

Object-based storage is a concept that was developed to help provide a solution to the ever-growing data storage needs that have accompanied the IT explosion since the late twentieth century. It acts as a counterpart to block-based storage, allowing large sets of files to be grouped together and to move the processing power for those files away from server and workstation CPUs and closer to the storage itself. This processing power is utilized to assist in the implementation of such features as fine-grained security policies, space management, and data abstraction.

Object ID

Since object-based storage is not addressed in blocks, like most of the storage used in everyday workstation and server environments, the object storage device (OSD) interface requires some way to find out how to address the data it contains. Objects are the individual pieces of data that are stored in a cloud storage system. They are composed of parts: an object data component, which is usually a file that is designated to be stored in the cloud storage system, and an object metadata component, which is a collection of values that describe object qualities. The OSD interface uses object IDs as a unique identifier for the combination of data and metadata that comprise each of the objects.

Metadata

Along with all the files that each object contains is an associated set of metadata that can be used to describe the data component of a specific object, and classify it or define relationships with other objects. This metadata is an extensible set of attributes that is either implemented by the OSD directly for some of the more common attributes or interpreted by higher-level storage systems that the OSD uses for its persistent storage.

Data BLOB

A binary large object, or BLOB, is a collected set of binary data that is stored as a single, discrete entity in a database management system. By gathering this binary data into larger collections, database administrators are able to better copy large amounts of data between databases with significantly reduced risk of error correction or data filtering.

Policies

Policies are similar to metadata in that they are attributes associated with the object. The difference is that policy tags contain information that is associated with a particular security mechanism.

Replicas

One of the primary uses of object-based storage is the practice of working with replicas. Replicas are essentially copies of one large set of data, often associated with a virtual hard drive or virtual machine. They are used to both increase availability and reduce the amount of risk associated with keeping a large amount of data in one location. Replicas are good candidates for object-based storage for several reasons:

- They are large datasets that require a copying mechanism that can run efficiently without requiring expensive error correction or filtering.
- They do not affect user performance SLAs if they are faced with I/O latency, which is often associated with object-based storage.

CERTIFICATION SUMMARY

The definitions of cloud computing are always changing. Understanding the similarities and differences between the cloud models is key to passing the CompTIA Cloud+ exam. It is equally important to grasp how the cloud can benefit an organization. Cloud computing is a growing industry, and IT professionals are going to be required to grow with it.

KEY TERMS

Use the list below to review the key terms that were discussed in this chapter. The definitions can be found within this chapter and in the glossary.

Infrastructure as a Service (IaaS)   Cloud model where the cloud consumer outsources responsibility for their infrastructure to an external cloud provider that owns the equipment, such as storage, servers, and connectivity domains

Platform as a Service (PaaS)   Cloud model that provides the infrastructure to create applications and host them with a cloud provider

Software as a Service (SaaS)   Cloud model that allows a cloud consumer the ability to use on-demand software applications delivered by the cloud provider via the Internet

Database as a Service (DBaaS)   Cloud model that delivers database operations as a service to multiple cloud consumers over the Internet

Communication as a Service (CaaS)   Allows a cloud consumer to utilize enterprise-level voice over IP (VoIP), virtual private networks (VPNs), private branch exchange (PBX), and unified communications using a cloud model

Business Process as a Service (BPaaS)   Any business process that is delivered as a service by utilizing a cloud solution

Anything as a Service (XaaS)   Cloud model that delivers IT as a service through hybrid cloud computing and works with a combination of SaaS, IaaS, PaaS, CaaS, DBaaS, and/or BPaaS

Private cloud   Cloud delivery model that is owned and maintained by a single organization; it is implemented behind the corporate firewall that enables an organization to centrally access IT resources

Public cloud   A pool of computing resources and services delivered over the Internet by a cloud provider

Hybrid cloud   Cloud model that utilizes both private and public clouds to perform distinct functions within the same organization

Community cloud   Cloud model where the infrastructure is shared between several organizations from a specific group with common computing needs and objectives

Elasticity   Allows an organization to dynamically provision and de-provision processing, memory, and storage resources to meet the demands of the network

On-demand self-service/just-in-time service   Gives cloud consumers access to cloud services through an online portal allowing them to acquire computing resources automatically and on demand without human interaction from the cloud provider

Pay-as-you-grow   A concept in cloud computing where you pay for cloud resources as an organization needs those resources

Chargeback   An accounting strategy that attempts to decentralize the costs of IT services and apply them directly to the teams or divisions that utilize those services

Ubiquitous access   Allows a cloud service to be widely accessible via a web browser from anywhere allowing for the same level of access either from home or work

Metering   The ability of a cloud platform to track the use of its IT resources focused primarily on measuring usage by cloud consumers

Multitenancy   Architecture providing a single instance of an multiple clients or tenants

Cloud bursting Allows an application running in a private cloud to burst into a public cloud on an on-demand basis

Object ID Unique identifier used to name an object

Metadata Data about data, used to describe particular attributes of data including how the data is formatted

Data BLOB Collection of binary data stored as a single entity

Policies Rule sets by which users and administrators must abide

Replicas Used to create a mirrored copy of data between two redundant hardware devices

✓ # TWO-MINUTE DRILL

Cloud Service Models

❑ A cloud service model is a set of IT-related services offered by a cloud provider.

❑ Infrastructure as a Service (IaaS) is a cloud service model that offers server storage, infrastructure, and connectivity domains to a cloud consumer.

❑ Platform as a Service (PaaS) allows developers to develop and test applications without worrying about the underlying infrastructure.

❑ Software as a Service (SaaS) provides on-demand applications to the cloud consumer over the Internet.

❑ Communications as a Service (CaaS) allows a cloud consumer to outsource enterprise-level communication services such asVoIP and PBX.

❑ Anything as a Service (XaaS) is a generic term used to describe the distribution of different cloud components.

Cloud Delivery Models and Services

❑ A private cloud is a cloud delivery model that is owned and operated by a single organization, implemented behind the corporate firewall, and maintained by the internal IT department.

❑ A public cloud is a pool of computing services and resources that are delivered to a cloud consumer over the Internet by a cloud provider.

❑ A hybrid cloud is a combination of a public and private cloud that allows an organization to move resources between the local data center and a public cloud.

❑ A community cloud shares cloud resources and infrastructure between organizations for a specific group that has common computing needs or objectives.

❑ Orchestration software allows for an automated approach to managing cloud resources by providing for automatic deployment of virtual machines and other infrastructure.

Cloud Characteristics and Terms

❑ Elasticity allows an organization to dynamically provision and de-provision compute resources to meet the demands of their network.

❑ Demand-driven service allows a cloud consumer to provision cloud resources on demand whenever they need to.

❑ Pay-as-you-grow allows a cloud consumer to pay only for the resources they are using and does not require a large up-front investment.

❑ Metering allows a cloud consumer to track who is using IT resources and charge the correct department for those resources.

❑ Cloud bursting allows a cloud consumer to "burst" an application running in a private cloud into a public cloud when demand gets too high for their internal resources.

Object Storage Concepts

❑ Metadata uses attributes in the file to describe the data.

❑ A data BLOB is a collected set of binary data that is stored together as a single, discrete entity in a database.

❑ Replicas are copies of a large set of data used to increase availability and reduce the amount of risk associated with keeping a large amount of data in one location.

SELF TEST

The following questions will help you measure your understanding of the material presented in this chapter.

Cloud Service Models

1. Which of the following would be considered an example of IaaS?
   A. Google Apps
   B. Salesforce
   C. Amazon Web Services
   D. AppScale

2. Which term is used to define the increasing number of services delivered over the Internet?
   A. XaaS
   B. CaaS
   C. MaaS
   D. C-MaaS

3. Voice over IP (VoIP) is an example of what type of cloud service?
   A. IaaS
   B. PaaS
   C. MaaS
   D. CaaS

4. Which of the following cloud solutions provides only hardware and network resources to make up a cloud environment?
   A. SaaS
   B. CaaS
   C. PaaS
   D. IaaS

5. Which of the following is usually accessed via a web browser?
   A. IaaS
   B. SaaS
   C. PaaS
   D. Virtual machines

Cloud Delivery Models and Services

6. What type of computing solution would be defined as a platform that is implemented within the corporate firewall and is under the control of the IT department?

   A. Private cloud

   B. Public cloud

   C. VLAN

   D. VPN

7. A cloud deployment has been created explicitly for the finance department. What type of cloud deployment would this be defined as?

   A. Public cloud

   B. Hybrid cloud

   C. Community cloud

   D. Private cloud

8. Which of the following statements would be used to explain a private cloud but not a public cloud?

   A. Used as a service via the Internet

   B. Dedicated to a single organization

   C. Requires users to pay a monthly fee to access services

   D. Provides incremental scalability

9. Which of the following statements is a benefit of a hybrid cloud?

   A. Data security management

   B. Requirement of a major financial investment

   C. Dependency of internal IT department

   D. Complex networking

Cloud Characteristics and Terms

10. Which of the following would be considered an advantage of cloud computing?

   A. Increased security

   B. Ability to scale to meet growing usage demands

   C. Ease of integrating equipment hosted in other data centers

   D. Increased privacy for corporate data

11. Which statement defines chargeback?
   A. The recovery of costs from consumers of cloud services
   B. The process of identifying costs and assigning them to specific cost categories
   C. A method of ensuring that cloud computing becomes a profit instead of a cost
   D. A system for confirming that billing occurs for the cloud services being used

12. When you run out of computer resources in your internal data center and expand to an external cloud on demand, this is an example of what?
   A. SaaS
   B. Hybrid cloud
   C. Cloud bursting
   D. Elasticity

Object Storage Concepts

13. A website administrator is storing a large amount of multimedia objects in binary format for the corporate website. What type of storage object is this considered to be?
   A. BLOB
   B. Replica
   C. Metadata
   D. Object ID

SELF TEST ANSWERS

Cloud Service Models

1. Which of the following would be considered an example of IaaS?
- A. Google Apps
- B. Salesforce
- C. Amazon Web Services
- D. AppScale

☑ **C.** Amazon Web Services is an example of IaaS because it provides hardware resources over the Internet.
☒ **A, B,** and **D** are incorrect. **A** and **B** are examples of SaaS. AppScale is an example of PaaS.

2. Which term is used to define the increasing number of services delivered over the Internet?
- A. XaaS
- B. CaaS
- C. MaaS
- D. C-MaaS

☑ **A.** XaaS is a collective term that means "Anything as a Service" (or "Everything as a Service").
☒ **B, C,** and **D** are incorrect. Communications as a Service (CaaS), Monitoring as a Service (MaaS), and Cloud Migration as a Service (C-MaaS) are all examples of XaaS.

3. Voice over IP (VoIP) is an example of what type of cloud service?
- A. IaaS
- B. PaaS
- C. MaaS
- D. CaaS

☑ **D.** Voice over IP is an example of CaaS.
☒ **A, B,** and **C** are incorrect. VoIP is not an example of any of these cloud services.

4. Which of the following cloud solutions provides only hardware and network resources to make up a cloud environment?
- **A.** SaaS
- **B.** CaaS
- **C.** PaaS
- **D.** IaaS

☑ **D.** In a cloud service model IaaS providers offer computers and other hardware resources. Organizations would outsource the equipment needed to support their business.

☒ **A, B,** and **C** are incorrect. SaaS allows applications to be hosted by a service provider and made available to the organization over the Internet. CaaS provides network communication such as VoIP. PaaS offers a way to rent hardware, operating systems, storage, and network capacity over the Internet.

5. Which of the following is usually accessed via a web browser?
- **A.** IaaS
- **B.** SaaS
- **C.** PaaS
- **D.** Virtual machines

☑ **C.** PaaS provides a platform to allow developers to build applications and services over the Internet. PaaS is hosted in the cloud and accessed with a web browser.

☒ **A, B,** and **D** are incorrect. In a cloud service model IaaS providers offer computers and other hardware resources. Organizations would outsource the equipment needed to support their business. SaaS allows applications to be hosted by a service provider and made available to the organization over the Internet. Virtual machines would not be accessed via a web browser.

Cloud Delivery Models and Services

6. What type of computing solution would be defined as a platform that is implemented within the corporate firewall and is under the control of the IT department?
- **A.** Private cloud
- **B.** Public cloud
- **C.** VLAN
- **D.** VPN

☑ **A.** A private cloud is a cloud computing solution that is implemented behind a corporate firewall and is under the control of the internal IT department.

☒ **B, C,** and **D** are incorrect. A public cloud is a cloud computing solution that is based on a standard cloud computing model where a service provider makes the resources available over the Internet. A VLAN (virtual LAN) is a broadcast created by switches. A VPN (virtual private network) extends a private network over a public network such as the Internet.

7. A cloud deployment has been created explicitly for the finance department. What type of cloud deployment would this be defined as?

   A. Public cloud

   B. Hybrid cloud

   C. Community cloud

   D. Private cloud

☑ **C.** A community cloud is a cloud solution that provides services to a specific or limited number of individuals who share a common computing need.

☒ **A, B,** and **D** are incorrect. A public cloud is a cloud computing solution that is based on a standard cloud computing model where a service provider makes the resources available over the Internet. A hybrid cloud is a cloud computing model where some of the resources are managed by the internal IT department and some are managed by an external organization. A private cloud is a cloud computing solution that is implemented behind a corporate firewall and is under the control of the internal IT department.

8. Which of the following statements would be used to explain a private cloud but not a public cloud?

   A. Used as a service via the Internet

   B. Dedicated to a single organization

   C. Requires users to pay a monthly fee to access services

   D. Provides incremental scalability

☑ **B.** A private cloud is dedicated to a single organization and is contained within the corporate firewall.

☒ **A, C,** and **D** are incorrect. These all describe features of a public cloud, not a private cloud. A public cloud is used as a service over the Internet, requires a monthly fee to access and use its resources, and is highly scalable.

9. Which of the following statements is a benefit of a hybrid cloud?

   A. Data security management

   B. Requirement of a major financial investment

   C. Dependency of internal IT department

   D. Complex networking

> ☑ **A.** A hybrid cloud offers the ability to keep the organization's mission-critical data behind a firewall and outside of the public cloud.
> ☒ **B, C,** and **D** are incorrect. These are all disadvantages of a hybrid cloud.

Cloud Characteristics and Terms

10. Which of the following would be considered an advantage of cloud computing?

   A. Increased security

   B. Ability to scale to meet growing usage demands

   C. Ease of integrating equipment hosted in other data centers

   D. Increased privacy for corporate data

> ☑ **B.** One of the benefits of cloud computing is the ability to easily scale and add resources to meet the growth of the organization.
> ☒ **A, C,** and **D** are incorrect. These are all disadvantages of cloud computing. The organization loses some control of their environment, has more difficulty integrating equipment hosted in multiple data centers, and deals with the uncertainty of whether other organizations have access to their data.

11. Which statement defines chargeback?

   A. The recovery of costs from consumers of cloud services

   B. The process of identifying costs and assigning them to specific cost categories

   C. A method of ensuring that cloud computing becomes a profit instead of a cost

   D. A system for confirming that billing occurs for the cloud services being used

> ☑ **A.** The purpose of a chargeback system is to measure the costs of IT services, hardware, or software and recover them from the business unit that used them.
> ☒ **B, C,** and **D** are incorrect. None of these options is the main focus of a chargeback system.

12. When you run out of computer resources in your internal data center and expand to an external cloud on demand, this is an example of what?
    A. SaaS
    B. Hybrid cloud
    C. Cloud bursting
    D. Elasticity

    ☑ **C.** Cloud bursting allows you add additional resources from an external cloud on an on-demand basis. The internal resource is the private cloud and the external resource is the public cloud.
    ☒ **A, B,** and **D** are incorrect. SaaS allows applications to be hosted by a service provider and made available to the organization over the Internet. A hybrid cloud is a cloud computing model where some of the resources are managed by the internal IT department and some are managed by an external organization. Elasticity provides fully automated scalability. It implies an ability to shift resources across infrastructures.

Object Storage Concepts

13. A website administrator is storing a large amount of multimedia objects in binary format for the corporate website. What type of storage object is this considered to be?
    A. BLOB
    B. Replica
    C. Metadata
    D. Object ID

    ☑ **A.** A BLOB is a collection of binary data that is stored as a single entity. BLOBs are primarily used to store images, videos, and sound.
    ☒ **B, C,** and **D** are incorrect. A replica is a complete copy of the data. Metadata describes information about the set of data, including who created the data and when it was collected. It is data about the data. An object ID identifies an object in a database.

2

Disk Storage Systems

S torage devices are the foundation of a storage network and are the building blocks of storage in a disk subsystem and stand-alone server. Disk system performance is a key factor to the overall health of the cloud environment, and you need to understand the different types of disks that are available and the benefits of each. Once an organization chooses the type of disk to use in their cloud environment, they need to protect the data that is stored on the disk. Along with describing the different types of disks and how to connect those disks to the system, this chapter illustrates how data can remain protected and performing at optimal levels by utilizing the various levels of RAID.

CERTIFICATION OBJECTIVE 2.01

Disk Types and Configurations

Disk drive technology has advanced at an astonishing rate over the past few years, making terabytes of storage available at a relatively low cost to consumers. Evaluating what types of disks to buy requires careful planning and evaluation of the purpose of the disk. If an organization is looking for a type of drive to support their database environment, they would be interested in a drive with high disk I/O as opposed to a drive that supports a file share on a test network (in which case the need is for disk space over disk I/O). In the following sections we examine each of the different disk types and clarify these distinctions.

Rotational Media

Disk storage is a generic term used to describe storage mechanisms where data is digitally recorded by various electronic, magnetic, optical, or mechanical methods on a rotating disk, or media. A disk drive is a device that uses this storage mechanism with fixed or removable media. Removable media refers to a compact disk, floppy disk, or USB drive, and fixed or nonremovable media refers to a hard disk drive.

A hard disk drive (HDD) uses rapidly rotating disks called platters coated with a magnetic material known as ferrous oxide to store and retrieve digital information. An HDD retains the data on the drive even when the drive is powered off. The data on an HDD is read in a random-access manner. What this means is that an individual block of data can be stored or retrieved in any order rather than only being accessible sequentially, as in the case of data that might exist on a tape.

An HDD contains one or more platters with read/write heads arranged on a moving arm that floats above the ferrous oxide surface to read and write data to the drive. HDDs have been the primary storage device for computers since the 1960s. Today the most common sizes for HDDs are the 3.5 inch, which is used primarily in desktop computers, and the 2.5 inch, which is used primarily in laptop computers. The primary competitors of the HDD are the solid state drive (SSD) and flash memory cards. HDDs should remain the dominating medium for secondary storage, but SSDs are replacing rotating hard drives in portable electronic devices because of their speed and ruggedness.

e x a m

ⓦ **a t c h** *Hard disk drives are used when speed is less important than total storage space.*

Interface Types

HDDs interface with a computer in a variety of ways, including ATA, SATA, Fibre Channel, SCSI, SAS, and IDE. Here we look at each of these interface technologies in greater detail. HDDs connect to a host bus interface adapter with a single data cable. Each HDD has its own power cable that is connected to the computer's power supply.

- **Advanced technology attachment (ATA)** is an interface standard for connecting storage devices in computers. ATA is often referred to as parallel ATA (or PATA).

- **Integrated drive electronics (IDE)** is the integration of the controller and the hard drive itself, which allows the drive to connect directly to the motherboard or controller. IDE is also known as ATA.

- **Serial ATA (SATA)** is used to connect host bus adapters to mass storage devices. Designed to replace PATA, it offers several advantages over its predecessor, including reduced cable size, lower cost, native hot swapping, faster throughput, and more efficient data transfer.

- **Small computer system interface (SCSI)** is a set of standard electronic interfaces accredited by the American National Standards Institute (ANSI) for connecting and transferring data between computers and storage devices. SCSI is faster and more flexible than earlier transfer interfaces. It uses a bus interface type, and every device in the chain requires a unique ID.

- **Serial attached SCSI (SAS)** is a data transfer technology that was designed to replace SCSI and to transfer data to and from storage devices. SAS is backward compatible with SATA drives.

■ **Fibre Channel** is a high-speed network technology used in storage networking. Fibre Channel is well suited to connect servers to a shared storage device such as a storage area network (SAN) due to its high-speed transfer rate of up to 16 gigabits per second.

Table 2-1 explains the different connection types and some of the advantages and disadvantages of each interface.

e x a m
ⓦatch   *Understanding the* | *each connector and the benefits of that*
differences in the interface types is key | *connector.*
for the test. You need to know when to use

TABLE 2-1   HDD Interface Types

Connector	Advantages	Disadvantages
Integrated drive electronics (IDE)	■ Lower cost ■ Large capacity	■ Only one device is able to read/write at a time if used in the typical master/slave configuration.
Serial ATA (SATA)	■ Lower cost ■ Large capacity ■ Faster transfer rates than ATA ■ Easy configuration	■ Slower transfer rates than SCSI ■ No native support in older operating systems
Small computer system interface (SCSI)	■ Faster speeds ■ Greater scalability ■ Compatible with older SCSI devices ■ Reliability ■ Appropriate for large amounts of data	■ Higher cost ■ Large variety of interfaces ■ Higher RPM, causing more noise and heat ■ More difficult configuration
Serial attached SCSI (SAS)	■ Compatibility with SATA ■ Higher transfer speeds ■ Serial communication vs. parallel ■ Increased availability	■ Higher cost ■ Use of SCSI command set

Access Speed

Just knowing the types of hard disks and the interface is not enough to calculate which drive type is best for a particular application. Understanding the speed at which a drive can access the data that is stored on that drive is critical to the performance of the application. A hard drive's speed is measured by the amount of time it takes to access the data that is stored on the drive. Access time is the response time of the drive and is a direct correlation of seek time and latency. Seek time is the measure of how long it takes the drive to find the data being accessed, whereas latency is the measure of the time delay that it takes for the drive to properly position the sector under the read/write head.

The access time of an HDD can be improved by either increasing the speed of the drive or reducing the time the drive has to spend seeking the data. Seek time generally falls in the range of 3 to 15 milliseconds (MS). The faster the disk can spin, the faster it can find the data and the lower the latency for that drive will be. Table 2-2 lists the average latency based on some common hard disk speeds.

Solid State Drive (SSD)

A solid state drive (SSD) is a high-performance storage device that contains no moving parts. It includes either dynamic random-access memory (DRAM) or flash memory boards, a memory bus board, a central processing unit (CPU), and sometimes a battery or separate power source. The majority of SSDs use "not and" (NAND)–based flash memory, which is a nonvolatile memory type, meaning the drive can retain data without power. SSDs produce the highest possible I/O rates because they contain their own CPUs to manage data storage. SSDs are less susceptible to shock or being dropped, are much quieter, and have a faster access time and lower latency than HDDs. SSDs and traditional hard disks have the same I/O interface, allowing SSDs to easily replace a traditional hard disk drive without changing the computer hardware.

TABLE 2-2	Rotational Speed (RPM)	Latency (MS)
Hard Disk Speed and Latency	3600	8.3
	4200	7.1
	5400	5.6
	7200	4.2
	10000	3
	15000	2

While SSDs can be used in all types of scenarios, they are especially valuable in a system where I/O response time is critical, such as a database server, a server hosting a file share, or any application that has a disk I/O bottleneck. Another example of where an SSD is a good candidate is in a laptop. SSDs are shock resistant; they also use less power and provide a faster startup time than HDDs. Since an SSD has no moving parts, both sleep response time and system response time are improved. SSDs are currently more expensive than traditional hard disk drives but are less of a risk for failure and data loss. Table 2-3 shows you some of the differences between SSDs and traditional hard disk drives.

TABLE 2-3 SSD versus HDD

Drive Characteristic	Solid State Drive (SSD)	Hard Disk Drive (HDD)
Startup Time	Almost instantaneous. There are no moving parts to start on an SSD.	Disk spin-up can take a few seconds. If a system has multiple hard disks, it might stagger spin-up to limit power usage.
Fragmentation	Very small. Defragmenting an SSD could actually cause wear by making additional writes to the memory.	Files that are frequently written become fragmented over time. Defragmentation is required to ensure optimum performance.
Noise	Virtually none, since an SSD has no moving parts.	Noise levels vary between different models and manufacturers.
Temperature Control	Able to tolerate higher temperatures than an HDD. Special cooling usually not required.	Ambient temperatures above 95°F can shorten life. Additional cooling could be required.
Susceptibility to Failure	Extremely resistant to shock and vibrations because it has no moving parts.	Susceptible to shock and vibrations due to moving heads above rapidly rotating platters.
Reliability and Expected Lifetime	Not as likely to have a mechanical failure since it has no moving parts. Reliability varies across manufacturers.	Potential for mechanical failure from normal use due to moving parts.
Power Consumption	Flash-based on average requires half the power of an HDD. High-performance DRAM requires as much power as an HDD.	Anywhere from 0.35 watts to 20 watts, depending on size and performance.
Cost	More expensive per GB compared to HDD.	Less expensive per GB than SSD.
Installation	Not sensitive to location or orientation. No exposed circuitry.	Circuits can be exposed and should not come in contact with other metal parts. Needs to be mounted to protect against vibrations.
Data Transfer Rate	Delivers consistent read/write speed. Sleep recovery is greatly improved compared to an HDD, due to no moving parts.	Slower response time because of constant seeking to read files from various locations on the disk.

USB Drive

A universal serial bus (USB) drive is an external plug-and-play storage device that can be plugged into a computer's USB port, and is recognized by the computer as a removable drive and assigned a drive letter by the computer. Unlike an HDD or SSD, a USB drive does not require a special connection cable and power cable to connect to the system, because it is powered via the USB port of the computer. Since a USB drive is portable and retains the data stored on it as it is moved between computer systems, it is a great device for transferring files quickly between computers or servers. There are many external storage devices that use USB, such as hard drives, flash drives, and DVD drives.

Tape

A tape drive is a storage device that reads and writes data to a magnetic tape. Using tape as a form of storage has been around for a long time. The role of tape has changed tremendously over the years and is still changing. Tape is now finding a niche in the market for longer-term storage and archiving of data, and it is the medium of choice for storage at an off-site location.

Tape drives provide sequential access to the data, whereas an HDD provides random access to the data. A tape drive has to physically wind the tape between reels to read any one particular piece of data. As a result it has a slow seek time, having to wait for the tape to be in the correct position to access the data. Tape drives have a wide range of capacity and allow for data to be compressed to a size smaller than that of the files stored on the disk.

CERTIFICATION OBJECTIVE 2.02

Tiering

In the previous section we discussed the different types of disks and the benefits of each of those disk types. Now that you understand the benefits of each disk, you know that storing data on the appropriate disk type can increase performance and decrease the cost of storing that data. Having flexibility in how and where to store an application's data is key to the success of cloud computing.

Tiered storage permits an organization to adjust where their data is being stored based on performance, availability, cost, and recovery requirements of an application. For example, data that is stored for restoration in the event of loss or corruption would be stored on the local drive so that it can be recovered quickly, whereas data that is stored for regulatory purposes would be archived to a lower-cost disk like tape storage.

Tiered storage can refer to an infrastructure that has a simple two-tier architecture, consisting of SCSI disks and a tape drive, or to a more complex scenario of three or four tiers. Tiered storage helps organizations plan their information life cycle management, reduce costs, and increase efficiency. Tiered storage requirements can also be determined by functional differences, for example, the need for replication and high-speed restoration.

With tiered storage, data can be moved from fast, expensive disks to slower, less expensive disks. Hierarchical storage management (HSM), which is discussed in the next section, allows for automatically moving data among four different tiers of storage. For example, data that is frequently used and stored on highly available, expensive disks can be automatically migrated to less expensive tape storage when it is no longer required on a day-to-day basis. One of the advantages of HSM is that the total amount of data that is stored can be higher than the capacity of the disk storage system currently in place.

Performance Levels of Each Tier

Data tiers are determined by the level of access required and the performance and reliability needed for that particular data. Organizations can save time and money by implementing a tiered storage infrastructure. Each tier has its own set of benefits and usage scenarios based on a variety of factors. Organizations and IT departments need to define each type of data and determine how to classify it. For example: Is the data critical to the day-to-day operation of the organization? Is there an archiving requirement for the data after so many months or years? And so on. Once the data has been classified, the organization can then move it to the appropriate tier.

Tier 1

Tier 1 data is defined as mission-critical, recently accessed, or secure files and should be stored on expensive and highly available disks such as RAID with parity. Tier 1 storage systems have better performance, capacity, reliability, and manageability.

Tier 2

Tier 2 data is data that runs major business applications, for example, e-mail and ERP. Tier 2 is a balance between cost and performance. Tier 2 data does not require sub-second response time but still needs to be reasonably fast.

Tier 3

Tier 3 data includes financial data that needs to be kept for tax purposes but is not accessed on a daily basis and so does not need to be stored on the expensive tier 1 or tier 2 storage systems.

Tier 4

Tier 4 data is data that is used for compliance requirements for keeping e-mails or data for long periods of time. Tier 4 data can be a large amount of data but does not need to be instantly accessible.

Policies

A multitiered storage system provides an automated way to move data between more expensive and less expensive storage systems, as an organization can implement policies that define what data fits into each tier and then manage how that data migrates between the tiers. For example, when financial data is more than a year old, the policy could be to move that data to a tier 4 storage solution, much like the HSM defined earlier.

Tiered storage provides IT departments with the best solution for managing the organization's data while also saving time and money. Tiered storage helps IT departments meet their service level agreements at the lowest possible cost and the highest possible efficiency.

CERTIFICATION OBJECTIVE 2.03

Redundant Array of Independent Disks (RAID)

So far in this chapter you have learned about the different disk types and how those disk types connect to a computer system. The next thing you need to understand is how to make the data that is stored on those disk drives as redundant as possible while maintaining a high-performance system. Redundant array of independent disks (RAID) is a storage technology that combines multiple hard disk drives into a single logical unit so that the data can be distributed across the hard disk drives for both improved performance and increased security according to their various RAID levels. How the data is distributed across the disks depends on both the redundancy and the performance requirements for the application, service, or dataset that is being delivered. The basic idea behind RAID is to combine multiple inexpensive disk drives into an array that displays as one large logical storage unit to the server.

There are two different options available when implementing RAID: software RAID and hardware RAID using a RAID controller. Software RAID is implemented on a server by using software that groups multiple logical disks into a single virtual disk. Most modern operating systems have built-in software that allows for the configuration of a software-based RAID array. Hardware RAID controllers are physical cards that are added to a server to off-load the overhead of RAID and do not require any CPU resources; they allow an administrator to boot straight to the RAID controller to configure the RAID levels. Hardware RAID is the most common form of RAID due to its tighter integration with the device and better error handling.

Now that you understand what RAID is and how it is implemented, you need to become familiar with the various RAID levels and when to choose each of them. Choosing the correct RAID level based upon what the application is being used for is critical to the performance of the application. This section describes the most common RAID levels in use today.

RAID 1

When drives are configured using RAID 1, they are said to be configured in a mirrored set. It is called "mirrored" because the data is exactly the same on both disks, as the drive creates a mirror image of disk 1 on disk 2 in the set. As you might expect, RAID 1 requires a minimum of two disks in order to establish a volume partition on a basic disk. Read requests sent to that volume can be serviced by either disk 1 or disk 2, and write requests will always update both disks. Each disk in a RAID 1 configuration contains a complete, identical copy of the data for the drive, and can be accessed independently. RAID 1 provides its data protection without a parity check, calculates data in two drives, and stores it on a separate drive.

RAID 1 is a particularly useful configuration when read performance and reliability are more important than storage capacity. A RAID 1 array can only be as big as the smallest disk. While RAID 1 can protect against the failure of a single hard drive, it does not protect against data corruption or file deletions since any changes would be instantly mirrored or copied to every drive in the array. In case of a disk controller failure or data corruption, an organization should still plan on implementing a proper backup strategy to complement the data protection already provided by the RAID 1 array configuration. Figure 2-1 shows an example of how the disks are configured in a RAID 1 array.

RAID 0

RAID 0 is a configuration that provides increased performance but has no redundancy built into it. This configuration requires a minimum of two disks. It "stripes" writes across both disks in the array to increase performance by getting access to multiple physical spindles, instead of just one, and splitting the data into blocks. Then it writes that data across all the drives in the array. If any of the drives fails, however, the entire array is irreparably damaged. RAID 0 offers low cost of implementation and is typically used for noncritical data that is regularly backed up and requires high write speed. Figure 2-2 shows an example of how the disks are configured in a RAID 0 array.

FIGURE 2-1

A graphical concept of RAID 1 mirroring.

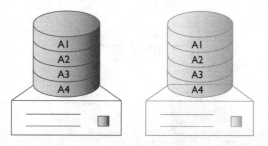

FIGURE 2-2

A RAID 0 striping
configuration.

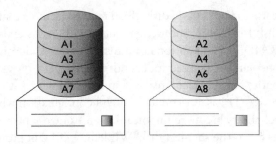

RAID 1+0

Raid 1+0 consists of a top-level RAID 0 array that is in turn composed of two or more RAID 1 arrays. It incorporates both the performance advantages of RAID 0 and the data protection advantages of RAID 1. Although its official designation is RAID 1+0, it is often referred to as RAID 10. If a single drive fails in a RAID 10 array, the lower-level mirrors will enter into a degraded mode while the top-level stripe can continue to perform as normal because both of its drives are still working as expected.

The drawback to RAID 10 is that it cuts your usable storage in half since everything is mirrored. It is also a very expensive configuration to implement. RAID 10 could be used if an application requires both high performance and reliability and the organization is willing to sacrifice capacity to get it. Some examples where this configuration might make sense are for enterprise servers, database servers, and high-end application servers. Figure 2-3 shows an example of how the disks are configured in a RAID 10 array.

FIGURE 2-3

RAID 1+0
mirroring and
striping, no parity.

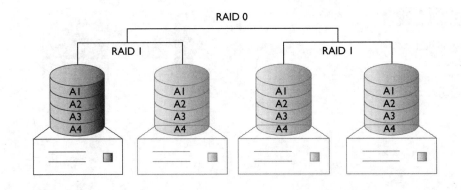

Recently we did some work for a small business that specializes in photography. They had been storing all their images on an older device and backing it up to tape every night. They realized that if the system went down they could possibly lose data, which in their line of work could be disastrous. (After all, you can't go back and retake pictures of a graduation ceremony!) They decided to implement a RAID 10 solution to give them redundancy and increase performance so that they would not lose irreplaceable data.

RAID 0+1

RAID 0+1 arrays are made up of a top-level RAID 1 mirror containing two or more RAID 0 stripe sets. This configuration is similar to RAID 10, as it provides both the advantages of RAID 0 and RAID 1. A single drive failure in RAID 0+1 results in one of the lower-level stripes completely failing since RAID 0 is not a fault-tolerant configuration. However, the top-level mirror continues to operate as normal, so there is no interruption to data access. In the case of this type of failure, the drive must be replaced and the stripe set has to be rebuilt as an empty stripe set, after which the mirror is rebuilt on the empty stripe set; therefore, it has a longer recovery period than RAID 10.

Again, similar to RAID 10, the RAID 0+1 configuration is recommended for applications requiring both high performance and reliability that also have the ability to sacrifice capacity. Figure 2-4 shows an example of how the disks are configured in a RAID 0+1 array.

RAID 5

RAID 5 is one of the most commonly used RAID implementations, as it provides a good balance of data protection, performance, and cost-effectiveness. A RAID 5 array uses block-level striping for a performance enhancement with distributed parity for data protection. A RAID 5 array distributes parity and the data across all drives and requires that all drives but one be present in order to operate. This means that

FIGURE 2-4

Example of a RAID 0+1 configuration.

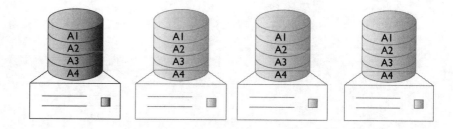

a RAID 5 array is not destroyed by a single drive failure, regardless of which drive is lost. When a drive fails, the RAID 5 array is still accessible to read and write data. After the failed drive has been replaced, the array enters into data recovery mode, which means that the parity data in the array is used to rebuild the missing data from the failed drive back onto the new hard drive.

RAID 5 uses the equivalent of one hard disk to store the parity, which means you "lose" or sacrifice the storage space equivalent to one of the drives that is part of the array. A RAID 5 array requires a minimum of three disks and provides good performance and redundancy at a low cost. RAID 5 delivers the ideal combination of good performance, fault tolerance, high capacity, and storage efficiency. RAID 5 is best suited for transaction processing, for example, a database application. It is great for storing large files where data is read sequentially. Figure 2-5 shows an example of how the disks are configured in a RAID 5 array.

RAID 6

RAID 6 can be viewed essentially as an extension of RAID 5, as it uses the same striping and parity block distribution across all the drives in the array. The difference is that RAID 6 adds an additional parity block, allowing it to use block-level striping with two parity blocks distributed across all the disks. The inclusion of this second parity block allows the array to tolerate the loss of two hard disks instead of the one failure that RAID 5 can tolerate. RAID 6 causes no performance hit on read operations but does have a lower performance rate on write operations due to the overhead associated with the parity calculations.

FIGURE 2-5

RAID 5 striping with parity.

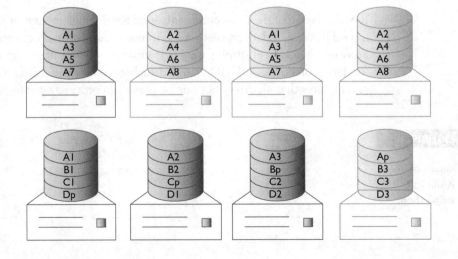

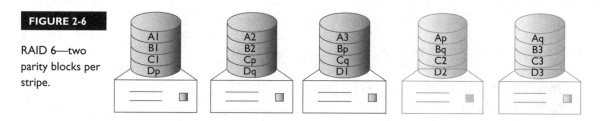

FIGURE 2-6

RAID 6—two parity blocks per stripe.

RAID 6 is ideal for supporting applications where additional fault tolerance that is not achievable with RAID 5 is required. The additional fault tolerance supplied by the second parity block in RAID 6 makes it a good candidate for deployment in environments where IT support is not readily available or spare parts may take a significant amount of time to be delivered on-site. Figure 2-6 shows an example of how the disks are configured in a RAID 6 array.

Table 2-4 compares the different RAID configurations to give you a better understanding of the advantages and requirements of each RAID level.

e x a m
ⓦatch
You need to understand the difference between each RAID level and when each particular level is appropriate to use.

TABLE 2-4   RAID Level Benefits and Requirements

Level	Description	Minimum Number of Disks	Fault Tolerance	Storage Efficiency
RAID 1	Blocks are mirrored. No striping or parity.	2	1 drive	50% or $n/2$
RAID 0	Blocks are striped. No mirror or parity.	2	None	100%
RAID 1+0 (or RAID 10)	Blocks are mirrored and striped.	4	1 drive per span up to maximum of 2	50%
RAID 0+1	Blocks are striped across two disks and mirrored on the third disk.	4	1 drive per span up to a maximum of 2	50%
RAID 5	Blocks are striped. Distributed parity.	3	1 drive	Number of drives −1
RAID 6	Blocks are striped with double distributed parity.	4	2 drives	Number of drives −2

EXAM AT WORK

Microsoft SQL Server RAID Configuration

Recently we were brought in to a customer site to help them plan for a new SQL server installation. The client was a medium-sized company with a fairly large SQL implementation. They wanted to use physical hardware instead of virtualizing their SQL server. Our job was to help them identify what hardware configuration to use for their environment.

How to design the hardware for an SQL server is a complex undertaking and one that is usually misunderstood. The DBAs generally let the system administrators design the server and the disk arrays, which is a common mistake. Setting up disk arrays for an SQL server is much different than doing it for a file or print server. A firm understanding of the various RAID levels and the advantages of each is of paramount importance, because misconfigured RAID levels can have a massive impact on the performance of an SQL server.

For this particular customer we recommended that they place the operating system on a RAID 1 (mirror) array. The client wanted to put the operating system on a RAID 5 array, which is usually a mistake in this type of environment. The operating system does not require a RAID 5 array and in fact its performance is reduced on a RAID 5 array because of the constant writing of the page file. It is typically not desirable to have the operating system calculating parity for data that is only going to be on the disk for a short period

of time. For that reason we recommended a RAID 1 array for their operating system.

The final three considerations for RAID levels and SQL servers were the log files, the database files, and the tempdb files. First we needed to break down the system databases. Each of the system databases had slightly different requirements. Since most of the databases were read requests and not write requests, RAID 5 was recommended for the system databases. Next we needed to evaluate the user database files. Most of the client's databases were read requests with very few write requests. Because of this, we recommended using RAID 5. (If the user database files are written at a high rate, then RAID 0+1 or RAID 1+0 would most likely be recommended.) Then we needed to evaluate the transaction logs. Because transaction logs are very write intensive, they should usually be placed on a RAID 1 or RAID 0+1 array, depending on the organization's cost structure. Since our client was looking to save cost on storage, RAID 1 was recommended. The last consideration was the tempdb placement. Again, tempdb is very write intensive, so we recommended the RAID 1 array.

From this example you can see that deciding which RAID level to use requires careful consideration and is critical to the overall performance of an application.

CERTIFICATION OBJECTIVE 2.04

File System Types

After choosing a disk type and configuration, an organization needs to be able to store data on those disks. The file system is responsible for storing, retrieving, and updating a set of files on a disk. It is the software that accepts the commands from the operating system to read and write data to the disk. It is responsible for how the files are named and stored on the disk.

The file system is also responsible for managing access to the file's metadata ("the data about the data") and the data itself and for overseeing the relationships to other files and file attributes. It also manages how much available space the disk has. The file system is responsible for the reliability of the data on the disk and for organizing that data in an efficient manner. It organizes the files and directories and tracks which areas of the drive belong to a particular file and which areas are not currently being utilized.

This section explains the different file types that will be covered on the CompTIA Cloud+ exam. Each file type has its own set of benefits and scenarios under which its use is appropriate.

Unix File System

The Unix file system (UFS) is the primary file system for Unix and Unix-based operating systems. UFS uses a hierarchical file system structure where the highest level of the directory is called the root (/, pronounced "slash") and all other directories span from that root. Under the root directory, files are organized into subdirectories and can have any name the user wishes to assign. All files on a Unix system are related to one another in a parent-child relationship, and they all share a common parental link to the top of the hierarchy.

Figure 2-7 shows an example of the structure of a Unix file system. The root directory has three subdirectories called bin, tmp, and users. The user's directory has two subdirectories of its own called Nate and Scott.

Extended File System

The extended file system (EXT) is the first file system created specifically for Linux. The metadata and file structure is based on the Unix file system. EXT is the default file system for most Linux distributions. EXT is currently on version 4, or EXT4,

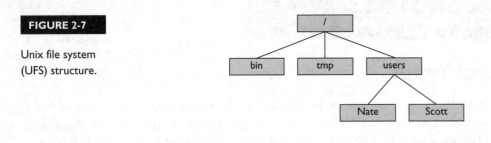

FIGURE 2-7

Unix file system
(UFS) structure.

which was introduced in 2008 and supports a larger file and file system size. EXT4 is backward compatible with EXT3 and EXT2, which allows for mounting an EXT3 and EXT2 partition as an EXT4 partition.

File Allocation Table

The file allocation table (FAT) file system is a legacy file system that provides good performance but does not deliver the same reliability and scalability as some of the newer file systems. The FAT file system is still supported by most operating systems for backward compatibility reasons but has mostly been replaced by NTFS (more on this in a moment) as the preferred file system for the Microsoft operating system. If a user has a drive running a FAT32 file system partition, however, they can connect it to a computer running Windows 7 and retrieve the data from that drive because Windows 7 still supports the FAT32 file system.

The FAT file system is used by a variety of removable media, including floppy disks, solid state memory cards, flash memory cards, and portable devices. The FAT file system does not support the advanced features of NTFS like encryption, VSS, and compression.

New Technology File System

The new technology file system (NTFS) is a proprietary file system developed by Microsoft to support the Windows operating systems. It first became available with Windows NT 3.1 and has been used on all of Microsoft's operating systems since then. NTFS was Microsoft's replacement for the FAT file system. NTFS has many advantages over FAT, including improved performance and reliability, larger partition sizes, and enhanced security.

Starting with version 1.2, NTFS added support for file compression, which is ideal for files that are written to on an infrequent basis. However, compression can lead to slower performance when accessing the compressed files; therefore, it is not recommended for .exe or .dll files, or for network shares that contain roaming profiles due to the extra processing required to load roaming profiles.

NTFS version 3.0 added support for volume shadow copy service (VSS), which keeps a historical version of files and folders on an NTFS volume. Shadow copies allow you to restore a file to a previous state without the need for backup software. The VSS creates a copy of the old file as it is writing the new file so the user has access to the previous version of that file. It is best practice to create a shadow copy volume on a separate disk to store the files.

An encrypting file system (EFS) provides an encryption method for any file or folder on an NTFS partition and is transparent to the user. EFS encrypts a file by using a file encryption key (FEK), which is associated with a public key that is tied to the user who encrypted the file. The encrypted data is stored on an alternate location from the encrypted file. To decrypt the file, EFS uses the private key of the user to decrypt the public key that is stored in the file header. If the user loses access to their key, a recovery agent can still access the files. NTFS does not support encrypting and compressing the same file.

Disk quotas allow an administrator to set disk space thresholds for users. This gives an administrator the ability to track the amount of disk space each user is consuming and limit how much disk space each user has access to. The administrator can set a warning threshold and a deny threshold and deny access to the user once they reach this threshold.

Virtual Machine File System

The virtual machine file system (VMFS) is VMware's cluster file system. It is used with VMware ESX server and vSphere and was created to store virtual machine disk images, including virtual machine snapshots. It allows for multiple servers to read and write to the file system simultaneously, while keeping individual virtual machine files locked. VMFS volumes can be logically increased by spanning multiple VMFS volumes together.

Z File System

The Z file system (ZFS) is a combined file system and logical volume manager designed by Sun Microsystems. The ZFS file system provides protection against data corruption and support for high storage capacities. ZFS also provides volume management, snapshots, and continuous integrity checking with automatic repair.

TABLE 2-5	File System Characteristics

File System	Maximum File Size	Maximum Volume Size	Encryption	Resizable Volumes
Unix file system (UFS)	32 PB	1 YB	No	Offline but cannot be shrunk
File allocation table (FAT32)	4 GB	2 TB	No	Offline
New technology file system (NTFS)	16 TB	256 TB	Yes	Online
Virtual machine file system (VMFS)	2 TB	64 TB	No	Offline but cannot be shrunk*
Z file system (ZFS)	16 EB	16 EB	Yes	Online but cannot be shrunk

* Newest version of VMFS allows dynamic resizing but must be supported by the OS for it to be utilized without a reboot or additional sizing tools.

ZFS was created with data integrity as its primary focus. It is designed to protect the user's data against corruption. ZFS is currently the only 128-bit file system. It uses a pooled storage method, which allows space to be used only as it is needed for data storage.

Table 2-5 compares the different file system types, lists their maximum file and volume sizes, and describes some of the benefits of each system.

exam

⚲atch *You should know the maximum volume size of each file system type for the exam. For example, if the requirement is a 3 TB partition for a virtual machine drive, you would not be able to use the FAT file system; you would need to use NTFS.*

CERTIFICATION SUMMARY

Understanding how different storage technologies affect the cloud is a key part of the CompTIA Cloud+ exam. This chapter discussed the various physical types of disk drives and how those drives are connected to systems and each other.

It also covered the concept of tiered storage as well as looking in depth at RAID storage technology. Knowing how to choose the correct RAID level in any given circumstance is important not only for the exam but also for the day-to-day operations of an IT administrator. We closed the chapter by giving an overview of the different file system types and the role proper selection of these systems plays in achieving scalability and reliability. It is critical to have a thorough understanding of all these issues as you prepare for the exam.

KEY TERMS

Use the list below to review the key terms that were discussed in this chapter. The definitions can be found within this chapter and in the glossary.

Solid state drive (SSD)   High-performance storage device that contains no moving parts

Hard disk drive (HDD)   Uses rapidly rotating aluminum or nonmagnetic disks called platters coated with a magnetic material known as ferrous oxide to store and retrieve digital information in any order rather than only being accessible sequentially, as in the case of data on a tape

USB drive   External plug-and-play storage device that is plugged into a computer's USB port and recognized by the computer as a removable drive and assigned a drive letter

Tape   Storage device for saving data by using digital recordings on magnetic tape

Advanced technology attachment (ATA)   Disk drive implementation that integrates the drive and the controller

Fibre Channel (FC)   Technology used to transmit data between computers at data rates of up to 10 Gbps

Serial ATA (SATA)   Used to connect host bus adapters to mass storage devices

Serial attached SCSI (SAS)   Data transfer technology that was designed to replace SCSI and to transfer data to and from storage devices

Integrated drive electronics (IDE)   Integrates the controller and the hard drive, allowing the manufacturer to use proprietary communication and storage methods without any compatibility risks for connecting directly to the motherboard

Small computer system interface (SCSI)   Set of standard electronic interfaces accredited by the American National Standards Institute (ANSI) for connecting and transferring data between computers and storage devices

Hierarchical storage management (HSM)   Allows for automatically moving data among four different tiers of storage

Redundant Array of Independent Disks (RAID)   Storage technology that combines multiple hard disk drives into a single logical unit so that the data can be distributed across the hard disk drives for both improved performance and increased security according to their various RAID levels

Unix file system (UFS)   Primary file system for Unix and Unix-based operating systems that uses a hierarchical file system structure where the highest level of the directory is called the root (/, pronounced "slash") and all other directories span from that root

Extended file system (EXT)   First file system created specifically for Linux where the metadata and file structure is based on the Unix file system

New technology file system (NTFS)   Proprietary file system developed by Microsoft to support the Windows operating systems; it was originally derived from a joint effort with IBM to provide a common OS called OS2, which used the HPFS or High Performance File

Encrypted file system (EFS)   A feature of the NTFS file system that provides file-level encryption

File allocation table (FAT)   Legacy file system used in Microsoft operating systems and is still used today by a variety of removable media

Virtual machine file system (VMFS)   VMware's cluster file system used with VMware ESX server and vSphere and created to store virtual machine disk images, including virtual machine snapshots

Z file system (ZFS)   Combined file system and logical volume manager designed by Sun Microsystems that provides protection against data corruption and support for high-storage capacities

✓ TWO-MINUTE DRILL

Disk Types and Configurations

❏ A solid state drive (SSD) is a high-performance drive that contains no moving parts, uses less power than a traditional hard disk drive (HDD), and provides a faster startup time than an HDD.

❏ A USB drive is an external plug-and-play storage device that provides a quick and easy way to move files between computer systems.

❏ A tape drive reads and writes data to a magnetic tape and differs from an HDD because it provides sequential access rather than random access to data.

❏ HDDs connect to a computer system in a variety of ways, including ATA, SATA, FC, SCSI, SAS, and IDE.

❏ The speed at which an HDD can access data stored on it is critical to the performance of the server and the application it is hosting.

Tiering

❏ Tiered storage allows data to be migrated between storage devices based on performance, availability, cost, and recovery requirements.

❏ There are four levels of tiered storage. The tiers range from tier 1, which is mission-critical data stored on expensive disks, to tier 4, which stores data for compliance requirements on less expensive disks.

Redundant Array of Independent Disks (RAID)

❏ RAID is a storage technology that combines multiple hard disk drives into a single logical unit to provide increased performance, security, and redundancy.

❏ RAID is implemented using either software RAID or hardware RAID via a RAID controller.

❏ RAID 1, or mirroring, uses two disks and provides data protection without parity or striping.

❏ RAID 0 requires two disks and provides increased performance without redundancy.

❏ RAID 1+0 requires four disks and incorporates the speed advantage of RAID 0 and the redundancy advantage of RAID 1.

❏ RAID 5 is one of the most common RAID implementations and uses three disks to provide block-level striping for performance and distributed parity for data protection.

❏ RAID 6 is an extension of RAID 5 that requires four disks because it uses two parity blocks distributed across all the disks.

File System Types

❏ The file system is responsible for storing, retrieving, and updating files on a disk.

❏ UFS is the file system that is predominantly used in Unix-based computers.

❏ The EXT file system is the first file system created specifically for Linux.

❏ FAT is a legacy file system that provides good performance but without the scalability and reliability of newer file systems.

❏ NTFS was developed by Microsoft to replace FAT and provides improved performance and reliability, larger partition sizes, and enhanced security.

❏ VMFS is VMware's cluster file system and is used with ESX server and vSphere.

❏ ZFS was developed by Sun Microsystems and provides protection against data corruption with larger storage capacities.

SELF TEST

The following questions will help you measure your understanding of the material presented in this chapter.

Disk Types and Configurations

1. A(n) _____ is a storage device that has no moving parts.
   A. HDD
   B. SSD
   C. Tape
   D. SCSI

2. Which type of storage device would be used primarily for off-site storage and archiving?
   A. HDD
   B. SSD
   C. Tape
   D. SCSI

3. You have been given a drive space requirement of 2 terabytes for a production file server. Which type of disk would you recommended for this project if cost is a primary concern?
   A. SSD
   B. Tape
   C. HDD
   D. VLAN

4. Which of the following storage device interface types is the most difficult to configure?
   A. IDE
   B. SAS
   C. SATA
   D. SCSI

5. If price is not a factor, which type of storage device interface would you recommend for connecting to a corporate SAN?
   A. IDE
   B. SCSI
   C. SATA
   D. FC

Tiering

6. Which data tier would you recommend for a mission-critical database that needs to be highly available all the time?
   A. Tier 1
   B. Tier 2
   C. Tier 3
   D. Tier 4

7. Which term describes the ability of an organization to store data based on performance, cost, and availability?
   A. RAID
   B. Tiered storage
   C. SSD
   D. Tape drive

8. Which data tier would you recommend for data that is financial in nature, is not accessed on a daily basis, and is archived for tax purposes?
   A. Tier 1
   B. Tier 2
   C. Tier 3
   D. Tier 4

Redundant Array of Independent Disks (RAID)

9. What RAID level would be used for a database file that requires minimum write requests to the database, a large amount of read requests to the database, and fault tolerance for the database?
   A. RAID 10
   B. RAID 1
   C. RAID 5
   D. RAID 0

10. Which of the following statements can be considered a benefit of using RAID for storage solutions?
    A. It is more expensive than other storage solutions that do not include RAID.
    B. It provides degraded performance, scalability, and reliability.
    C. It provides superior performance, improved resiliency, and lower costs.
    D. It is complex to set up and maintain.

11. True or False. Even with the proper RAID configuration an organization should still have an appropriate backup plan in place in case of a failure.
   A. True
   B. False

File System Types

12. Which of the following file systems is used primarily for Unix-based operating systems?
   A. NTFS
   B. FAT
   C. VMFS
   D. UFS

13. Which of the following file systems was designed to protect against data corruption and is a 128-bit file system?
   A. NTFS
   B. UFS
   C. ZFS
   D. FAT

14. The following file system was designed to replace the FAT file system:
   A. NTFS
   B. ZFS
   C. EXT
   D. UFS

15. Which of the following file systems was the first to be designed specifically for Linux?
   A. FAT
   B. NTFS
   C. UFS
   D. EXT

SELF TEST ANSWERS

Disk Types and Configurations

1. A(n) _____ is a storage device that has no moving parts.
   A. HDD
   B. SSD
   C. Tape
   D. SCSI

   ☑ **B.** A solid state drive is a drive that has no moving parts.
   ☒ **A, C,** and **D** are incorrect. A hard disk drive has platters that rotate. A tape drive writes data to a magnetic tape. SCSI is an interface type.

2. Which type of storage device would be used primarily for off-site storage and archiving?
   A. HDD
   B. SSD
   C. Tape
   D. SCSI

   ☑ **C.** Tape storage is good for off-site storage and archiving because it is less expensive than other storage types.
   ☒ **A, B,** and **D** are incorrect. HDD and SSD have different advantages and would normally not be used for off-site or archiving of data. SCSI is an interface type.

3. You have been given a drive space requirement of 2 terabytes for a production file server. Which type of disk would you recommended for this project if cost is a primary concern?
   A. SSD
   B. Tape
   C. HDD
   D. VLAN

   ☑ **C.** You should recommend using an HDD because of the large size requirement. An HDD would be considerably cheaper than an SSD. Also, since it is a file share the faster boot time provided by an SSD is not a factor.
   ☒ **A, B,** and **D** are incorrect. While an SSD can work in this situation, the fact that cost is the primary concern rules it out. Although tape storage is considered cheap, it is not fast enough to support the requirements. VLAN is not a type of storage.

4. Which of the following storage device interface types is the most difficult to configure?

    A. IDE

    B. SAS

    C. SATA

    D. SCSI

> ☑ **D.** SCSI is relatively difficult to configure as the drives must be configured with a device ID and the bus has to be terminated.
>
> ☒ **A, B,** and **C** are incorrect. All of these interface types are relatively easy to configure.

5. If price is not a factor, which type of storage device interface would you recommend for connecting to a corporate SAN?

    A. IDE

    B. SCSI

    C. SATA

    D. FC

> ☑ **D.** Fibre Channel delivers the fastest connectivity method with speeds of up to 16 Gbps, but it is more expensive than the other interface types. If price is not a factor, FC should be the recommendation for connecting to a SAN.
>
> ☒ **A, B,** and **C** are incorrect. While IDE is the least expensive of the group, it does not deliver the speed that FC would. SCSI would be a good choice if price were a limitation. Since price is not a limiting factor in this case, FC would be the better choice. SATA is similar to SCSI, as it delivers a viable option when price is the primary concern for connecting to a SAN. Since price is not a factor, FC is the better choice.

Tiering

6. Which data tier would you recommend for a mission-critical database that needs to be highly available all the time?

    A. Tier 1

    B. Tier 2

    C. Tier 3

    D. Tier 4

☑ **A.** Tier 1 data is defined as data that is mission-critical, highly available, and secure data.

☒ **B, C,** and **D** are incorrect. Tier 2 data is not mission-critical data and does not require the same response time as tier 1. Tier 3 data is data that is not accessed on a daily basis. Tier 4 data is used for archiving and is kept for compliance purposes.

7. Which term describes the ability of an organization to store data based on performance, cost, and availability?
   A. RAID
   B. Tiered storage
   C. SSD
   D. Tape drive

☑ **B.** Tiered storage refers to the process of moving data between storage devices based on performance, cost, and availability.

☒ **A, C,** and **D** are incorrect. RAID is the process of making data highly available and redundant. It does not allow you to move data between storage devices. SSD and tape drive are types of storage devices.

8. Which data tier would you recommend for data that is financial in nature, is not accessed on a daily basis, and is archived for tax purposes?
   A. Tier 1
   B. Tier 2
   C. Tier 3
   D. Tier 4

☑ **C.** Tier 3 storage would be for financial data that you want to keep for tax purposes and is not needed on a day-to-day basis.

☒ **A, B,** and **D** are incorrect. Tier 1 storage is used for data that is mission-critical, highly available, and secure data. Tier 2 data is not mission-critical data but, like tier 1, is considerably more expensive than tier 3. Tier 4 data is used for archiving data and is kept for compliance purposes.

Redundant Array of Independent Disks (RAID)

9. What RAID level would be used for a database file that requires minimum write requests to the database, a large amount of read requests to the database, and fault tolerance for the database?

A. RAID 10
B. RAID 1
C. RAID 5
D. RAID 0

> ☑ **C.** RAID 5 is best suited for a database or system drive that has a lot of read requests and very few write requests.
>
> ☒ **A, B,** and **D** are incorrect. RAID 10 would be used for a database that requires a lot of write requests and needs high performance. RAID 1 is used when performance and reliability are more important than storage capacity and is generally used for an operating system partition. RAID 0 provides no fault tolerance and would not be recommended.

10. Which of the following statements can be considered a benefit of using RAID for storage solutions?

A. It is more expensive than other storage solutions that do not include RAID.
B. It provides degraded performance, scalability, and reliability.
C. It provides superior performance, improved resiliency, and lower costs.
D. It is complex to set up and maintain.

> ☑ **C.** Using RAID can provide all these benefits over conventional hard disk storage devices.
>
> ☒ **A, B,** and **D** are incorrect. RAID can be a more expensive solution compared to conventional storage because of the loss of storage space to make up for redundancy. This is not a benefit of RAID. RAID does not provide degraded performance, scalability, or reliability. RAID can be more complex to configure and maintain, so this would not be a benefit of implementing RAID.

11. True or False. Even with the proper RAID configuration an organization should still have an appropriate backup plan in place in case of a failure.

A. True
B. False

> ☑ **A.** A proper backup plan is recommended even if you have implemented RAID. You may need to store the data off-site, or the machine itself may have a failure. Also, it is possible, although unlikely, that all drives can fail at the same time.
>
> ☒ **B** is incorrect. Although RAID does provide redundancy, it does not allow for off-site storage. Because you need some form of off-site storage, having no backup plan in place is not recommended.

File System Types

12. Which of the following file systems is used primarily for Unix-based operating systems?

A. NTFS
B. FAT
C. VMFS
D. UFS

☑ **D.** UFS is the primary file system in a Unix-based computer.

☒ **A, B,** and **C** are incorrect. NTFS is a proprietary Microsoft file system and is used on Microsoft-based operating systems. FAT is a legacy file system used to support older operating systems. VMFS is used for VMware's cluster file system.

13. Which of the following file systems was designed to protect against data corruption and is a 128-bit file system?

A. NTFS
B. UFS
C. ZFS
D. FAT

☑ **C.** ZFS was developed by Sun Microsystems and is focused on protecting the user's data against corruption. It is currently the only 128-bit file system.

☒ **A, B,** and **D** are incorrect. The other file systems were not designed for protecting against data corruption and are not 128-bit file systems.

14. The following file system was designed to replace the FAT file system:

A. NTFS
B. ZFS
C. EXT
D. UFS

☑ **A.** NTFS was designed by Microsoft as a replacement for FAT.

☒ **B, C,** and **D** are incorrect. The other file system types were designed for operating systems other than Microsoft Windows.

15. Which of the following file systems was the first to be designed specifically for Linux?
   A. FAT
   B. NTFS
   C. UFS
   D. EXT

☑ **D.** EXT was the first file system designed specifically for Linux.

☒ **A, B,** and **C** are incorrect. These file systems were not designed for Linux and are used primarily in other operating systems.

3

Storage
Networking

S torage is the foundation of a successful infrastructure. The traditional method of storing data is changing with the emergence of cloud storage. Servers and storage that were once sold separately are now being bundled together in a cloud storage environment, sometimes referred to as Storage as a Service. Organizations can now purchase storage that connects directly to a blade server, making the need for a separate storage network obsolete.

Understanding the advantages and disadvantages of each storage technology is a key concept for an IT administrator. It is their responsibility to help the organization understand the risks and the benefits of moving to cloud storage.

CERTIFICATION OBJECTIVE 3.01

Storage Technologies

Storage technologies are the instruments that are used to record and play back the bits and bytes that the compute resources process to provide their functions for delivering applications. Just as there are many different environments in which computers are used, there are many types of storage to accommodate the needs of each of those environments based on factors such as cost, performance, and data security. Figure 3-1 displays a graphical comparison of the three storage technologies DAS, NAS, and SAN, which we explore in more detail directly.

FIGURE 3-1

DAS, NAS, and SAN: Three major storage technologies.

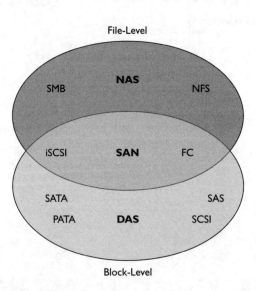

Direct Attached Storage (DAS)

Direct attached storage (DAS) is the type of storage that most administrators are first exposed to. Some storage protocols that are used to access these storage devices are IDE, SATA, and SCSI. This is the storage technology that is most frequently utilized by desktops, laptops, and single or small server environments. It is the least expensive storage option available for online storage. As its name suggests, this type of storage is directly attached to the computer that utilizes it and does not have to traverse any sort of network to be accessed. Direct attached storage is made available only to that local computer and cannot be used as shared storage. DAS has the ability to provide both block-level and file-level access to data for the clients using the operating system. As a result, DAS is typically limited in its ability to provide high-availability solutions.

Storage Area Network (SAN)

A storage area network (SAN) is a high-performance option that is employed by many data centers as a high-end storage solution with data security capabilities and a very high price tag to go along with it. A SAN is a storage device that resides on its own network and provides block-level access to computers that are attached to it. The disks that are part of a SAN are divided into subdivisions called logical unit numbers, or LUNs, that provide the block-level access to specified computers. LUNs are often similar in theory to a disk drive. SANs are capable of very complex configurations, allowing administrators to divide storage resources and access permissions very granularly and with very high performance capabilities. Because of the complex options available in SANs, because each SAN solution is vendor specific, and because of the critical nature of their deployment, SANs require specialized training to support them effectively, along with constant monitoring and attention. All of these administrative requirements add to the cost of deploying a SAN solution.

SANs are also able to provide shared storage or access to the same data at the same time by multiple computers. This is critical for enabling high availability in data center environments that employ virtualization solutions requiring access to the same virtual machine files by multiple hosts. Shared storage allows them to perform migrations of virtual machines without any downtime, as discussed in more detail in Chapter 5.

Computers require a special adapter to communicate with a SAN, much like they need a network card to access their data networks. The network that a SAN utilizes is referred to as a fabric and can be comprised of fiber-optic cables, Ethernet adapters, or specialized SCSI cables. A host bus adapter (HBA) is usually a PCI add-on card that can be inserted into a free spot in a host and then connected either to the SAN disk array directly or, as is more often the case, to a storage area networking switch. Another option is to use a virtual HBA, which emulates a physical HBA and allocates portions of the physical HBA to virtual machines. Storage data is transferred from the disk array over the storage area network to the host via the HBA, which prepares it for processing by the host's compute resources. Each HBA has a unique World Wide Name (WWN), which is an 8-byte identifier similar to an Ethernet MAC address on a network card. There are two types of WWNs on an HBA: a node WWN (WWNN), which can be shared by either some or all of the ports of a device, and a port WWN (WWPN), which is unique to each port.

In addition to SANs, organizations have the ability to use a virtual storage area network (VSAN), which can consolidate separate physical SAN fabrics into a single larger fabric, allowing for easier management while maintaining security. A VSAN allows for identical Fibre Channel IDs to be used at the same time within different VSANs. VSANs allow for user-specified IDs that are used to identify the VSAN.

HBAs usually have the capability to increase performance significantly by off-loading the processing required for the host to consume the storage data without having to utilize its own processor cycles. This means that an HBA enables greater efficiency for its host by allowing its processor to focus on running the functions of its operating system and applications instead of on storage I/O.

Network Attached Storage (NAS)

Network attached storage (NAS) offers an alternative to storage area networks for providing network-based shared storage options. NAS devices utilize TCP/IP networks for sending and receiving storage traffic in addition to data traffic. A NAS provides file-level data storage that can be connected to and accessed from a TCP/IP network. Because NAS utilizes TCP/IP networks instead of a separate SAN fabric, many IT organizations are able to utilize existing infrastructure components to support both their data and storage networks. This use of common infrastructure can greatly cut costs while providing similar shared storage capabilities. Expenses are reduced for a couple of reasons:

- Data networking infrastructure costs significantly less than storage networking infrastructure.

- Shared configurations between data and storage networking infrastructure enable administrators to support both with no additional training or specialized skill sets.

One way to differentiate a NAS from a SAN is that a NAS appears to the client operating system as a file server, whereas a SAN appears to the client operating system as a disk (typically a LUN) that is visible in disk management utilities. This allows a NAS to use Universal Naming Convention addressable storage. Network attached storage leverages protocols such as TCP/IP and iSCSI, both of which are discussed later in this chapter in more detail.

e**x**a**m**

wa**t**c**h**   *Storage area networking (SAN) provides much better performance than network attached storage (NAS).*

CERTIFICATION OBJECTIVE 3.02

Access Protocols and Applications

Now that you have learned about the various storage technologies that are available, we now turn our attention to the access protocols and applications that utilize these technologies to transmit, shape, and prioritize storage information between hosts and their storage devices.

Fibre Channel (FC)

Fibre Channel is a technology for transmitting data between computers at data rates of up to 10 Gbps. IT organizations have made Fibre Channel the technology of choice for interconnecting storage controllers and drives when architecting infrastructures that have high performance requirements. Fibre Channel architecture is comprised of many interconnected individual units, which are called nodes. Each of these nodes has multiple ports, and these ports connect the nodes in a storage unit architecture using one of three different interconnection topologies: point-to-point, arbitrated loop, and switched fabric. Fibre Channel also has the capability to transmit over long distances. When deployed using optical fiber, it can transmit between devices up to about six miles apart. While Fibre Channel is the transmission medium, it still utilizes SCSI or IP riding on top of it for its commands.

e**x**a**m**

wa**t**c**h**   *Fibre Channel is deployed when the highest levels of performance are required.*

Fibre Channel Protocol

The SCSI commands that ride atop the Fibre Channel transport are sent via the Fibre Channel protocol (FCP). In order to increase performance, this protocol takes advantage of hardware that can utilize protocol off-load engines (POEs). This assists the host by offloading processing cycles from the CPU, thereby improving system performance. The frames in the Fibre Channel Protocol consist of three components: an encapsulating header called the start-of-frame (SOF) marker, the data frame itself, and the end-of-frame (EOF) marker. This encapsulated structure enables the FC frames to be transported across other protocols, such as TCP, if desired.

Fibre Channel over Ethernet (FCoE)

Fibre Channel over Ethernet (FCoE) enables the transport of Fibre Channel traffic over Ethernet networks by encapsulating Fibre Channel frames over Ethernet networks. Fibre Channel over Ethernet is able to utilize the new high-speed Ethernet, and can fully utilize 10 Gbit Ethernet networks (or higher speeds) while still preserving the FC protocol.

Ethernet

Ethernet is an established standard for connecting computers to a local area network (LAN). Ethernet is a relatively inexpensive and reasonably fast LAN technology, with speeds ranging from 10 MB/s to 10 GB/s. Because it enables high-speed data transmission and is relatively inexpensive, Ethernet has become ubiquitous in IT organizations and the Internet. Ethernet technology operates at the physical and data link layers of the OSI model (layers 1 and 2). Although it is capable of high speeds, it is limited by both the length and the type of cables over which it travels. The Ethernet standard divides its data traffic into groupings called frames. These frames are utilized by storage protocols to deliver their data from one point to another, such as from a NAS device to a server.

Internet Protocol (IP)

Internet protocol (IP) is a protocol that operates at the network layer of the OSI model (layer 3) and provides unique addresses and traffic routing capabilities. Computers utilizing the Internet protocol are addressed using dotted decimal notation with four octets divided by dots. As the name suggests, IP is the protocol that enables the Internet. Like Ethernet networks, it is ubiquitous in IT departments and provides a proven and relatively inexpensive and well-understood technology on which to build storage networks.

Internet Small Computer System Interface (iSCSI)

iSCSI is a protocol that utilizes serialized IP packets to transmit SCSI commands across IP networks and enables servers to access remote disks as if they were locally attached. iSCSI "initiator" software running on the requesting entity converts disk block-level I/O into SCSI commands that are then serialized into IP packets that traverse any IP network to their targets. At the destination storage device, the iSCSI packets are interpreted by the storage device array into the appropriate commands for the disks it contains. Figure 3-2 shows an example of how multiple servers can leverage iSCSI to connect to shared storage over an IP network.

iSCSI is limited by the transmission speeds of the Ethernet network it travels over; when administrators design iSCSI networks, they should pay close attention to the design so that the storage traffic is isolated from the data network traffic. Although its performance is not as high as Fibre Channel SAN, iSCSI on a NAS device can be an inexpensive entry into shared storage for IT departments or a training ground using repurposed equipment for administrators who want to get hands-on experience with storage networking.

FIGURE 3-2

Using iSCSI over an IP network.

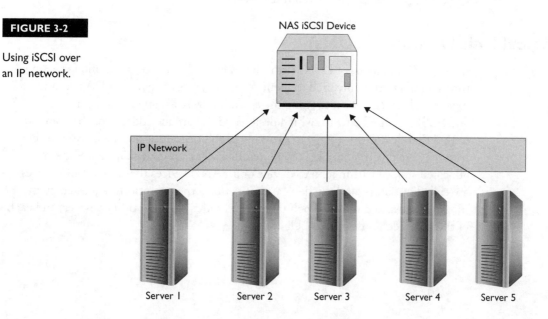

on the
Job

While working at a small IT shop that wanted to explore the use of virtualization, our focus was to create some solutions for our customers that promised higher availability. We needed to get some shared storage that we could use to enable some of the automatic migration and performance tuning capabilities of our virtualization platform. We didn't, however, have much of a budget to spend on research and development. We wound up repurposing a gigabit Ethernet switch, some category 6 Ethernet cable, and a couple of retired servers to set up our test environment with very little cost. Using the built-in capabilities of the operating system and some open-source software, we had everything we needed to build out an entire lab and evaluate the capabilities of our proposed solutions.

CERTIFICATION OBJECTIVE 3.03

Storage Provisioning

Now that you understand the technologies, protocols, and applications for moving storage data around networks, we will explore the ways in which that data is presented to computers. Data can be made available to computers in a number of ways, with varying degrees of availability and security.

Logical Unit Numbers (LUNs)

Logical unit numbers, or LUNs (introduced earlier), have been around for a long time and were originally used to identify SCSI devices as part of a DAS solution for higher-end servers. Devices along the SCSI bus were assigned a number from 0 to 7 and SCSI 2 utilized 0 to 15, which designated the unique address for the computer to find that device. In storage networking LUNs operate as unique identifiers, but now they are much more likely to represent a virtual hard disk from a block of allocated storage within a NAS device or a SAN. Devices that request I/O process are called initiators, and the devices that perform the operations requested by the initiators are called targets. Each target can hold up to eight other devices, and each of those devices is assigned a LUN.

Network Shares

Network shares are storage resources that are made available across the network and appear as if they are a resource on the local machine. Traditionally network shares are implemented using the server message block (SMB) protocol when using Microsoft products. They are typically in the form of NFS in Linux, and they appear as shared folders in both operating systems. Access to these shares happens within an addressable file system as opposed to using block storage.

Zoning and LUN Masking

SANs are designed with high availability and performance in mind. In order to provide the flexibility that system administrators demand for designing solutions that utilize those capabilities, servers need to be able to mount and access any drive on the SAN. This flexible access can create several problems, including disk resource contention and data corruption. To mitigate these problems, storage devices can be isolated and protected on a SAN by utilizing zoning and LUN masking, which allow for dedicating storage devices on the SAN to individual servers.

Zoning controls access from one node to another. It enables isolation of a single server to a group of storage devices or a single storage device, or associates a set of multiple servers with one or more storage devices. Zoning is implemented at the hardware level on Fibre Channel switches and is configured with what is referred to as "hard zoning" on a port basis or "soft zoning" using a World Wide Name (WWN). In Figure 3-3, the fibre switch is controlling access for the red server and the blue

FIGURE 3-3

Zoning using a
Fibre Channel
switch.

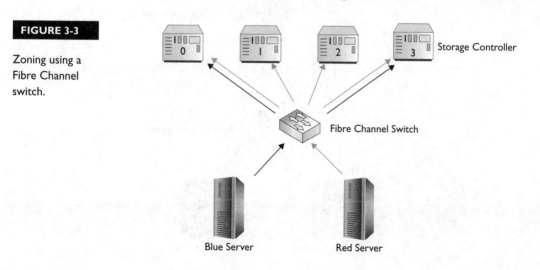

Storage Controller

0   1   2   3

Fibre Channel Switch

Blue Server   Red Server

server to connect to the storage controllers 0–3. It grants access for the blue server to the LUNs on controllers 0 and 3, while the red server is granted access to all LUNs on all storage controllers.

LUN masking is executed at the storage controller level instead of at the switch level. By providing LUN-level access control at the storage controller, the controller itself enforces access policies to the devices. LUN masking provides more detailed security than zoning because LUNs allow for sharing storage at the port level. In Figure 3-4, LUN masking is demonstrated as the blue server is granted access from the storage controller to LUNs 0 and 3, while the red server is granted access to all LUNs.

Multipathing

Whereas zoning and LUN masking are configuration options that limit access to storage resources, multipathing is a way of making data more available or fault tolerant to the computers that need to access it. Multipathing does exactly what its name suggests, in that it creates multiple paths for the computer to reach the

FIGURE 3-4

LUN masking using the storage controller.

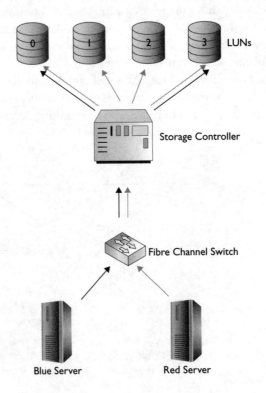

storage resources it is attempting to contact. These multiple paths are created by a combination of hardware and software resources. The hardware resources are multiple network interface cards (NICs) or multiple HBAs deployed to a single computer. These multiple adapters provide options for the software to run in multipath mode, which allows it to use either of the adapters to send traffic over in case one of them were to fail.

Setting up multipathing on the computer, however, is not enough to ensure high availability of the applications designed to run on it. The entire network infrastructure that the data traffic travels upon should be redundant so that a failure of any one component will not interrupt the storage data traffic. This means that in order to implement an effective multipath solution, redundant cabling, switches, routers, and ports on the storage devices must be considered as well. Enabling this kind of availability may be necessary to meet the business requirements of the applications being hosted, but such a configuration can be very expensive.

CERTIFICATION SUMMARY

Storage networking is a key component of the CompTIA Cloud+ exam. Storage is the foundation of a successful infrastructure. Understanding when to use the different storage types is important for optimizing a cloud deployment. For purposes of the exam, you need to know the three major storage technologies presented in this chapter (DAS, SAN, and NAS) and when it is appropriate to use each.

After choosing the proper storage type, an organization must decide how to connect their cloud environment to that storage and how to configure the storage to meet the needs of their cloud deployment. Understanding the benefits of each connection type (FC, FCP, FCoE, Ethernet, IP, and iSCSI) and the use of LUNs and zoning for configuration is required for doing well on the exam.

KEY TERMS

Use the list below to review the key terms that were discussed in this chapter. The definitions can be found within this chapter and in the glossary.

Direct attached storage (DAS)   Storage system that is directly attached to a server or workstation and cannot be used as shared storage

Storage area network (SAN)   Storage device that resides on its own network and provides block-level access to computers that are attached to it

Logical unit numbers (LUNs)   Unique identifier used to identify a logical unit or collection of hard disks in a storage device

Host bus adapter (HBA)   A network card that allows a device to communicate directly with a storage area network (SAN) or a SAN switch

World Wide Name (WWN)   Unique identifier used in storage technologies similar to Ethernet MAC addresses on a network card

Network attached storage (NAS)   Provides file-level data storage to a network over TCP/IP

Fibre Channel   Technology used to transmit data between computers at data rates of up to 10 Gbps

Fibre Channel protocol (FCP)   Transport protocol that transports SCSI commands over a Fibre Channel network

Fibre Channel over Ethernet (FCoE)   Enables the transport of Fibre Channel traffic over Ethernet networks by encapsulating Fibre Channel frames over Ethernet networks

Internet small computer system interface (iSCSI)   The communication protocol that leverages standard IP packets to transmit typical SCSI commands across an IP network; it then translates them back to standard SCSI commands, which enables servers to access remote disks as if they were locally attached

Network shares   Storage resources that are made available across a network and appear as if they are a resource on the local machine

Server message block (SMB)   Network protocol used to provide shared access to files and printers

Zoning   Controls access from one node to another in a storage network and enables isolation of a single server to a group of storage devices or a single storage device

LUN masking   Makes a LUN available to some hosts and unavailable to others

Multipathing   Creates multiple paths for a computer to reach a storage resource

✓ TWO-MINUTE DRILL

Storage Technologies

- ❑ A direct attached storage (DAS) system is a storage system that is directly attached to a server or workstation and does not have a storage network between the two devices.
- ❑ A storage area network (SAN) is a storage device that resides on its own network and provides block-level access to computers that are attached to the SAN.
- ❑ A host bus adapter (HBA) is a special network card that allows a device to communicate with a SAN directly or a SAN switch.
- ❑ Network attached storage (NAS) is a file-level data storage device that is connected to a computer network and provides data access to a group of clients.
- ❑ A SAN can provide better performance than a NAS.

Access Protocols and Applications

- ❑ Fibre Channel (FC) can be used to connect servers to shared storage devices with speeds of up to 10 Gbps.
- ❑ Fibre Channel frames can be encapsulated over Ethernet networks by utilizing Fibre Channel over Ethernet (FCoE).
- ❑ Ethernet is an established standard for connecting computers to a local area network (LAN). It is relatively inexpensive and can provide data speeds ranging from 10 MB/s to 10 GB/s.
- ❑ Internet small computer system interface (iSCSI) utilizes serialized IP packets to transmit SCSI commands across IP networks, and enables servers to access remote disks as if they were locally attached.

Storage Provisioning

- ❑ A logical unit number (LUN) is a unique identifier assigned to an individual hard disk device or collection of devices (a "logical unit") as addressed by the SCSI, iSCSI, or FC protocol.

❏ A LUN identifies a specific logical unit, which can be a portion of a hard disk drive, an entire hard disk, or several hard disks in a storage device like a SAN.

❏ A network share provides storage resources that are accessible over the network.

❏ Multipathing creates multiple paths for a computer to reach storage resources, providing a level of redundancy for accessing a storage device.

SELF TEST

The following questions will help you measure your understanding of the material presented in this chapter.

Storage Technologies

1. Which type of storage system is directly attached to a computer and does not use a storage network between the computer and the storage system?
   A. NAS
   B. SAN
   C. DAS
   D. Network share

2. Which of the following characteristics describe a network attached storage (NAS) deployment?
   A. Requires expensive equipment to support
   B. Requires specialized skillsets for administrators to support
   C. Delivers the best performance of any networked storage technologies
   D. Provides great value by utilizing existing infrastructure

3. Which statement would identify the primary difference between a NAS and a DAS?
   A. A NAS cannot be shared and accessed by multiple computers.
   B. A DAS provides fault tolerance.
   C. A DAS does not connect to networked storage devices.
   D. A NAS uses an HBA and a DAS does not.

4. Which storage type can take advantage of Universal Naming Convention addressable storage?
   A. SAN
   B. NAS
   C. DAS
   D. SATA

5. Which storage type provides block-level storage?
   A. SAN
   B. NAS
   C. DAS
   D. SATA

6. Which of the following connects a server and a SAN and improves performance?
    A. NIC teaming
    B. Host bus adapter (HBA)
    C. Ethernet
    D. SCSI

Access Protocols and Applications

7. Which of the following protocols allows Fibre Channel to be transmitted over Ethernet?
    A. HBA
    B. FCoE
    C. iSCSI
    D. SAN

8. Which of the following is considered a SAN protocol?
    A. FCP
    B. IDE
    C. SSD
    D. DTE

9. Which of the following allows you to connect a server to storage devices with speeds of 10 Gbps?
    A. Ethernet
    B. iSCSI
    C. Fibre Channel
    D. SAS

10. Which of the following uses IP networks that enable servers to access remote disks as if they were locally attached?
    A. SAS
    B. SATA
    C. iSCSI
    D. Fibre Channel

Storage Provisioning

11. Warren is a systems administrator working in a corporate data center, and he has been tasked with hiding storage resources from a server that does not need access to the storage device hosting the storage resources. What can you configure on the storage controller to accomplish this task?
    A. Zoning
    B. LUN masking
    C. Port masking
    D. VLANs

12. Which of the following would increase availability from a virtualization host to a storage device?
    A. Trunking
    B. Multipathing
    C. Link aggregation
    D. VLANs

13. Which of the following allows you to provide security to the data contained in a storage array?
    A. Trunking
    B. LUN masking
    C. LUN provisioning
    D. Multipathing

SELF TEST ANSWERS

Storage Technologies

1. Which type of storage system is directly attached to a computer and does not use a storage network between the computer and the storage system?
   A. NAS
   B. SAN
   C. DAS
   D. Network share

   ☑ **C.** A DAS is a storage system that directly attaches to a server or workstation without a storage network in between the devices.

   ☒ **A, B,** and **D** are incorrect. A NAS provides file-level storage that is connected to a network and supplies data access to a group of devices. A SAN is a dedicated network and provides access to block-level storage. A network share is a piece of information on a computer that can be accessed remotely from another computer.

2. Which of the following characteristics describe a network attached storage (NAS) deployment?
   A. Requires expensive equipment to support
   B. Requires specialized skillsets for administrators to support
   C. Delivers the best performance of any networked storage technologies
   D. Provides great value by utilizing existing infrastructure

   ☑ **D.** Network attached storage can utilize existing Ethernet infrastructures to deliver a low-cost solution with good performance.

   ☒ **A, B,** and **C** are incorrect. Expensive and often proprietary hardware and software along with systems administrators with specialized skillsets are required to run storage area networks. Storage area networks, although more expensive to build and support, provide the best possible performance for storage networking.

3. Which statement would identify the primary difference between a NAS and a DAS?
   A. A NAS cannot be shared and accessed by multiple computers.
   B. A DAS provides fault tolerance.
   C. A DAS does not connect to networked storage devices.
   D. A NAS uses an HBA and a DAS does not.

☑ **C.** A DAS is a storage system that directly attaches to a server or workstation without a storage network in between the devices.

☒ **A, B,** and **D** are incorrect. A NAS can be shared and accessed by multiple computers over a network. A DAS would not provide fault tolerance since it is connected to a single server, and neither NAS nor DAS technologies utilize HBAs as a part of their solution.

4. Which storage type can take advantage of Universal Naming Convention addressable storage?
   A. SAN
   B. NAS
   C. DAS
   D. SATA

☑ **B.** A NAS appears to the client operating system as a file server, which allows it to use Universal Naming Convention addressable storage.

☒ **A, C,** and **D** are incorrect. A DAS is directly attached to a server and is accessed directly from an indexed filesystem. A SAN only provides storage at a block level, and SATA is an interface technology, not a storage type.

5. Which storage type provides block-level storage?
   A. SAN
   B. NAS
   C. DAS
   D. SATA

☑ **A.** A SAN is a storage device that resides on its own network and provides block-level access to computers that are attached to it.

☒ **B, C,** and **D** are incorrect. A NAS provides file-level storage. A DAS is not accessible over a storage network. SATA is an interface technology, not a storage type.

6. Which of the following connects a server and a SAN and improves performance?
   A. NIC teaming
   B. Host bus adapter (HBA)
   C. Ethernet
   D. SCSI

☑ **B.** An HBA card connects a server to a storage device and improves performance by off-loading the processing required for the host to consume the storage data without having to utilize its own processor cycles.

☒ **A, C,** and **D** are incorrect. NIC teaming teams multiple NICs into a single interface and provides redundancy. Ethernet and SCSI would not improve performance because they cannot off-load the processing for the host computer to connect to the storage device.

Access Protocols and Applications

7. Which of the following protocols allows Fibre Channel to be transmitted over Ethernet?
   A. HBA
   B. FCoE
   C. iSCSI
   D. SAN

☑ **B.** Fibre Channel over Ethernet (FCoE) enables the transport of Fibre Channel traffic over Ethernet networks by encapsulating Fibre Channel frames over Ethernet networks.

☒ **A, C,** and **D** are incorrect. iSCSI is a protocol that utilizes serialized IP packets to transmit SCSI commands across IP networks and enables servers to access remote disks as if they were locally attached. A SAN is a storage technology and an HBA is an adapter used to improve the performance of a SAN. They are not protocols.

8. Which of the following is considered a SAN protocol?
   A. FCP
   B. IDE
   C. SSD
   D. DTE

☑ **A.** The Fibre Channel protocol is a transport protocol that transports SCSI commands over a Fibre Channel network. These networks are used exclusively to transport data in FC frames between storage area networks and the HBAs attached to servers.

☒ **B, C,** and **D** are incorrect. IDE is used to connect devices to a computer. SSD is a type of hard drive. DTE stands for "data terminal equipment." A computer is an example of DTE.

9. Which of the following allows you to connect a server to storage devices with speeds of 10 Gbps?
   A. Ethernet
   B. iSCSI
   C. Fibre Channel
   D. SAS

> ☑ **C.** You can use Fibre Channel (FC) to connect servers to shared storage devices with speeds of up to 10 Gbps.
> ☒ **A, B,** and **D** are incorrect. While Ethernet can run at 10 Gbps, it is not normally used to directly connect to a storage device like Fibre Channel.

10. Which of the following uses IP networks that enable servers to access remote disks as if they were locally attached?
   A. SAS
   B. SATA
   C. iSCSI
   D. Fibre Channel

> ☑ **C.** iSCSI utilizes serialized IP packets to transmit SCSI commands across IP networks and enables servers to access remote disks as if they were locally attached.
> ☒ **A, B,** and **D** are incorrect. SAS and SATA do not allow you to connect to remote disks as if they were locally attached to the system. Fibre Channel utilizes the Fibre Channel protocol to transmit data packets to SANs across a fabric of fiber optic cables, switches, and HBAs.

Storage Provisioning

11. Warren is a systems administrator working in a corporate data center, and he has been tasked with hiding storage resources from a server that does not need access to the storage device hosting the storage resources. What can you configure on the storage controller to accomplish this task?
   A. Zoning
   B. LUN masking
   C. Port masking
   D. VLANs

☑ **B.** LUN masking is executed at the storage controller level instead of at the switch level. By providing LUN-level access control at the storage controller, the controller itself enforces access policies to the devices, making it more secure. This is the reason that physical access to the same device storing the LUNs remains "untouchable" by the entity using it.

☒ **A, C,** and **D** are incorrect. LUN masking provides more detailed security than zoning because LUNs allows for sharing storage at the port level. Port masking occurs at the switch level instead of the controller, and VLANs are virtualized local area networks that are also not modified at the controller.

12. Which of the following would increase availability from a virtualization host to a storage device?
    A. Trunking
    B. Multipathing
    C. Link aggregation
    D. VLANs

☑ **B.** Multipathing creates multiple paths for the computer to reach the storage resources it is attempting to contact, improving fault tolerance and possibly speed.

☒ **A, C,** and **D** are incorrect. Trunking provides network access to multiple clients by sharing a set of network lines instead of providing them individually. Link aggregation combines multiple network connections in parallel to increase throughput. VLANs are virtual local area networks that do not have any effect on increasing availability to storage resources.

13. Which of the following allows you to provide security to the data contained in a storage array?
    A. Trunking
    B. LUN masking
    C. LUN provisioning
    D. Multipathing

☑ **B.** LUN masking enforces access policies to storage resources, and these storage policies make sure that the data on those devices is protected from unauthorized access.

☒ **A, C,** and **D** are incorrect. Trunking provides network access to multiple clients by sharing a set of network lines instead of providing them individually. LUN provisioning does the opposite of LUN masking by making LUNs available for data access, and multipathing creates multiple paths for the computer to reach the storage resources that it is attempting to contact.

4

Network Infrastructure

N etwork configuration is an integral piece of cloud computing and is key to cloud computing performance. One of the factors an organization must consider is the impact of networking on cloud computing performance and the differences that exist between their current network infrastructure and what would be utilized in a cloud computing infrastructure.

This chapter introduces you to networking components that are used in cloud computing. After reading this chapter, you should understand the different types of networks and how to optimize an organization's network for cloud computing. You will also learn how network traffic is routed between the various cloud models and how to secure that traffic. And you will find out about the different network protocols used in cloud computing and when to use those protocols. It is important for you to have a thorough understanding of these topics for the exam.

CERTIFICATION OBJECTIVE 4.01

Network Types

A network is defined as a group of interconnected computers and peripherals that are capable of sharing resources, including software, hardware, and files. The purpose of a network is to provide users with accessibility to information that multiple people might need to perform their day-to-day job functions.

There are numerous advantages for an organization to construct a network. It allows users to share files so that multiple users can access them from a single location. An organization can share resources such as printers, fax machines, storage devices, and even scanners, thus reducing the total number of resources they have to purchase and maintain. A network also allows for applications to be shared by multiple users as long as the application is designed for this and the appropriate software licensing is in place.

There are three types of networks: Intranet, Internet, and Extranet. They all rely on the same Internet protocols but have different levels of access for users inside and outside the organization. This section describes each of these network types and when to use them.

Intranet

An Intranet is a private network based on the Internet protocol (IP) that is configured and controlled by a single organization and is only accessible to users that are internal to that particular organization. An Intranet allows an organization to share information and websites within the organization and is protected from external access by a firewall or a network gateway. For example, an organization may want to share announcements, the employee handbook, confidential financial information, or organizational procedures with its employees but not with people outside the organization. An Intranet can host multiple private websites and is usually the focal point for internal communication.

An Intranet is very similar to the Internet except an Intranet is on an isolated network. For example, a web page that is designed for the Intranet may have a similar look and feel as any other website that is on the Internet, the only difference being who is authorized to access the web page. Public web pages that are accessible over the Internet are typically available to everyone, whereas an Intranet is owned and controlled by the organization and that organization decides who can access that web page. Figure 4-1 shows an example of an Intranet configuration.

Internet

The Internet is a global system of interconnected computer networks that use the same Internet protocols (TCP/IP) as an Intranet network uses. Unlike an Intranet, which is controlled by and serves only one organization, the Internet is not controlled by a single organization and serves billions of users around the world. The Internet is

FIGURE 4-1

An Intranet network configuration, where access is private.

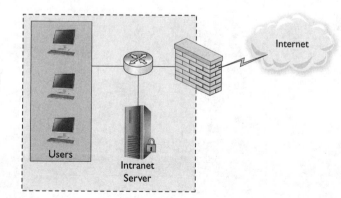

a network of multiple networks relying on network devices and common protocols to transfer data from one intermediate destination (sometimes called a hop) to another until it reaches its final destination.

Aside from a few countries that impose restrictions on what people in their country can view, the Internet is largely unregulated and anyone can post or read whatever they want on the Internet. The Internet Corporation for Assigned Names and Numbers (ICANN) is a nonprofit organization that was created to coordinate the Internet's system of unique identifiers, including domain names and IP addresses.

Extranet

An Extranet is an extension of an Intranet, with the primary difference that an Extranet allows controlled access from outside the organization. An Extranet permits access to outside users with the use of firewalls, access profiles, and privacy protocols. It allows an organization to securely share resources with other businesses. For example, an organization could use an Extranet to sell their products and services online or to share information with business partners.

Both Intranets and Extranets are owned and supported by a single organization. The way to differentiate between an Intranet and an Extranet is by who has access to the private network and the geographical reach of that network. Figure 4-2 shows an example configuration of an Extranet network.

exam

watch *The difference between an Intranet and an Extranet is that an Intranet does not allow access to resources from outside the organization.*

FIGURE 4-2

An Extranet network configuration, where outside access is limited.

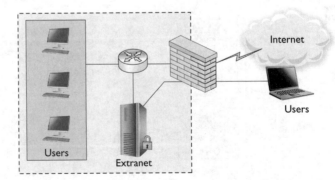

CERTIFICATION OBJECTIVE 4.02

Network Optimization

Now that you know about the different types of networks, you need to understand the components of those networks and how to optimize those components. In this section you will learn the components that make up Intranet and Extranet networks and how to configure them so that they perform in the most efficient manner.

Network optimization is the process of keeping a network operating at peak efficiency. To keep the network running at peak performance, an administrator must perform a variety of tasks, including updating the firmware and operating system on routers and switches, identifying and resolving data flow bottlenecks, and monitoring network utilization. By keeping the network optimized, a network administrator can more accurately meet the terms of the organization's SLA.

Network Topologies

How the different nodes, or devices, in a network are connected and how they communicate is determined by the network's topology. Network topology is the blueprint of the connections of a computer network and can be either physical or logical. Physical topology refers to the design of the network's physical components: computers, switches, cable installation, and so on. Logical topology can be thought of as a picture of how the data flows within a network.

A local area network (LAN) is a network topology that spans a relatively small area like an office building. A LAN is a great way for people to share files, devices, pictures, and applications and is primarily Ethernet based. There are three different data rates of modern Ethernet networks: Fast Ethernet, which can transfer data at a rate of 100 Mbit/s (megabits per second); Gigabit Ethernet, which transfers data at 1,000 Mbit/s; and 10 Gigabit Ethernet, which transfers data at 10,000 Mbit/s.

A metropolitan area network (MAN) is very similar to a LAN except that a MAN spans a city or a large campus. A MAN usually connects multiple LANs and is used to build networks with high data connection speeds for cities or college campuses. MANs are efficient and fast because they use high-speed data carriers such as fiber optics.

A wide area network (WAN) is a network that covers a large geographic area and can contain multiple LANs or MANs. WANs are not restricted by geographic areas. The Internet is an example of a WAN. A number of corporations use leased lines to create a corporate WAN that spans a large geographic area containing multiple states or even countries.

on the **!** Job

Working for a large organization with regional offices all across the United States, we were tasked with setting up a WAN. The company's offices ranged from 5 to 100 or more employees. To accommodate their needs, we set up a VPN connection using leased Internet lines at each location to connect into a central data center. This allowed every employee to connect into the data center and share resources no matter where their physical location.

As an IT professional, you need to understand the pros and cons of the different network topologies when you are building and designing a network. After evaluating the needs of the organization, you can then choose the most efficient topology for the intended purpose of the network. The primary physical topologies to be considered are bus, star, ring, mesh, and tree.

Bus

In a bus topology every node is connected to a central cable, referred to as the bus or backbone. In a bus topology only one device is allowed to transmit at any given time. Since bus topology uses a single cable, it is easy to set up and cost-effective. Bus topology is not recommended for large networks because of the limitations to the number of nodes that can be configured on a single cable. It should also be noted that troubleshooting a bus topology is much more difficult than troubleshooting a star topology, because in a bus topology you have to determine where the cable was broken or removed. Figure 4-3 shows an example of a network configured to use a bus topology.

Star

In a star topology each node is connected to a central hub or switch, and the nodes communicate by sending data through the central hub. In a star topology new nodes

FIGURE 4-3

Network configuration using a bus topology.

Backbone

can easily be added or removed without impacting the rest of the nodes on the network. Star topology offers improved performance over a bus topology and failure of one node does not affect the rest of the network. Problematic nodes can be easily isolated by unplugging that particular node; if the problem disappears it is obviously related to that node, making troubleshooting much simpler in a star topology. The main drawback to the star is that if the central hub or switch fails, all the nodes connected to it are disconnected and unable to communicate with the other nodes. Figure 4-4 shows an example of a network configured to use a star topology.

Ring

In a ring topology each node is connected to another, forming a circle or a ring. Each packet is sent around the ring until it reaches its target destination. The ring topology is hardly used in today's enterprise environment due to the fact that, if one of the links in the network path is broken, all network connectivity is lost. Figure 4-5 shows an example of a network configured to use a ring topology.

FIGURE 4-4

Network configuration using a star topology.

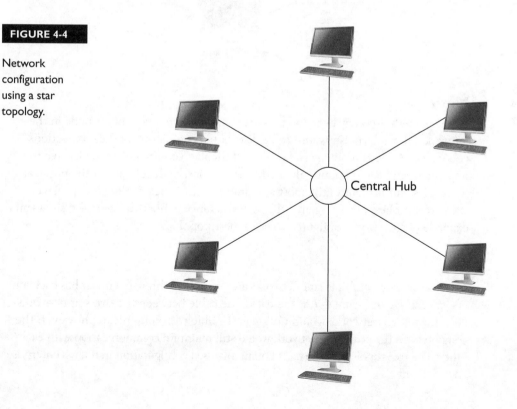

FIGURE 4-5

Network configuration using a ring topology.

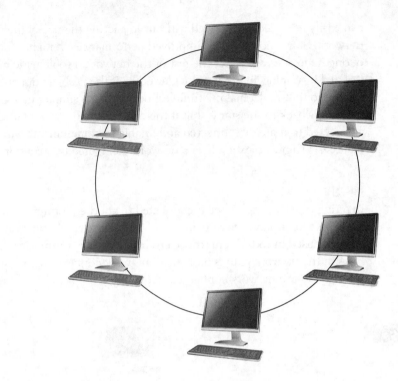

Mesh

In a true mesh topology every node is interconnected to every other node in the network, allowing transmissions to be distributed even if one of the connections goes down. A mesh topology is, however, difficult to configure and expensive to implement and is not commonly used. It is the most fault tolerant of the physical topologies, but it requires the most amount of cable. Since cabling is expensive, the cost must be weighed against the fault tolerance achieved. Figure 4-6 shows an example of a network configured to use a mesh topology.

Tree

In a tree topology multiple star networks are connected through a linear bus backbone. As you can see in Figure 4-7, if the backbone cable between the two star networks fails, those two networks would no longer be able to communicate; however, the computers on the same star network would still maintain communication with each other. The tree topology is the most commonly used configuration in today's enterprise environment.

Network
configuration
using a mesh
topology.

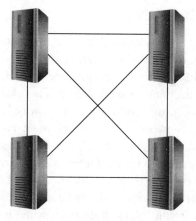

Network
configuration
using a tree
topology.

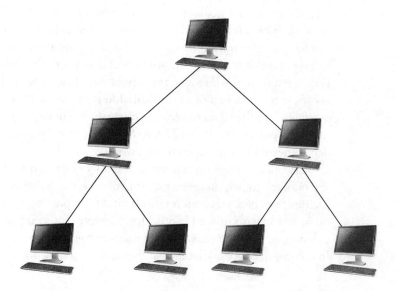

Bandwidth and Latency

Now that you understand the different network topologies that you can configure, you need to know what other factors affect network performance. When moving to the cloud, network performance is crucial to the success of your deployment because the data is stored off-site. Two of the necessities to determining network performance are bandwidth and network latency. Bandwidth is the speed of the network. Network latency is the time delay that is encountered while data is being sent from one point to another on the network.

There are two types of latency: low latency and high latency. A low-latency network connection is a connection that experiences very small delays while sending and receiving traffic. A high-latency network has long delays while sending and receiving traffic. Network latency, when it is excessive, can create bottlenecks that prevent data from using the maximum capacity of the network bandwidth, thereby decreasing the effective bandwidth.

Compression

Compression is defined as the reduction in the size of data that is traveling across the network, which is achieved by converting that data into a format that requires fewer bits for the same transmission. Compression is typically used to minimize required storage space or to reduce the amount of data transmitted over the network. When using compression to reduce the size of data that is being transferred, a network engineer sees a decrease in transmission times since there is more bandwidth available for other data to use as it traverses the network. Compression can result in higher processor utilization due to the fact that a packet must be compressed and decompressed as it traverses the network.

Network compression can automatically compress data before it is sent over the network to help improve performance, especially where bandwidth is limited. Maximizing the compression ratio is vital to improving application performance on networks with limited bandwidth. Compression can play a key role in cloud computing. As an organization migrates to the cloud network, compression is vital in controlling network latency and maximizing network bandwidth.

Caching

Caching is the process of storing frequently accessed data in a location closer to the device that is requesting the data. For example, a web cache could store web

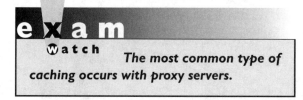

pages and web content either on the physical machine that is accessing the website or on a storage device like a proxy server. This would increase the response time of the web page and reduce the amount of network traffic required to access the website, thus improving network speed and reducing network latency.

There are multiple benefits to caching, including the cost savings that comes with the reduction of bandwidth needed to access information via the Internet and the improved productivity of the end users (because cached information loads significantly faster than noncached information). With your data now being stored in the cloud it is important to understand how caching works and how to maximize caching to improve performance and maximize your network bandwidth.

Load Balancing

Throughout this section we have discussed the importance of optimizing network traffic and infrastructure. In order to optimize network traffic, the data must be routed as efficiently as possible. For example, if an organization's network has five routers and three of them are running at 5 percent and the other two are running at 90 percent, the network utilization is not as efficient as it possibly could be. If each of the routers were running at 20 percent utilization, it would improve network performance and limit network latency. The same could be said for a website that is getting thousands of hits every minute; it would be more efficient if the traffic were split between multiple web servers that are part of a web farm. This would increase performance and remove the single point of failure connected with having only one server respond to the requests.

Load balancing is the process of distributing incoming HTTP or application requests evenly across multiple devices or web servers so that no single device is overwhelmed. Load balancing allows for achieving optimal resource utilization and maximizing throughput without overloading a single device. Load balancing increases reliability by creating redundancy for your application or website by using dedicated hardware or software. Figure 4-8 shows an example of how load balancing works for web servers.

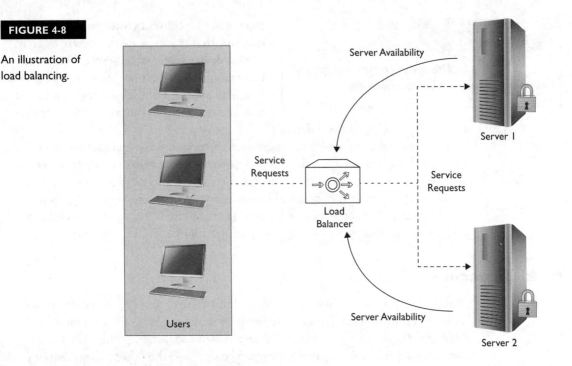

FIGURE 4-8

An illustration of
load balancing.

Server Availability

Server 1

Service
Requests

Load
Balancer

Service
Requests

Users

Server Availability

Server 2

CERTIFICATION OBJECTIVE 4.03

Routing and Switching

Now that you understand the different options and configurations that are available
for setting up a network, you are ready to learn how to route traffic over the network.
Knowing how a network operates is the most important piece to understanding
routing and switching. In the previous section you learned that a network operates
by connecting computers and devices in a variety of different physical configurations.
Routers and switches are the networking devices that enable other devices on the
network to connect and communicate with each other and with other networks.
They are placed on the same physical network as the other devices.

While routers and switches may give the impression they are rather similar, the
devices are responsible for very different operations on a network. A switch is used
to connect multiple devices on the same network or LAN. For example, a switch

connects computers, printers, servers, and a variety of other devices and allows those devices to share network resources with each other. This makes it possible for users to share resources, saving valuable time and money for the organization. A router, on the other hand, is used to connect multiple networks together and allows a network to communicate with the outside world. An organization would use a router to connect their network to the Internet, thus allowing their users to share a single Internet connection. A router can analyze the data that is being sent over the network and change how it is packaged so that it can be routed to another network or even over a different type of network.

Network Address Translation (NAT)

Now that you know a router can allow users to share a single IP address when browsing the Internet, you need to understand how that process works. Network address translation, or NAT, allows a router to modify packets so that multiple devices can share a single public IP address. Most organizations require Internet access for their employees but do not have enough valid public IP addresses to allow each individual to have their own public address to locate resources outside of their network. The main purpose of NAT is to limit the number of public IP addresses an organization needs.

For example, most organizations use a private IP address range, which allows the devices on the network to communicate with all the other devices on the network and in turn makes it possible for users to share files, printers, and the like. But if those users need to access anything outside the network, they would require a public IP address. If Internet queries originate from various internal devices, the organization would be required to have a valid public IP address for each device. NAT consolidates the addresses needed for each internal device to a single valid public IP address, allowing all of the organization's employees to access the Internet with the use of a single public IP address.

To fully understand this concept, you first need to know what makes an IP address private and what makes an IP address public. Any IP address that falls into one of the IP address ranges that are reserved for private use by the Internet Engineering Task Force (IETF) is considered to be a private IP address. Table 4-1 lists the different private IP address ranges.

TABLE 4-1	Address Range	Usable IPs	Network Class
Private IP Addresses	10.0.0.0–10.255.255.255	16,777,216	Class A network
	172.16.0.0–172.31.255.255	1,048,576	Class B network
	192.168.0.0–192.168.255.255	65,536	Class C network
	169.254.0.0–169.254.255.255	65,534	Class B network

A private network that adheres to the Internet Engineering Task Force (IETF) published standard, (RFC) 1918, is a network address space not used or allowed on the public Internet. These addresses are commonly used in a home or corporate network or LAN when a public IP address or globally routed address is not required on each device. Because these address ranges are not made available as public IP addresses, and consequently are never assigned specifically for use to any organization, they receive the designation of "private" IP addresses. IP packets that are addressed by private IPs cannot be transmitted onto the public Internet over the backbone. There are two reasons for the recent surge in using RFC 1918 addresses: one is that Internet Protocol version 4 (IPv4) address space is rapidly diminishing; and the other is that a significant security enhancement is achieved by providing address translation, whether it is NAT or PAT (described shortly) or a combination of the two. A perpetrator on the Internet cannot directly access a private IP address without the administrator taking significant steps to relax the security. A NAT router is sometimes referred to as a poor man's firewall. In reality it is not a firewall at all, but it shields the internal network (individuals using private addresses) from attacks and from what is sometimes referred to as IBR (Internet background radiation).

In order to access resources that are external to their network, an organization is required to have at least one "routable" or public IP address. This is where NAT comes into play. NAT allows a router to change the private IP address into a public IP address so that the organization can access resources that are external to them; then the NAT router tracks those IP address changes. When the external information being requested comes back to the router, it changes the IP address from a public IP address to a private IP address so that it can forward the traffic back to the requesting device. NAT allows a single device like a router to act as an agent or a go-between for a private network and the Internet. NAT provides the benefits of saving public IP addresses, higher security, and ease of administration.

In addition to public and private IP addresses, there is also automatic private IP addressing (APIPA; sometimes called Autonet), which gives a dynamic host configuration protocol (DHCP) client the ability to receive an IP address even if it cannot communicate with a DHCP server. APIPA addresses are "nonroutable" over the Internet and allocate an IP address in the private range of 169.254.0.1–169.254.255.254. APIPA uses address resolution protocol (ARP) to verify that the IP address is unique in the network.

Port Address Translation (PAT)

Similar to NAT, port address translation (PAT) allows for mapping of private IP addresses to public IP addresses as well as for mapping multiple devices on a network to a single public IP address. Its goal is the same as that of NAT: to conserve public IP addresses. PAT enables the sharing of a single public IP address between multiple clients trying to access the Internet.

A good example of PAT is a home network where multiple devices are trying to access the Internet at the same time. In this instance your ISP would assign your home network's router a single public IP address. On this network you could have multiple computers or devices trying to access the Internet at the same time by means of the same router. When device Y logs on to the Internet, it is assigned a port number that is appended to the private IP address. This gives device Y a unique IP address. If device Z were to log on to the Internet at the same time, the router would assign the same public IP address to device Z but with a different port number. The two devices are sharing the same public IP address to browse the Internet, but the router distributes the requested content to the appropriate device based on the port number the router has assigned to that particular device.

Subnetting and Supernetting

Subnetting is the practice of creating subnetworks, or subnets. A subnet is a logical subdivision of an IP network. Using subnets may be useful in large organizations where it is necessary to allocate address space efficiently. They may also be utilized to increase routing efficiency, and offer improved controls for network management when different networks require separation of administrator control for different entities in a large or multi-tenant environment. Inter-subnet traffic is exchanged by routers, just as it would be exchanged between physical networks.

All computers that belong to a specific subnet are addressed with the use of two separate bit groups in their IP address, with one group designating the subnet and the other group designating the specific host on that subnet. The routing prefix of the address can be expressed in either classful or classless inter-domain routing, or CIDR, notation. CIDR has become the most popular routing notation method in recent years. This notation is written as the first address of a network, followed by a slash (/), then finishing with the bit length of the prefix. To use a common example, 192.168.1.0/24 is the prefix of the network starting at the given address, having 24 bits allocated for the network prefix and the remaining 8 bits reserved for host addressing. An allocation of 24 bits is equal to the subnet mask for that network, which you may recognize as the familiar 255.255.255.0.

As subnetting is the practice of dividing one network into multiple networks, supernetting does the exact opposite, combining multiple networks into one larger network. Supernetting is most often utilized to combine multiple class C networks. It was created to solve the problem of routing tables growing too large for administrators to manage by aggregating networks under one routing table entry. It also provided a solution to the problem of class B network address space running out.

In much the same fashion as subnetting, supernetting takes the IP address and breaks it down into a network bit group and a host identifier bit group. It also uses CIDR notation. The way to identify supernetted networks is that the network prefix is always lower than 23, which allows for a greater number of hosts (on the larger network) to be specified in the host bit group.

Virtual Local Area Network (VLAN)

A virtual local area network, or VLAN, is the concept of partitioning a physical network to create separate, independent broadcast domains that are part of the same physical network. VLANs are very similar to physical LANs but add the ability to break up physical networks into logical groupings of networks all within the same physical network. VLANs were conceived out of the desire to create logical separation without the need for additional physical hardware (i.e., network cards, wiring, and routers). VLANs can even traverse physical networks, forming a logical network or VLAN even if the devices exist on separate physical networks. With the use of a virtual private network (VPN), which extends a private network over a public network such as the Internet, a VLAN can even traverse the entire Internet. A VLAN is usually associated with an IP subnet, so all the devices in that IP subnet belong to the same VLAN. In order to configure a VLAN you must first create a

VLAN and then bind the interface and IP address to it. VLANs must be routed and switch ports must be assigned membership to a particular VLAN on a port-by-port basis. For example, you could implement a VLAN to place only certain end users inside the VLAN to help control broadcast traffic.

VLAN tagging is the process of inserting a 4-byte header directly after the destination address and source address of the Ethernet frame header. There are two types of VLAN tagging mechanisms: ISL, which is proprietary to Cisco equipment; and IEEE 802.1q, which is supported by everyone including Cisco and is usually the VLAN option of choice. Utilizing the IEEE 802.1q protocol, approximately 4,095 different VLAN IDs can be achieved on the same physical network segment (depending on what is supported by the switch and router devices).

on the
Job

One of the organizations we worked for was a small college that had multiple training rooms and wanted to control broadcast traffic. This was a perfect situation for a VLAN. We set up a separate VLAN for each of the classrooms so that none of the classrooms would cause unnecessary broadcast traffic to the others.

Broadcasts by their very nature are processed and received by each member of the broadcast domain. VLANs can improve network performance by segmenting the network into groups that share broadcast traffic. For example, each floor of a building might have its own subnet. It might make sense to create a VLAN for that subnet to control broadcasts to other floors of the building, thus reducing the need to send broadcasts to unnecessary destinations (in this case another floor of the building). The general rule for VLANs is to keep the resources that are needed for the VLANs and that are consumed by members of the VLAN on that same VLAN. Latency issues will occur whenever a packet must cross a VLAN, as it must be routed. This situation should be avoided if possible.

The type of port that supports a VLAN is called an access link. When a device connects using an access link, it is unaware of any VLAN membership. It behaves as if it were a component of a broadcast domain. All VLAN information is removed by switches from the frame before it gets to the device connected to the access link. No communication or interaction can take place between the access link devices and the devices outside of their designated VLAN. This communication is only made possible when the packet is routed through a router, or a VSM in Cisco nomenclature. A trunk link, also known just as a "trunk," is a port that transports packets for any VLAN. These trunk ports are usually found in connections between switches, and require the ability to carry packets from all available VLANs because those VLANs span over multiple switches. Trunk ports are typically VLAN 0 or VLAN 1, but there is nothing magical about those numbers. It is up to the manufacturer to determine which ID is designated as the trunk port. Specifications are spelled out in the 802.1q protocol, but just like any other "blueprint" some manufacturers will make their own interpretation of how they should be implemented.

For the purpose of cloud VLANs it is important to understand another type of VLAN known as a private VLAN, or PVLAN. PVLANs contain switch ports that cannot communicate with each other but can access another network. PVLANs restrict traffic through the use of private ports so that they communicate only with a specific uplink trunk port. A good example of the use of a PVLAN is in a hotel setting. Each room of the hotel has a port that can access the Internet, but it is not advantageous for the rooms to communicate with each other.

Routing Tables

A routing table is a data table stored on a router that the router uses to determine the destination of network packets it is responsible for routing. A routing table is a database that is stored in the router's memory and managed by the router's hardware. It contains information about the network topology that is located adjacent to the router hosting the routing table.

CERTIFICATION OBJECTIVE 4.04

Network Ports and Protocols

Now that you understand how to select the physical network configuration and segment and route network traffic, you need to learn about the different ports and protocols that are used in cloud computing. A network port is an application-specific endpoint to a logical connection. It is how a client program finds a specific service on a device. A network protocol, on the other hand, is an understood set of rules agreed upon by two or more parties that determine how network devices exchange information over a network. In this section we discuss the different protocols used to securely connect a network to the Internet so that it can communicate with the cloud environment.

Hypertext Transfer Protocol (HTTP) and Hypertext Transfer Protocol Secure (HTTPS)

Hypertext transfer protocol (HTTP) is an application protocol built on TCP used to distribute hypertext markup language (HTML) files, text, images, sound, videos, multimedia, and other types of information over the Internet. HTTP typically allows for communication between a web client or web browser and a web server hosting a website. HTTP defines how messages between a web browser and a web server are formatted and transmitted and which actions the web server and browser should take when they are issued specific commands. For example, when you type http://www.comptia.org into your web browser, it uses the HTTP protocol to send an HTTP command to the web server that hosts the website. The HTTP command tells the web server to retrieve and transmit the web page http://www.comptia.org to your computer via the HTTP protocol to your web browser.

By default, HTTP uses port 80 to communicate between the web server and the web client, but any other port not in use can be used. A common example is to use 8080. HTTP is considered a stateless protocol because each command is executed independently without any awareness of the commands that were issued prior to the current command; essentially after the request is made the client and the server forget about each other. In this situation neither the web client nor web browser nor web server can retain information between different HTTP requests across the web page.

Hypertext transfer protocol secure (HTTPS) is an extension of the HTTP protocol that provides secure communication over the Internet. HTTPS is not a separate protocol from HTTP; it simply layers the security capabilities of secure sockets layer (SSL) or transport layer security (TLS) on top of the HTTP protocol in order to provide security to the standard HTTP protocol, since HTTP communicates in plain text. Web browsers understand how to translate this information, and most modern web browsers display some kind of icon to notify the user that the web page is secure. For example, Internet Explorer displays a padlock icon along with https:// in the address bar. HTTPS encrypts a communication by using information obtained in a digital certificate (i.e., the public key) to encrypt the session between the web client and the web server. HTTPS uses port 443 by default instead of the standard port 80 used by HTTP. When a web client first accesses a website using the HTTPS protocol, the server sends a certificate with its embedded public key to the web client. The client generates a session key (sometimes called a symmetric key) and encrypts the session key with the server's public key. The server has the private key, which is the other half of the public-private key pair, and is able to decrypt the session key, which allows for a covert and confidential exchange of a very fast session key. No entity other than the server has access to the private key.

During the normal process of authentication, the client then verifies that the certificate is in its trusted root store, thus trusting the certificate was signed by a trusted certificate authority. After the client is able to verify the certificate is coming from the correct web server, it creates a session key that is only accessible by that web client. It encrypts the session key using the public key it received from the web server in the form of a certificate with an embedded public key. The sending server is the only entity that should have a copy of the private key so that it is able to decrypt the sent session key. Now both entities have a copy of the very fast session key, and the server receives it securely. Once both the web client and the web server know the session key, the SSL handshake is complete and the session is encrypted. As part of the protocol either the client or the server can ask that the key be "rolled" at any time. Rolling the key is simply asking the browser to generate a new 40-, 128-, or 256-bit key or above, forcing a would-be attacker to shoot at a moving target.

on the

ⓘo b

A good example of using HTTPS comes from an experience working for a large retail firm. The employer needed an e-commerce web page that could receive credit card payments over the Internet, which in turn required a secure form of transmission for data as it traveled over the Internet. So the organization had to purchase a certificate from a trusted certificate authority (e.g., VeriSign), and deploy it on their internal web servers. Once the certificate was purchased and deployed to the servers, customers were able to use HTTPS to communicate with the web page and thus have the ability to purchase products using their credit card information in a secure manner.

File Transfer Protocol (FTP) and File Transfer Protocol Secure (FTPS)

Unlike HTTP, which is used to view web pages over the Internet, the file transfer protocol (FTP) is used to download and transfer files over the Internet. FTP is a standard network protocol that allows for access to and transfer of files over the Internet using either the command-line or graphical-based FTP client. An organization hosts files on an FTP server so that people from outside the organization can download those files to their local computers. Figure 4-9 shows an example of a graphical-based FTP client.

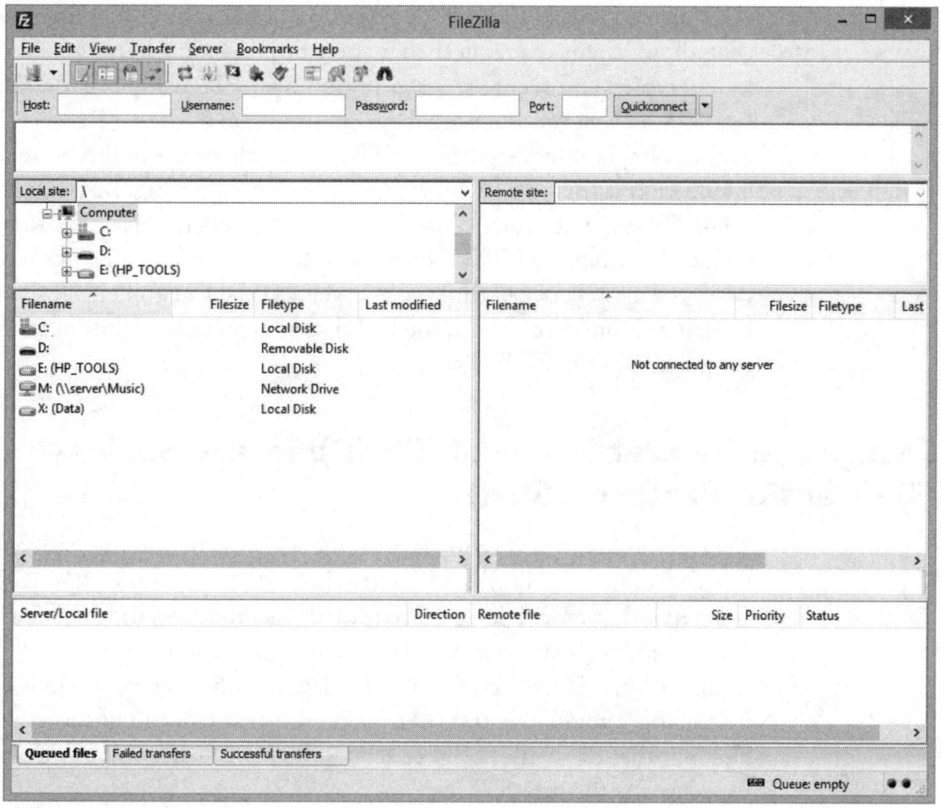

FIGURE 4-9

Screenshot of a graphical-based FTP client.

The FTP protocol is built on a client-server architecture and provides a data connection between the FTP client and the FTP server. The FTP server is the computer that stores the files and authenticates the FTP client. The FTP server listens on the network for incoming FTP connection requests from FTP clients. The clients, on the other hand, use either the command-line or FTP client software to connect to the FTP server. After the FTP server has authenticated the client, the client has the ability to download files, rename files, upload files, and delete files on the FTP server based on the client's permissions. The FTP client software has an interface that allows you to explore the directory of the FTP server, just like you would use Windows Explorer to explore the content of your local hard drive on a Microsoft Windows–based computer.

Similar to how HTTPS is an extension of HTTP, FTPS is an extension of FTP that allows clients to request that their FTP session be encrypted. FTPS allows for encrypted and secure transfer of files over FTP using SSL or TLS. There are two different methods for securing client access to the FTP server: implicit and explicit. Implicit mode gives an FTPS-aware client the ability to require a secure connection with an FTPS-aware server without affecting the FTP functionality of non-FTPS-aware clients. With explicit mode, a client must explicitly request a secure connection from the FTPS server; then the security and encryption method must be agreed upon between the FTPS server and the FTPS client. If the client does not request a secure connection, the FTPS server can either allow or refuse the client's connection to the FTPS server.

Secure File Transfer Protocol (SFTP)/Secure Shell File Transfer Protocol (SSH)

Two methods for transferring files securely across the Internet are secured file transfer protocol (FTPS) and secure shell file transfer protocol (SFTP), which is a network protocol designed to provide secure access to files, file transfers, file editing, and file management over the Internet using a secure shell (SSH) session. Unlike FTP, SFTP encrypts both the data and the FTP commands, preventing the information from being transmitted in clear text over the Internet. SFTP differs from FTPS in that SFTP uses SSH to secure the file transfer and FTPS uses SSL or TLS to secure the file transfer.

SFTP clients are functionally similar to FTP clients, except SFTP clients use SSH to access and transfer files over the Internet. An organization cannot use standard FTP client software to access an SFTP server, nor can they use SFTP client software to access FTP servers. There are a few things to consider when deciding on which method should be used to secure FTP servers. SFTP is generally more secure and superior to FTPS. If the organization is going to connect to a Linux or Unix FTP server, SFTP is the better choice because it is supported by default on these operating systems. If one of the requirements for the FTP server is that it needs to be accessible from personal devices, such as tablets and smartphones, then FTPS would be the better option since most of these devices natively support FTPS but may not support SFTP.

e x a m

W a t c h   *It is important to understand that FTPS and SFTP are not the same thing. FTPS uses SSL or TLS and certificates to secure FTP communication, and SFTP uses SSH keys to secure FTP communication.*

Domain Name System (DNS) and Dynamic Host Configuration Protocol (DHCP)

DNS distributes the responsibility for both the assignment of domain names and the mapping of those names to IP addresses to the authoritative name servers within each domain. An authoritative name server is responsible for maintaining its specific domain name and can also be authoritative for subdomains of that primary domain. For example, if you want to go to a particular web page like http://www.comptia.org, all you do is type the name of the web page into your browser and it displays the web page. In order for your web browser to display that web page by name, it needs to be able to locate it by IP address. This is where the domain name system (DNS) comes into play. DNS translates Internet domain or host names into IP addresses. So DNS would automatically convert the name http://www.comptia.org into an IP address for the web server hosting that web page. In order to store the entire name and address information for all the public hosts on the Internet, DNS uses a distributed hierarchical database. DNS databases reside in a hierarchy of database servers where no one DNS server contains all the information.

DNS distributes the responsibility of assigning domain names and mapping those domain names to IP addresses through the use of authoritative name servers within each domain. An authoritative name server is responsible for maintaining a particular domain name and can be authoritative for subdomains of the primary domain. For example, we own the domain name coursewareexperts. com and host the DNS for that domain on a server in our data center, making our DNS servers authoritative for that domain. So any time anyone types http://www.coursewareexperts.com into their web browser, it's going to query a chain of DNS servers until it gets an authoritative response for that domain name. The client checks with the local DNS server first to see if it receives an authoritative response for the coursewareexperts.com domain. If it does not, it queries the next level of DNS servers until it gets to the root DNS server to find the server that is authoritative for the coursewareexperts.com domain name. Figure 4-10 shows an example of how a client performs a DNS search.

DNS consists of a tree of domain names. Each branch of the tree has a domain name and contains resource records for that domain. Resource records describe specific information about a particular object. The DNS zone at the top of the tree is called the root zone. Each zone under the root zone has a unique domain name or multiple domain names, and the owner of that domain name is considered authoritative for that DNS zone. Figure 4-11 shows the DNS hierarchy for the coursewareexperts.com example.

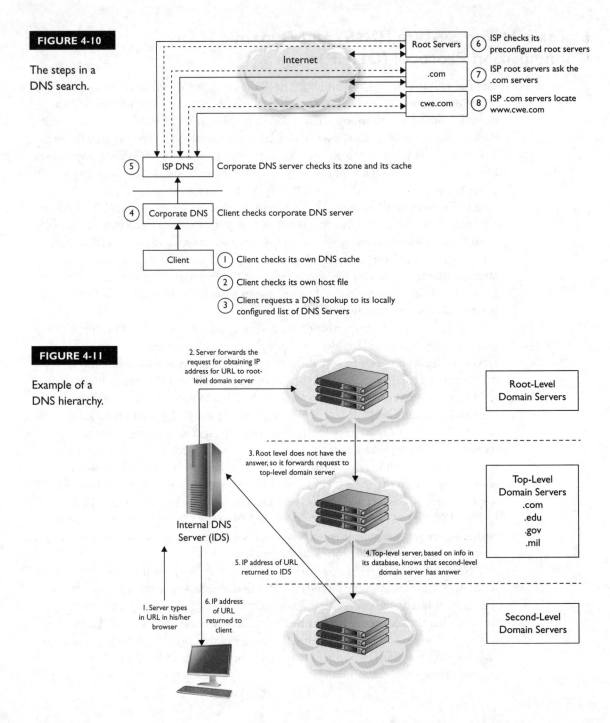

FIGURE 4-10

The steps in a DNS search.

Root Servers
Internet
.com
cwe.com

⑥ ISP checks its preconfigured root servers

⑦ ISP root servers ask the .com servers

⑧ ISP .com servers locate www.cwe.com

⑤ ISP DNS — Corporate DNS server checks its zone and its cache

④ Corporate DNS — Client checks corporate DNS server

Client

① Client checks its own DNS cache

② Client checks its own host file

③ Client requests a DNS lookup to its locally configured list of DNS Servers

FIGURE 4-11

Example of a DNS hierarchy.

2. Server forwards the request for obtaining IP address for URL to root-level domain server

Root-Level Domain Servers

Internal DNS Server (IDS)

3. Root level does not have the answer, so it forwards request to top-level domain server

Top-Level Domain Servers
.com
.edu
.gov
.mil

5. IP address of URL returned to IDS

4. Top-level server, based on info in its database, knows that second-level domain server has answer

1. Server types in URL in his/her browser

6. IP address of URL returned to client

Second-Level Domain Servers

Dynamic host configuration protocol (DHCP) is a network protocol allowing a server to automatically assign IP addresses from a predefined range of numbers called a scope to computers on a network. DHCP is responsible for assigning IP addresses to computers, and DNS is responsible for resolving those IP addresses to names. A DHCP server can register and update resource records on a DNS server on behalf of a DHCP client. A DHCP server is used any time an organization does not wish to use static IP addresses (IP addresses that are manually assigned).

DHCP servers maintain a database of available IP addresses and configuration options. The DHCP server leases an IP address to a client based on the network to which that client is connected. The DHCP client is then responsible for renewing their lease or IP addresses before the lease expires. DHCP supports both IPv4 and IPv6. It can also be used to create a static IP address mapping by creating a reservation that assigns a particular IP address to a computer based on that computer's media access control (MAC) address.

If an organization's network has only one IP subnet, clients can communicate directly with the DHCP server. If the network has multiple subnets, the company can still use a DHCP server to allocate IP addresses to the network clients. To allow a DHCP client on a subnet that is not directly connected to the DHCP server to communicate with the DHCP server, the organization can configure a DHCP relay agent in the DHCP client's subnet. A DHCP relay agent is an agent that relays DHCP communication between DHCP clients and DHCP servers on different IP subnets. DNS and DHCP work together to help clients on an organization's network communicate as efficiently as possible, and allow the clients to discover and share resources located on the network.

Simple Mail Transfer Protocol (SMTP)

Documents and videos are not the only pieces of information that you might want to share and communicate over the Internet. While HTTP and FTP allow you to share files, videos, and pictures over the Internet, SMTP is the protocol that allows you to send electronic messages (e-mail) over the Internet. SMTP uses port 25 and provides a standard set of codes that help to simplify the delivery of e-mail messages between e-mail servers. Almost all e-mail servers that send e-mail over the Internet use SMTP to send messages from one server to another. After the e-mail server has received the message, the user can view that e-mail using an e-mail client, such as

Microsoft Outlook. The e-mail client also uses SMTP to send messages from the client to the e-mail server.

Well-Known Ports

Ports are used in a transmission control protocol (TCP) or user datagram protocol (UDP) network to specify the endpoint of a logical connection and how the client can access a specific application on a server over the network. Port binding is used to determine where and how a message is transmitted. Link aggregation can also be implemented to combine multiple network connections to increase throughput. The well-known ports are assigned by the Internet Assigned Numbers Authority (IANA) and range from 0 to 1023. The IANA is responsible for maintaining the official assignments of port numbers for a specific purpose. You do not need to know all of the well-known ports for the CompTIA Cloud+ exam, so we are going to focus only on the ports that are relevant to the exam. Table 4-2 specifies the server process and its communication port.

e x a m

ⓦatch   *Make sure you know the ports listed in Table 4-2 and which service uses each port.*

TABLE 4-2	Service Name	Port Number	Description
Well-Known Ports	FTP	21	File transfer protocol, used to transfer data via the FTP protocol
	SSH	22	Secure shell, used for secure logins, file transfers, and port forwarding
	Telnet	23	Telnet, used to send unencrypted text messages
	SMTP	25	Simple mail transfer protocol, used to route e-mails between mail servers
	Domain	53	Domain name server (DNS)
	BOOTP	68	Bootstrap protocol client, used by dynamic host configuration protocol (DHCP)
	HTTP	80	World Wide Web hypertext transfer protocol (HTTP)
	HTTPS	443	HTTP over secure sockets layer (SSL)

CERTIFICATION SUMMARY

A network's physical topology is a key factor in its overall performance. This chapter explained the various physical topologies and when to use each of them. It also discussed how traffic is routed across the network, which is key to understanding how to implement cloud computing. Since most information is accessed over an Internet connection, it is very important to know how to properly configure a network and how it is routed.

There are a variety of different ways to reduce network latency and improve network response time and performance, including caching, compression, load balancing, and maintaining the physical hardware. These issues are critical for ensuring that an organization meets the terms of its SLA.

KEY TERMS

Use the list below to review the key terms that were discussed in this chapter. The definitions can be found within this chapter and in the glossary.

Intranet   Private network that is configured and controlled by a single organization and is only accessible to users that are internal to that organization

Extranet   Extension of an Intranet with the difference being an Extranet allows access to the network from outside the organization

Internet   Global system of interconnected computer networks that is not controlled by a single organization or country.

Local area network (LAN)   Network topology that spans relatively small areas like an office building and allows people to share files, devices, printers, and applications

Metropolitan area network (MAN)   Network topology connecting multiple LANs together to span a large area like a city or a large campus

Wide area network (WAN)   Network that covers a large geographic area and can contain multiple LANs or MANs

Bus   Communication system used to transfer data between the components inside of a computer motherboard, processor, or network device. It gets its name from the concept of a bus line where it stops and allows people to get off and board. It is a communication system that is attached at many points along the bus line

Star   Network topology where each node is connected to a central hub or switch and the nodes communicate by sending data through the central hub

Ring   Network topology where each node is connected to another forming a circle or a ring

Mesh   Network topology where every node is interconnected to every other node in the network

Tree   Network topology containing multiple star networks that are connected through a linear bus backbone

Bandwidth   The amount of data that can be transferred from one network location to another in a specific amount of time

Latency   The delay in time calculated from the time a service request is made until that request is fulfilled. Typically used to describe network and hard drive speeds.

Compression   Reduction in the size of data being traversed across the network

Caching   Process of transparently storing data at a quicker response location so that any future requests for that data can be accessed faster than through the slower medium

Load balancing   Distributes workloads across multiple computers to optimize resources and throughput for preventing a single device from being overwhelmed

Router   Device that connects multiple networks together and allows a network to communicate with the outside world

Switch   Network device that connects multiple devices together on the same network or LAN

Network address translation (NAT)   Allows a router to modify packets so that multiple devices can share a single public IP address

Port address translation (PAT)   Mapping of both ports and IP addresses from a private to a public system

Subnetting   Creates subnetworks through the logical subdivision of IP networks

Supernetting   Combines multiple networks into one larger network

Virtual local area network (VLAN)   Partitions a physical network to create separate, independent broadcast domains that are part of the same physical network

Routing tables   Data table stored on a router used by the router to determine the destination of network packets it is responsible for routing

Hypertext transfer protocol (HTTP)   Protocol used to distribute HTML files, text, images, sound, videos, multimedia files, and other information over the Internet

Hypertext transfer protocol secure (HTTPS)   An extension of the HTTP protocol that provides secure communication over the Internet using secure sockets layer (SSL) or transport layer security (TLS)

File transfer protocol (FTP)   Network protocol that allows for access to and the transfer of files over the Internet using either the command-line or graphical-based FTP client

File transfer protocol secure (FTPS)   Uses secure sockets layer (SSL) or transport layer security (TLS) to secure the transfer of files over FTP

Secure file transfer protocol (SFTP)   Provides secure access to files, file transfers, file editing, and file management over the Internet using secure shell (SSH)

Secure shell file transfer protocol (SSH)   Used to secure logins, file transfers, and port forwarding

Domain name system (DNS)   Translates Internet domain or host names into IP addresses

Dynamic host configuration protocol (DHCP)   Network protocol that automatically assigns IP addresses from a predefined range of numbers called a scope to computers on a network

Simple mail transfer protocol (SMTP)   Protocol used to send electronic messages (e-mail) over the Internet

Ports   Application-specific endpoint to a logical connection

✓ TWO-MINUTE DRILL

Network Types

❏ A network is a group of interconnected computers and peripherals capable of sharing resources.

❏ An Intranet is a private network that is controlled by a single organization and is only accessible to users who are internal to the organization.

❏ The Internet is a global system of interconnected computer networks and, unlike an Intranet, is not controlled by a single organization.

❏ An Extranet is similar to an Intranet in the fact that it is controlled by a single organization, but it also allows controlled access from outside the organization.

Network Optimization

❏ A LAN is a network that connects computers to each other and allows them to communicate over a short distance. Similar to a LAN, a MAN connects computers to one another, but a MAN spans a city or a large campus.

❏ A WAN can contain multiple LANs and MANs and spans large geographic areas.

❏ A network's topology determines how computers communicate.

❏ Network latency is the time delay that is encountered while data is being transferred over a network.

❏ Compression converts data into a smaller format and works to reduce network latency.

❏ Caching stores frequently accessed information closer to the device that is requesting it.

❏ Load balancing allows for distribution of incoming HTTP requests across multiple web servers to improve network performance and response time.

Routing and Switching

❏ NAT allows a router to modify packets so that multiple devices can share a single public IP address.

❏ PAT is similar to NAT, except PAT allows for mapping multiple devices to a single public IP address by changing its port number.

❑ Subnetting allows a network to be divided into smaller networks to ease administration.

❑ A VLAN makes it possible to divide a large network into smaller networks, even if every device physically does not connect to the same switch.

❑ A router has a built-in database called a routing table that stores information about the network's topology and the devices that are connected to the router.

Network Ports and Protocols

❑ HTTP allows for communication between a web client and a web server over the Internet using port 80 by default.

❑ HTTPS is an extension of the HTTP protocol that uses port 443 and secures the communication between the web client and the web server.

❑ The FTP protocol uses port 21 by default and allows you to download and transfer files over the Internet using either the command-line or graphical-based FTP client.

❑ FTP communication can be secured using FTPS or SFTP. FTPS uses SSL or TLS to encrypt FTP communication, while SFTP uses SSH keys to encrypt FTP communication.

❑ DHCP is used to automatically assign IP addresses to computers based on a predefined scope. DNS then translates those addresses into readable and easily recognized host names.

❑ E-mail is transferred over the Internet between mail servers using the SMTP protocol over port 25.

SELF TEST

The following questions will help you measure your understanding of the material presented in this chapter.

Network Types

1. Which network type is not accessible from outside the organization by default?
   A. Internet
   B. Extranet
   C. Intranet
   D. LAN

2. Which of the following statements describes the difference between an Extranet and an Intranet network configuration?
   A. An Intranet does not require a firewall.
   B. An Extranet requires less administration than an Intranet.
   C. An Intranet is owned and operated by a single organization.
   D. An Extranet allows controlled access from outside the organization.

3. Which of the following is a network of multiple networks relying on network devices and common protocols to transfer data from one destination to another until it reaches its final destination and is accessible from anywhere?
   A. Intranet
   B. Extranet
   C. Internet
   D. LAN

Network Optimization

4. Which of the following terms defines the amount of data that can be sent across a network at a given time?
   A. Network latency
   B. Bandwidth
   C. Compression
   D. Network load balancing

5. Which of the following causes network performance to deteriorate and delays network response time?

  A. Network latency

  B. Caching

  C. Network bandwidth

  D. High CPU and memory usage

6. After taking a new job at the state university, you are asked to recommend a network topology that best fits the large college campus. The network needs to span the entire campus. Which network topology would you recommend?

  A. LAN

  B. WAN

  C. MAN

  D. SAN

7. You administer a website that receives thousands of hits per second. You notice the web server hosting the website is operating at close to capacity. What solution would you recommend to improve the performance of the website?

  A. Caching

  B. Network load balancing

  C. Compression

  D. Network bandwidth

Routing and Switching

8. Which process allows a router to modify packets so that multiple devices can share a single public IP address?

  A. NAT

  B. DNS

  C. VLAN

  D. Subnetting

9. Which of the following IP addresses is in a private IP range?

  A. 12.152.36.9

  B. 10.10.10.10

  C. 72.64.53.89

  D. 173.194.96.3

10. Which of the following technologies allows you to logically segment a LAN into different broadcast domains?
    A. MAN
    B. WAN
    C. VLAN
    D. SAN

Network Ports and Protocols

11. Which of the following protocols and ports is used to secure communication over the Internet?
    A. HTTP over port 80
    B. SMTP over port 25
    C. FTP over port 21
    D. HTTPS over port 443

12. SFTP uses _____ to secure FTP communication.
    A. Certificates
    B. FTPS
    C. SSH
    D. SMTP

13. In a network environment _____ is responsible for assigning IP addresses to computers and _____ is responsible for resolving those IP addresses to names.
    A. DNS, DHCP
    B. DHCP, DNS
    C. HTTP, DNS
    D. DHCP, SMTP

14. Which of these ports is the well-known port for the Telnet service?
    A. 25
    B. 22
    C. 23
    D. 443

15. This protocol is responsible for transferring electronic mail messages from one mail server to another over the Internet.
    A. DNS
    B. HTTPS
    C. FTP
    D. SMTP

SELF TEST ANSWERS

Network Types

1. Which network type is not accessible from outside the organization by default?
A. Internet
B. Extranet
C. Intranet
D. LAN

☑ **C.** An Intranet is a private network that is configured and controlled by a single organization and is only accessible by users that are internal to that organization.

☒ **A, B,** and **D** are incorrect. An Extranet is similar to an Intranet, but it is accessible from outside the organization. The Internet is accessible from anywhere, and a LAN is part of an Intranet but is not a separate network type.

2. Which of the following statements describes the difference between an Extranet and an Intranet network configuration?
A. An Intranet does not require a firewall.
B. An Extranet requires less administration than an Intranet.
C. An Intranet is owned and operated by a single organization.
D. An Extranet allows controlled access from outside the organization.

☑ **D.** An Extranet is an extension of an Intranet with the primary difference being that an Extranet allows controlled access from outside the organization.

☒ **A, B,** and **C** are incorrect. An Extranet requires a little bit more administration due to the fact that you have to maintain access to resources outside the organization. Both an Intranet and an Extranet are owned by a single organization, so this is not a difference in the two network types.

3. Which of the following is a network of multiple networks relying on network devices and common protocols to transfer data from one destination to another until it reaches its final destination and is accessible from anywhere?
A. Intranet
B. Extranet
C. Internet
D. LAN

☑ **C.** The Internet is not controlled by a single entity and serves billions of users around the world.

☒ **A, B,** and **D** are incorrect. An Intranet is only accessible to users within a specific organization. An Extranet allows only controlled access from outside the organization. A LAN is part of an Intranet.

Network Optimization

4. Which of the following terms defines the amount of data that can be sent across a network at a given time?
   A. Network latency
   B. Bandwidth
   C. Compression
   D. Network load balancing

☑ **B.** Bandwidth is the amount of data that can traverse a network interface over a specific amount of time.

☒ **A, C,** and **D** are incorrect. Network latency is a time delay that is encountered while data is being sent from one point to another on the network and impacts network bandwidth. Compression is the reduction in the size of data brought about by converting it into a format that requires fewer bits and does not define the amount of data that can be sent over the network. Network load balancing is used to increase performance and provide redundancy for websites and applications.

5. Which of the following causes network performance to deteriorate and delays network response time?
   A. Network latency
   B. Caching
   C. Network bandwidth
   D. High CPU and memory usage

☑ **A.** Network latency is a time delay that is encountered while data is being sent from one point to another on the network and impacts network bandwidth and performance.

☒ **B, C,** and **D** are incorrect. Caching is the process of storing frequently accessed data in a location close to the device requesting the data and helps improve network performance. Network bandwidth is the amount of data that can traverse a network interface over a specific amount of time. CPU and memory are different compute resources that need to be monitored for performance but are separate from network performance.

6. After taking a new job at the state university, you are asked to recommend a network topology that best fits the large college campus. The network needs to span the entire campus. Which network topology would you recommend?

A. LAN

B. WAN

C. MAN

D. SAN

☑ **C.** A metropolitan area network (MAN) can connect multiple LANs and is used to build networks with high data connection speeds for cities or college campuses.

☒ **A, B,** and **D** are incorrect. A local area network (LAN) is a network that connects computers to each other and allows them to communicate over a short distance and would not satisfy the requirement of spanning a large campus. A wide area network (WAN) is a network that can contain multiple LANs and/or MANs and is not restricted by geographic area. A storage area network (SAN) would not allow you to connect different LANs throughout the campus as the question requires.

7. You administer a website that receives thousands of hits per second. You notice the web server hosting the website is operating at close to capacity. What solution would you recommend to improve the performance of the website?

A. Caching

B. Network load balancing

C. Compression

D. Network bandwidth

☑ **B.** Network load balancing is used to increase performance and provide redundancy for websites and applications.

☒ **A, C,** and **D** are incorrect. Caching is the process of storing frequently accessed data in a location close to the device requesting the data and helps improve network performance for the client, but it would not help improve the performance of the web server. Compression is defined as the reduction in the size of data, which is done by converting that data into a format that requires fewer bits and does not define the amount of data that can be sent over the network. Again, this is a technology that helps with the receiving end of the network traffic but will not alleviate performance issues on the hosting server. Network bandwidth is the amount of data that can traverse a network interface over a specific amount of time, and is a measurement but not a technique or mechanism for improving performance.

Routing and Switching

8. Which process allows a router to modify packets so that multiple devices can share a single public IP address?
   A. NAT
   B. DNS
   C. VLAN
   D. Subnetting

   ☑ **A.** NAT allows your router to change your private IP address into a public IP address so that you can access resources that are external to your organization; then the router tracks those IP address changes.

   ☒ **B, C,** and **D** are incorrect. DNS maps host names to IP addresses, but does not allow multiple hosts to operate from a single IP address. A VLAN allows you to logically segment a LAN into different broadcast domains, whereas subnetting allows you to divide one network into multiple networks.

9. Which of the following IP addresses is in a private IP range?
   A. 12.152.36.9
   B. 10.10.10.10
   C. 72.64.53.89
   D. 173.194.96.3

   ☑ **B.** 10.0.0.0–10.255.255.255 is a private class A address range.

   ☒ **A, C,** and **D** are incorrect. All of these are examples of public IP addresses. Only IP addresses that fall into the IP ranges listed in Table 4-1 are considered private IP addresses.

10. Which of the following technologies allows you to logically segment a LAN into different broadcast domains?
    A. MAN
    B. WAN
    C. VLAN
    D. SAN

☑ **C.** A VLAN allows you to configure separate broadcast domains even if the devices are plugged into the same physical switch.

☒ **A, B,** and **D** are incorrect. A MAN usually connects physically, not logically, separated LANs and is used to build networks with high data connection speeds for cities or college campuses. A WAN is a network that covers a large geographic area and can contain multiple physical, not logical, LANs and/or MANs. A SAN is a dedicated network used to provide access to block-level storage and not broadcast domains.

Network Ports and Protocols

11. Which of the following protocols and ports is used to secure communication over the Internet?
    A. HTTP over port 80
    B. SMTP over port 25
    C. FTP over port 21
    D. HTTPS over port 443

    ☑ **D.** HTTPS is an extension of the HTTP protocol that provides secure communication over the Internet and uses port 443 by default.

    ☒ **A, B,** and **C** are incorrect. HTTP uses port 80 by default and allows for communication between a web client or web browser and a web server hosting a website. SMTP uses port 25 by default to transfer e-mail messages over the Internet. FTP uses port 21 by default to download and transfer files over the Internet. None of these three protocols is a secure form of communication.

12. SFTP uses _____ to secure FTP communication.
    A. Certificates
    B. FTPS
    C. SSH
    D. SMTP

    ☑ **C.** SFTP uses SSH keys to secure FTP communication.

    ☒ **A, B,** and **D** are incorrect. FTPS uses SSL or TLS and certificates to secure FTP communication. SMTP is used to transfer e-mail messages over the Internet.

13. In a network environment _____ is responsible for assigning IP addresses to computers and _____ is responsible for resolving those IP addresses to names.

    A. DNS, DHCP

    B. DHCP, DNS

    C. HTTP, DNS

    D. DHCP, SMTP

    ☑ **B.** DHCP is responsible for assigning IP addresses to computers and DNS is responsible for resolving those IP addresses to names.

    ☒ **A, C,** and **D** are incorrect. HTTP allows for communication between a web client or web browser and a web server hosting a website. SMTP is used to transfer e-mail messages over the Internet.

14. Which of these ports is the well-known port for the Telnet service?

    A. 25

    B. 22

    C. 23

    D. 443

    ☑ **C.** Telnet uses port 23 by default for its communication.

    ☒ **A, B,** and **D** are incorrect. Port 25 is used by SMTP for transferring e-mail. Port 22 is used by SSH, and port 443 is used by HTTPS to provide secure communication over the Internet.

15. This protocol is responsible for transferring electronic mail messages from one mail server to another over the Internet.

    A. DNS

    B. HTTPS

    C. FTP

    D. SMTP

    ☑ **D.** SMTP is used to transfer e-mail messages from one e-mail server to another over the Internet.

    ☒ **A, B,** and **C** are incorrect. DNS translates Internet domain or host names into IP addresses. HTTPS is an extension of the HTTP protocol that provides secure communication over the Internet. FTP is a standard network protocol that allows access to and transfer of files over the Internet using either a command-line or graphical-based FTP client.

5

Virtualization Components

Virtualization technologies have grown substantially over the past five years. Prior to that, many major software vendors would not support their applications if they were being run in a virtualized environment. Now virtualization is the standard when it comes to creating an efficient data center, and almost all application vendors support their applications to run in a virtualized environment. Virtualization allows a cloud provider to deliver these same resources on demand to a cloud consumer as needed. This is the key element of cloud computing.

The IT world has shifted from an applications-to-hardware relationship of one-to-one to that of many-to-one. With the shift to one physical computer running multiple applications and operating systems, the IT industry has become more efficient and has allowed organizations to save thousands of dollars on hardware and data center costs. Virtualization plays a key role in cloud computing by empowering cloud providers to deliver lower-cost hosting environments to cloud consumers. With virtualization an organization can do more with less physical hardware and can deliver applications to their users faster than ever. When an organization implements virtualization, it allows them to get the most out of their physical hardware by running multiple virtual servers on one physical server. This helps them consolidate their infrastructure and reduce total cost of ownership by cutting data center space, power consumption, and administrative overhead.

One key piece of software that has allowed the shift to virtualization is the hypervisor. It is also a key piece of information to be familiar with for the exam. This chapter begins by looking at the various types of hypervisors and how they operate.

CERTIFICATION OBJECTIVE 5.01

Hypervisor

A hypervisor is a piece of software or hardware that creates and runs virtual machines. It is the entity that allows multiple operating systems to run on a single physical machine. The computer running the hypervisor is defined as the "host" computer. The virtual machines that are running on the host are called "guest" machines. The hypervisor is responsible for managing the guest operating system resources, including memory, CPU, and other resources that the guest operating system might need. There are currently two distinct types of hypervisors: type 1 and type 2. Understanding the two types of hypervisors is critical to creating a successful virtualization environment and integrating that environment with the cloud computing models discussed in Chapter 1.

Type 1

A type 1 hypervisor is one that is created and deployed on a bare metal installation. The first thing installed on a type 1 hypervisor is the hypervisor itself; for all intents and purposes it acts as the operating system for the bare metal machine. The software communicates directly with the physical server hardware and boots before the operating system. Almost all of the major virtualization distributors, including VMware, Citrix, and Microsoft, currently use type 1 hypervisors. Figure 5-1 shows an example of what a type 1 hypervisor looks like. The image is meant to give you a graphical representation of the layered design, with hardware layer building on top of hardware layer.

Type 2

Unlike a type 1 hypervisor that is loaded on a bare metal server, a type 2 hypervisor is loaded on top of an already existing operating system installation. For example, a system that is running Microsoft Windows 7 might have a VMware workstation installed on top of that operating system. Type 2 hypervisors create a layer they must

FIGURE 5-1

The layered design of a type 1 hypervisor.

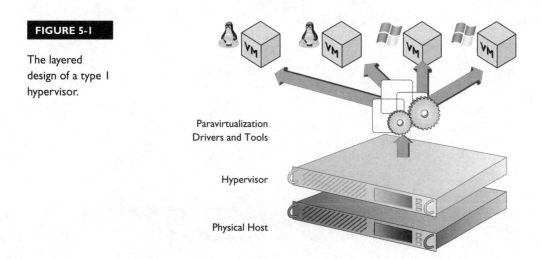

traverse as they are distributed to the guest virtual machines. A type 2 hypervisor relies on the operating system and cannot boot until the operating system is loaded and operational. Since type 2 relies heavily on the underlying operating system, if the system crashes or doesn't boot, all of the guest virtual machines are affected.

Type 1 is the hypervisor of choice for high performance, scalability, and reliability since it functions directly on top of the host hardware and exposes hardware resources to virtual machines. Because the type 2 hypervisor sits on top of the operating system, it makes the virtualized environment less scalable and more complex to manage. Figure 5-2 gives a graphical representation of a type 2 hypervisor. Notice the difference in layering as compared to the type 1 hypervisor.

e x a m

ᙡatch   **The primary difference between a type 1 hypervisor and a type 2 hypervisor is that type 1 is installed natively on the server and boots before** **the operating system, while type 2 is installed on top of or after the operating system.**

FIGURE 5-2

Image of a type 2 hypervisor.

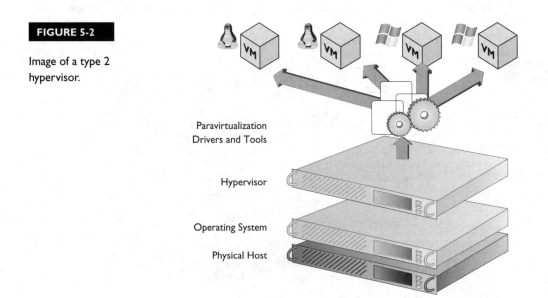

Proprietary

When a company is choosing which type of hypervisor to use, it is important that they understand the difference between a proprietary and an open-source hypervisor. A proprietary hypervisor is one that is developed and licensed under an exclusive legal right of the copyright holder. It is created and distributed under a license agreement to the customer. Microsoft's Hyper-V and VMware's ESX/ESXi are examples of proprietary hypervisors.

Open Source

Some say that the open-source market is growing and advancing faster than the proprietary products market. It can also be argued that the open-source hypervisors are more secure than the proprietary hypervisors because of the underlying operating system running the hypervisor. An open-source hypervisor is provided at no cost and delivers the same ability as a proprietary hypervisor to run multiple guest virtual machines on a single host. Some examples of open-source hypervisors are Citrix XenServer and the kernel-based virtual machine (KVM). Choosing between proprietary and open-source hypervisors can be a difficult decision. Some of the factors that need to be considered are security, trust of the manufacturer, and the operating systems that are supported by the hypervisor. Some organizations also choose not to use an open source because their IT staff is not familiar with the interface. For example, an organization may choose to use Microsoft Hyper-V over Citrix XenServer because their IT staff is already familiar with the Microsoft product line and will not have as big of a learning curve as they might if they used an open-source hypervisor.

Consumer versus Enterprise

The difference between enterprise and consumer-level hypervisors is minute in IT today. A lot of the new desktop operating systems come with a virtualization option already built in; for example, Microsoft Windows 8 now comes with Hyper-V, allowing desktop-level hardware to run a virtual environment. When comparing what a consumer would use for a hypervisor to what an enterprise might use, it is important to consider the goals of the user. An enterprise organization is most likely looking to run multiple operating systems on a single piece of physical hardware, and those operating systems are going to support a large amount of users and a variety of software. In an enterprise environment like this, a type 1 hypervisor is more suitable based on the advantages of type 1 that we have already discussed. In comparison a consumer looking to configure a virtual environment on a desktop is probably not looking to support a large number of users; more than likely they are looking to test a new operating system or application in an isolated environment that is separate from the operating system running their desktop. In this case a type 2 hypervisor is more likely to fit the need. Type 2 would allow the desktop to continue to run the original operating system and then virtually run the new operating system or application that the user is trying to test.

CERTIFICATION OBJECTIVE 5.02

Virtualization Host

Now that you understand what a hypervisor is and how it interacts with a computer, you need to understand the virtualization host that runs the hypervisor software. The virtualization host is the system that is installed first and then hosts or contains the guest virtual machines. The host server provides all of the underlying hardware and compute resources for the guest virtual machines, including memory, CPU, hard disk, and network I/O. Since the host machine provides the resources for the guest, it must contain at least enough hardware resources to meet the minimum requirements for its guest virtual machines.

A virtualization host computer allows different operating systems to coexist on the same host computer. For example, you could have a virtual machine running Microsoft Windows 2012 and another virtual machine running a Linux operating system. Before a computer system can become a virtualization host, there are a number of hardware prerequisites that a computer system must meet. These include BIOS configuration, memory, CPU, and NIC. Figure 5-3 shows an example of a virtualization host computer.

Hardware-Assisted Virtualization

Hardware-assisted virtualization enables efficient full virtualization, which is used to simulate a complete hardware environment or a virtual machine. It is basically a software that allows the hardware to provide architectural support for the host computer to support running guest virtual machines. Hardware-assisted

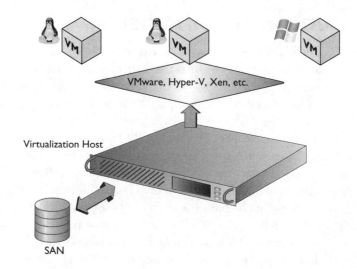

FIGURE 5-3

A graphical representation of a virtualization host.

virtualization helps make virtualization more efficient by utilizing the hardware capabilities built into the host computer's processor. Both AMD and Intel support hardware-assisted virtualization. If an organization wants to find out whether their hardware supports hardware-assisted virtualization, a good place to start is with the AMD and Intel websites. Both websites have a list of all the processors that support hardware-assisted virtualization. It should also be noted that all processors manufactured after 2003 have hardware-assisted virtualization built in. Some laptops were slow to allow access to it, but it was there.

If an organization has already purchased the hardware or wants to repurpose older hardware as a virtualization host, there are free software tools they can download and run that will check to see if their hardware supports hardware-assisted virtualization. For example, if a company is trying to use an older server as a virtualization host to run Microsoft Hyper-V, Microsoft has a free software tool that can determine if that server supports hardware-assisted virtualization and Microsoft Hyper-V.

ⓦatch   *Hardware-assisted virtualization enables efficient full virtualization using the hardware capabilities of the host computer.*

Basic Input/Output System (BIOS)

The BIOS is built-in software that comes with the computer and is usually stored on either a ROM chip or a flash memory chip. The BIOS determines what features a computer supports without having to access any additional software that is loaded on the computer. For example, the BIOS can contain the software that is needed to control the keyboard, the display settings, disk drives, USB settings, power options, and multiple other options. The BIOS allows a computer to boot itself and is available even if the hard disks in the computer fail or are corrupted.

So what does the BIOS have to do with virtualization? The BIOS plays a key role when enabling virtualization on a host computer. In order for a modern computer to act as a host and have the ability to host guest virtual machines, modern operating systems rely on the BIOS to support hardware-assisted virtualization. Some older computers do not have this feature available in the BIOS; others might need a firmware update to the BIOS before the feature can be enabled. However, most of the newer-model servers from most manufacturers, including the latest desktop computers, do support this feature. With the advancement in virtualization and desktop computers, it is no longer necessary to have a host machine running a server-class hardware. Much of the desktop hardware now natively supports hardware-assisted virtualization.

Firmware Configurations

Firmware is a set of instructions that is programmed for a specific hardware device. Firmware tells the hardware device how to communicate with the computer system. Firmware upgrades can be performed on a number of devices, including motherboards, network cards, and hard drives. Firmware upgrades are generally carried out so that the hardware can support new features and functionality. For example, you might do a firmware upgrade on a network card so that the card is supported in a new operating system.

In some cases it might be necessary to do a firmware upgrade to a computer's BIOS in order for it to support hardware-assisted virtualization. This would generally be done on older hardware, as most new hardware purchased today already supports hardware-assisted virtualization. Motherboard manufacturers place firmware updates and the software needed to update the BIOS firmware on their websites for customers to download.

Recently we were brought in to help a small company set up their virtualized environment. They did not budget for new server hardware to host the virtualization environment, and they brought us in to see if the current hardware would support virtualization. We checked the manufacturer's web page and found out the hardware would support virtualization but needed a firmware upgrade before hardware-assisted virtualization could be enabled.

Central Processing Unit (CPU) and Cores

Now that you understand the prerequisites to creating a host machine, you need to understand how to properly size a host machine. Making sure that the host machine can support at least the minimum number of guest virtual machines that the organization is trying to run is a critical step in creating a successful virtualization environment. One of the many benefits of virtualization is the ability to provision virtual machines on the fly as the organization's demands grow, making the purchase of additional hardware unnecessary. If the host computer is not sized correctly, however, it is not possible to add virtual machines without adding compute resources to the host computer.

The first step to sizing the host machine is purchasing the correct type and number of CPUs. Both AMD (AMD-V) and Intel (Intel VT) support virtualization, so the manufacturer is not as critical as is the number of CPU cores and the speed of the CPUs. A multicore processor is a single physical CPU with two or more independent CPUs called cores. Generally speaking, with virtualization a company is better off spending money on more cores with more cache rather than on faster CPU speed. So, for example, if the company has to choose between a system with a 12-core CPU running at 2.2 GHz or a system with a 6-core CPU running at 2.93 GHz, the 12-core CPU is the better choice. This is because with virtualization the company can spread the virtual machine load across more CPU cores, which translates into faster and more consistent virtual machine performance.

Once the organization has defined the processor for the host computer, they need to evaluate how to assign those CPU resources to the guest virtual machines. Not surprisingly, virtual machines use virtual CPUs (vCPUs), which can be added to a virtual machine when it is created. The number of vCPUs that the company should add is dependent on a number of factors, but it is possible to assign multiple vCPUs to a single virtual machine. It is also possible for an organization to assign more vCPUs to their virtual machines than they have physical CPU cores. However, assigning more vCPUs than CPU cores is a tricky proposition. Before undertaking such a move, the company should evaluate the workload of all the virtual machines on the server and whether or not that workload is processor intensive. Most of the time it is safe to assign four to six vCPUs for every CPU core on the server, but again evaluating the environment and the goal of that environment is key. For example, a heavily used Microsoft SQL server is going to be a very processor-intensive virtual machine, so in that scenario an organization would want a one-to-one CPU-to-vCPU assignment. VMware, Hyper-V, and Citrix all have calculators available to help determine exactly how to distribute vCPUs based on best practices for that particular virtualization product. Table 5-1 displays the maximum number of logical CPUs and virtual CPUs for some of the virtualization products currently available.

Memory Capacity and Configurations

Once the organization has decided which CPU and how many CPU cores they are going to purchase for the virtualization host, the next step is to plan the amount of random-access memory (RAM) that the host machine will need. Planning the amount of memory needed on a host machine is quite different from planning the number of CPUs. CPU resources can be oversubscribed (i.e., you can add more vCPUs than you have physical CPUs), but with memory it is much harder to oversubscribe. So planning for memory is critical. The more RAM and the faster the RAM speed, the better for a virtualization host.

Some virtualization platforms allow for adjusting virtual machine memory on the fly, essentially allowing one virtual machine to borrow memory from another virtual machine without shutting down the system. Each of the virtualization products supports virtual machine memory allocation a little bit differently, but the one thing that is consistent is that more memory on the host machine is always better. The job of the IT administrator is to maximize the cost savings of virtualization and the value it brings to the organization. Careful planning is required to provide

TABLE 5-1   Virtualization Host Maximum Resources

Component	VMware ESXi 5.1	Hyper-V 3.0	XenServer 6.1
Logical CPUs per Host	160	320	160
Virtual CPUs per Host	2048	2048	900
RAM per Host	2 TB	4 TB	1 TB
Virtual Machines per Host	512	1024	150
Network Cards per Host	32	No limits imposed by Hyper-V	16

enough memory on the host machine to dynamically provision virtual machines as the organization's needs grow and at the same time to make the most cost-efficient choices. Table 5-1 shows the maximum amount of memory that is allowed on a host machine for some of the virtualization products currently available.

Network Interface Cards (NICs)

While CPU and memory are a primary component when planning the hardware for a virtualization host, the type of network cards to use is just as important. Choosing the correct network configuration and type of card are critical to the success of a virtual environment. Network latency can diminish the speed of a virtual environment, so the organization needs to carefully plan which features their network cards on the host computer need to support.

The first step when planning the NICs for the host computer is to understand the physical aspects of the network. To achieve the best possible network performance on their host computer, the company should use only server-class NICs. It is also necessary to verify that the infrastructure between the source and destination NICs does not introduce a bottleneck. For example, if the organization is using a 10-gigabit NIC to connect to a 10-gigabit port on a switch, they must make sure that all the patch cables support 10-gigabit speeds and that the switch is configured to use 10 gigabits and is not hard coded to use 1-gigabit speeds. The network can only be as fast as the slowest link, so having a misconfigured switch or a bad cable can cause a bottleneck and result in slower performance.

There are some other key features to consider when purchasing NICs for the virtualization host computer. Table 5-2 lists those features and gives a brief description of each.

TABLE 5-2 NIC Hardware Features

Feature	Description
Checksum Off-Load	Off-loads the process of TCP packets to the network controller from the CPU
TCP Segmentation Off-Load (TSO)	Converts large chunks of data into smaller packets to be transmitted through the network
64-Bit Direct Memory Access (DMA) Addresses	Permits high-throughput and low-latency networking
Jumbo Frames (JF)	Extends Ethernet to 9,000 bytes, allowing for less packet overhead on the server and fewer server interrupts
Large Receive Off-Load (LRO)	Increases inbound throughput by reducing CPU overhead, aggregating multiple incoming packets from a single stream into a larger buffer

Virtual Machine

After carefully planning and designing the virtualization host computer, it is ready to support guest virtual machines. However, there is just as much planning, if not more, that needs to go into configuring the virtual machines. With virtualization comes the ability to maximize the physical server and no longer have "unused" resources. While this is a huge advantage and cost savings to an organization, it also requires more planning than the one-to-one way of thinking prior to virtualization. Before virtualization IT administrators were confined to the physical resources that were available on the server running a particular application. With virtualization an IT administrator now has the ability to add compute resources to a virtual machine without having to purchase additional hardware, as long as the virtualization host computer has been designed with this in mind.

The concept of a virtual machine is sometimes difficult to grasp. Think of a virtual machine in the same way you think of a physical server hosting an application. A virtual machine emulates a physical computer, with the only difference being that its compute resources are managed by a hypervisor that translates resource requests to the underlying physical hardware. You can think of a virtual machine as a portable file that can be moved, copied, and reassigned to a different virtualization host with minimal administration.

The guest operating system is unaware that it is running in a virtual environment, so it allows applications and software to be installed as if it were running on a physical server. Isolation of applications is just one of the many advantages of running a virtual environment. The applications can be installed on separate virtual machines, which provides complete isolation from other applications running on the host computer or another virtual machine. This is a great way to test new applications without interfering with existing applications, or to create a development environment that is completely segmented from the production environment. This section explains the compute resources that make up a virtual machine and how to manage and plan for those resources in a virtual environment.

Virtual Disks

Just like a physical server, a virtual machine needs to have a place to install an operating system and applications and to store files and folders. Simply put, a virtual disk is a file that represents a physical disk drive to the virtual machine. A virtual disk file resides on the host computer and is seen by the guest virtual machine. It contains the same properties and features of a physical drive, including disk partitions, a file system, and files and folders.

When creating a virtual disk, a few decisions need to be made, including the type of disk, the name and location of the disk, and the size of the disk. Each of the major virtualization manufacturers have different terms when describing virtual disk configurations. For example, if you are using Microsoft Hyper-V, you would have the options of making a dynamically expanding virtual disk, a fixed virtual disk, or a differencing virtual disk. If you are creating a fixed-size disk, you would specify the size of the disk when it is created. If you are creating a dynamically expanding virtual disk, the disk starts as a small size and adds storage as needed. On the other hand, if you are creating a virtual disk in VMware ESXi, you have the option of creating a thick disk or a thin disk. A thick disk is similar to a fixed disk in Microsoft Hyper-V in that the size is specified and allocated during the creation of the virtual disk. A thin disk is similar to a dynamically expanding disk in Microsoft Hyper-V in that the disk starts out small and adds space as required by the virtual machine.

While the different virtualization manufacturers use different terms to define their virtual disks, the concepts are similar. Whether you are using Hyper-V, ESXi, or XenServer, you still need to decide which type of disk to use for which application. If you are concerned about disk space, then using a thin disk or dynamically expanding disk would be the best option. If size is not a concern, then you could use a fixed-size or thick disk.

When planning for virtual disks, another concept that is critical to understand is thin provisioning. Thin provisioning allows virtual disks to allocate and commit storage space on demand and use only the space they currently require. With thin provisioning, a company can create multiple virtual disks and set the limits of those virtual disks to an amount greater than the total available storage space. This essentially allows them to overcommit the storage capacity. Careful monitoring must be implemented in this scenario to control the actual disk usage, but if configured correctly, thin provisioning can save an organization time and money.

When configuring a thick-provisioned or fixed-size virtual disk, the organization allocates the storage space while the initial disk is being created. This means that the virtual disk is guaranteed and consumes whatever amount of disk space the company specifies during creation of that virtual disk. When comparing thin and thick provisioning and which one works best in the organization's environment, it is important to keep a few things in mind. Thick provisioning provides better performance because the drive size is not being built as the application requires more drive space. Thin provisioning does not have the same performance level as a thick disk and needs to be monitored closely to prevent running out of available disk space since storage space is by definition overcommitted. The application can also help determine which type of virtual disk to choose. For example, an application that writes a lot of data to the drive, like Microsoft SQL, would not perform as well on a thin-provisioned disk. If the application is not writing to the virtual disk that often and space is a concern, then a thin-provisioned disk would be more appropriate. Table 5-3 shows the maximum number of virtual IDE and SCSI disks that are available for various types of virtual machines.

Virtual NICs

Configuring and planning the virtual network interface cards is just as important as planning the virtual disk configuration. The network interface card in a computer is what allows the computer to interact with other virtual machines and devices on the network. Proper configuration of the virtual NIC and network settings is a key component to minimizing bottlenecks in the virtual environment. A virtual network interface card does not have any physical components; it is a software component made up of software drivers that mimic a physical NIC. A virtual NIC allows an organization to change some of the properties of the NIC itself, including MAC address settings, network connections, and VLAN ID. This allows for greater control over the virtual NIC from within the hypervisor software. Once the settings

TABLE 5-3   Virtual Machine Limits

Components (per Virtual Machine)	VMware ESXi 5.1	Microsoft Hyper-V 3.0	Citrix XenServer 6.1
Memory	1 TB	1 TB	128 GB
Virtual CPUs	64	64	32
Virtual IDE Hard Disks	4	4	XenServer does not emulate SCSI or IDE and uses xvd devices with a maximum of 16
Virtual SCSI Disks	60	256	
Virtual NICs	10	12	7

are configured and the virtual NIC is installed on the virtual machine, it functions almost like a physical NIC installed on a physical server.

After attaching a virtual NIC to a virtual machine, the organization has the ability to add that virtual NIC to a virtual network. A virtual network is a group of network devices that are configured to access local or external network resources, and consists of virtual network links. In effect, a virtual network is the network where traffic between the virtual servers is routed using virtual switches and virtual routers. A virtual router is software-based router that allows a virtualization host to act like a hardware router over the network. A virtual network allows the virtual machine to interact with the rest of the LAN. In addition to configuring a virtual switch, an administrator has the option to configure bridged networking, which allows the virtual machine to communicate with the outside world using the physical NIC so it can appear as a normal host to the rest of the network. There are some options that need to be considered when configuring a virtual machine to communicate with the rest of the local area network. For example, the company might not want their virtual machine to communicate with anything on the LAN, in which case they can isolate it to communicate only with other virtual machines on the same host. In a different scenario they might want to bridge the connection between their virtual machine and the LAN used by the host computer so that the virtual machine can communicate with devices that are external to the host computer. Determining how the virtual NIC and virtual machine use virtual networks is an important piece of virtualization. Remember, one of the many benefits of virtualization is the ability to isolate applications for testing and deployment, but that is only possible if the virtual network and virtual NIC are configured properly.

After the virtual machine's operating system recognizes and installs the virtual NIC, it can be configured just like a physical NIC. It is possible to set the IP address, the DNS, the default gateway, netmask, the link speed, and so on. The actual network configuration of the virtual NIC is identical to that of a physical network adapter. So the virtual machine connects to the network in the same manner a physical machine would that has the same IP address and subnet mask configuration. A virtual machine can be configured to use one or more virtual Ethernet adapters, allowing each adapter to have its own MAC and IP address. Table 5-3 shows the maximum number of virtual NICs that are available on various types of virtual machines.

Virtual Switches

Once the organization has created and added a virtual NIC to their virtual machine, the next step in the process is to assign a virtual switch to the machine so that it can communicate with other network devices. Similar to a physical switch, a virtual switch makes it possible to connect other network devices together. A virtual switch controls how the network traffic flows between the virtual machines and the host computer as well as how network traffic flows between the virtual machine and other network devices in the organization. Virtual switches also allow the company to isolate network traffic to their virtual machines. A virtual switch can provide some of the same security features as a physical switch, including policy enforcement, isolation, traffic shaping, and simplified troubleshooting. It can support VLANs and is compatible with standard VLAN implementations. However, a virtual switch cannot be attached to another virtual switch; instead, more ports can be added to the existing switch.

An organization can create different types of virtual switches to control network connectivity to a virtual machine. An external virtual switch allows the virtual machine to communicate with other virtual machines on the same host and with other network devices located outside the host computer. An internal virtual switch allows the virtual machines and the host to communicate with each other, but the virtual machine is unable to communicate with network devices located outside the host computer.

Planning the virtual switch configuration is extremely important to a company's virtualization design. It is equally important for the organization to make sure the virtual switch that the virtual machine uses to communicate is configured correctly. Proper design of the virtual switch environment is critical to the virtual machine being able to communicate to the correct part of the network.

e x a m
ⓦ a t c h
You need to understand how to configure a virtual switch so that a virtual machine can communicate with the correct network devices.

Memory

Managing memory on a virtual machine is different than managing memory on a physical server. When dealing with a physical server, an organization has to decide at the time of purchase how much memory that server needs to have. When building or deploying a virtual machine, the company can change the memory on the fly as needed. A virtual machine only consumes memory if that virtual machine is running. Managing virtual machine memory is easier and allows the organization to maximize their resources for that virtual machine. They can set the initial size of the virtual machine's memory and change that setting after the virtual machine has been created and is operational. For example, they may have a virtual machine running file and print services and may be uncertain what the memory requirements ultimately will be. In this instance they can configure a low amount of memory to start and then monitor the virtual machine to determine its memory utilization. If it reaches 90 or 100 percent utilization, they can easily increase the amount of memory without having to purchase additional hardware. Keep in mind, however, that this is only possible if there is additional memory available on the virtualization host computer. The host computer must also have enough physical memory available to start the virtual machine; if there is not enough available physical memory, the virtual machine will not be allowed to start. Earlier in this chapter you learned how to plan memory allocation on the virtualization host; now you can see why planning the host computer resources is so important.

When an organization is creating a virtual machine and assigning memory for the first time, it is important to ensure, first of all, that the amount of memory meets the minimum recommendations for the operating system that the virtual machine is going to be running. In addition, the company must consider what types of applications the virtual machine will be running. If a specific application requires a lot of memory on a physical server, it will need the same setup on a virtual machine. The organization must also take into account what other virtual machines are running on the host computer that will be competing with this virtual machine for memory resources. And they need to consider what other applications are going to be running on the host computer that might need resources as well. This should not be a major factor on a type 1 hypervisor since it is best practice not to run any additional software on the host computer. However, if there are additional applications running on the host computer besides the hypervisor, the company should take that into consideration when planning memory size on a virtual machine. On a type 2 hypervisor other applications would be running on the host computer and would require memory, so those applications would need to be factored in when determining memory size for the virtual machine.

Memory can be assigned to a virtual machine in a couple of ways. One option is to configure a static amount of memory that is assigned to the virtual machine at all times. Static memory is a predefined amount of memory that is allocated to the virtual machine. If an organization uses this setting for all the virtual machines on a host computer, then the host computer must have at least enough physical memory to support those virtual machines. A second option is to use dynamic memory, which allows a company to assign a minimum and maximum amount of memory to a virtual machine. With dynamic memory, a virtual machine consumes memory based on its current workload. Dynamic memory also allows for overcommitting the host computer's physical memory so that more virtual machines can be run on that host computer. In addition, an organization can enable dynamic memory on a per-virtual-machine basis, targeting only those virtual machines that can benefit from it. One way for a company to determine if they should use static or dynamic memory is by taking into account the application the virtual machine will be running. For example, if they have a virtual machine that is running an application that uses a fixed amount of memory, it is better to use static memory and allocate exactly the amount of memory that virtual machine needs. Managing virtual machine memory is a key component to the performance of the virtualization environment and needs to be carefully planned and executed. Table 5-3 shows the maximum amount of memory that is available for various types of virtual machines.

Storage Virtualization

Planning where to store the virtual disks and configuration files for the virtual machine is something that needs careful consideration. Storage virtualization groups multiple network storage devices into a single storage unit that can be managed from a central console and used by a virtual machine or host computer. Storage virtualization usually occurs in a storage area network (SAN) where a high-speed collection of shared storage devices can be used. Managing storage devices can be a complex and tedious task for an administrator. Storage virtualization simplifies the administration of common storage tasks, such as archiving, recovery, backups, and the configuration of storage.

A virtualized storage environment has some distinct advantages over non-virtualized storage. In a non-virtualized storage environment, the host computers connect directly to the storage that is internal to the host or to an external array. In this scenario the server takes complete ownership of the physical storage, with an entire disk tied to a single server. Virtualized storage enables the use of shared storage devices and solves the issue of a single server owning the storage by allowing multiple host servers and virtual machines to simultaneously access the storage. Shared storage can present storage to a host computer, and the host computer in turn can present the storage to the virtual machine. Multiple host computers can access shared storage at the same time, which allows the virtual machines to migrate between host computers. Virtualization software supports all the common storage interconnects for block-based storage, including Fibre Channel, iSCSI, Fibre Channel over Ethernet (FCoE), and direct attached storage. The virtualization software provides an interface to simplify how the virtual machine accesses the storage. It also presents SCSI and IDE controllers to the virtual machines so that the operating system can recognize the storage. The virtual machine sees only a simple physical disk attached via the IDE or SCSI controller provided by the virtualization software. There are a number of advantages to presenting virtualized storage to a virtual machine, including ease of management, improved efficiency, and the ability to present storage types that the native operating system might not support.

If an organization uses Fibre Channel to connect to shared storage, they are taking advantage of N_port ID virtualization (NPIV), a technology that allows multiple host computers to share a single physical Fibre Channel port identification, or N_port. This allows a single host bus adapter to register multiple World Wide Names (WWNs) and N_port identification numbers. By using NPIV each host server can present a different WWN to the shared storage device, which allows each host computer to see its own storage.

In addition to storage virtualization, an organization might look to clustered storage to provide increased performance, capacity, and reliability for the storage environment that the virtual machines access. Clustered storage combines multiple storage devices together to distribute the workload between storage devices and provide access to the virtual machine files, regardless of the physical location of the files.

Guest Tools

Guest tools are software additions that are added to a virtual machine after the operating system has been installed. They enhance the performance of a virtual machine and improve the interaction between the virtual machine and the host computer. Guest tools also make it easier to manage a virtual machine by providing enhanced features, such as faster graphics performance, time synchronization between host and guest, increased network performance, and the ability to copy files between the virtual machine and the host computer. The guest tools are also responsible for integrating the drivers into the guest virtual machine operating system.

A guest virtual machine operating system can run without installing guest tools, but it loses a lot of the important functionality and ease of administration without them. Installing the guest tools is easy and straightforward on all major virtualization applications and is sometimes even built into the operating system. For example, a Windows Server 2012 virtual machine created using Microsoft Hyper-V has the virtual machine integration services already loaded. Most operating systems, including Microsoft Windows, Linux, Solaris, FreeBSD, NetWare, and Mac OS X, support installation of guest tools.

exam

ⓦatch　　*Guest tools help the virtual machine interact with the host machine. Some virtual machine features may not* *work without the guest tools being installed on that virtual machine.*

CERTIFICATION SUMMARY

Knowing how to plan a virtualization environment is of great importance to any organization wishing to adopt a cloud computing infrastructure. A virtualization host computer uses software called a hypervisor that allows a single physical computer to host multiple guests called virtual machines, which can run different operating systems and have different amounts of compute resources assigned to each guest. Understanding how a host computer and a guest virtual machine interact and share resources is a key concept not only to the CompTIA Cloud+ exam but to a successful cloud computing implementation.

KEY TERMS

Use the list below to review the key terms that were discussed in this chapter. The definitions can be found within this chapter and in the glossary.

Hypervisor   Piece of software or hardware that creates and runs a virtual machine and allows multiple operating systems to run on a single physical computer

Type I hypervisor   Hypervisor that is created and deployed on a bare metal installation

Type 2 hypervisor   Hypervisor loaded on top of an already existing operating system installation

Open source   Hypervisor software provided at no cost and delivers the same ability to run multiple guest virtual machines on a single host

Proprietary   Software that is developed and licensed under an exclusive legal right of the copyright holder

Virtualization host   System that hosts or contains guest virtual machines

Virtual machine/guest   Emulates a physical computer where the virtualization host translates requests for compute resources to the underlying physical hardware

Basic input/output system (BIOS)   Built-in software that allows the computer to boot without an operating system and controls the code required to manage the keyboard, display, disk drives, and a number of other functions

Firmware   Set of instructions that are programmed for a specific hardware device that instructs the hardware device how to communicate with the computer system

Hardware-assisted virtualization   Enables efficient full virtualization used to simulate a complete hardware environment or a virtual machine

Central processing unit (CPU)   Hardware device responsible for executing all of the instructions from the operating system and software

Virtual CPU (vCPU)   Used on a guest virtual machine and is similar to a physical CPU

Network interface card (NIC)   Computer component that is used to connect a computer to a computer network

Virtual NIC (vNIC)   Similar to a physical NIC and has the ability to connect to a virtual switch and be assigned an IP address, default gateway, and subnet mask

Virtual disk   Emulates a physical disk drive to a virtual machine

Thin provisioning   Allows a virtual disk to allocate and commit storage space on demand and use only the space it currently requires

Thick provisioning   Allocates the amount of disk space required when the virtual disk is created

Virtual switch   Similar to a physical switch, it allows network devices to be connected and is used to control how the network traffic flows between the virtual machines and the virtualization host

Storage virtualization   Groups multiple network storage devices into a single storage unit that can be managed from a central console and presented to a virtual machine or host computer as a single storage unit

Guest tools   Software additions that are added to a virtual machine after the operating system has been installed to improve the interaction between the virtual machine and the virtualization host

N_Port ID Virtualization (NPIV)   Allows multiple host computers to share a single physical Fibre Channel port identification or N_Port

✓ TWO-MINUTE DRILL

Hypervisor

- ❑ A hypervisor is software that allows a computer system to run multiple operating systems on a single piece of hardware.
- ❑ A computer that runs the hypervisor and hosts multiple operating systems is called the host computer.
- ❑ A type 1 hypervisor is deployed on a bare metal system and communicates directly with the physical server hardware.
- ❑ A type 2 hypervisor is loaded on top of a system that is already running an operating system. It relies on that operating system to load a guest virtual machine.
- ❑ An open-source hypervisor is provided at no cost, whereas a proprietary hypervisor is purchased by the customer under a licensed agreement.
- ❑ A consumer is more likely to use a type 2 hypervisor and an enterprise is more likely to use a type 1 hypervisor to host multiple guest virtual machines.

Virtualization Host

- ❑ In order for a computer to be configured as a host computer, the BIOS must support and have hardware-assisted virtualization enabled, which might require a firmware upgrade.
- ❑ Planning the resources a virtualization host requires to support the virtual environment is a key step to having a successful virtualization implementation.
- ❑ When planning how many CPUs to have in a host computer, the number of CPU cores is more important than the speed of the CPU.
- ❑ When purchasing NICs for a host computer, it is important that they support some of the advanced features, like TCP off-load, jumbo frames, checksum off-load, and large receive off-load.

Virtual Machine

- ❑ A virtual machine is very similar to a physical computer, with the primary difference being a virtual machine's compute resources are managed by a hypervisor.

❑ A virtual environment allows you to isolate a virtual machine from the rest of the network for testing and development of new applications and operating systems.

❑ A virtual disk emulates a physical disk and is managed by the virtual machine in the same manner a physical disk would be.

❑ A virtual disk can be either thick or thin. A thin-provisioned disk starts out small and grows as data is written to it, whereas a thick disk size is defined when the disk is created.

❑ A virtual NIC (vNIC) is similar to a physical NIC and can be assigned an IP address, default gateway, and subnet mask.

❑ A vNIC is connected to a virtual switch, and the virtual switch dictates how the vNIC and virtual machine communicate on the network.

❑ A virtual machine has the ability to use dynamic memory, which allows the virtual machine to start with a smaller amount of memory and increase it based on the load on the virtual machine.

❑ Storage virtualization groups multiple network storage devices into a single storage unit that can be managed from a central console and presented to a virtual machine or host computer as a single storage unit.

❑ Guest tools are software additions that provide features and enhancements to a virtual machine, along with improving the interaction between a virtual machine and a host computer.

SELF TEST

The following questions will help you measure your understanding of the material presented in this chapter.

Hypervisor

1. Which of the following hypervisors would provide the best performance for a host machine?
   A. Type 1
   B. Type 2
   C. Open source
   D. Proprietary

2. You are investigating which technology is best suited for virtualizing a server operating system for personal use on a desktop computer. Which of the following technologies would you recommend?
   A. Type 1
   B. Type 2
   C. SAN
   D. RAID 6

3. Which of the following hypervisors runs on a bare metal system?
   A. Open source
   B. Proprietary
   C. Type 1
   D. Type 2

4. What type of hypervisor is provided to an enterprise to use without cost?
   A. Proprietary
   B. Open source
   C. Type 1
   D. Type 2

5. An administrator is testing a variety of operating systems while performing other functions like surfing the Internet and word processing. What type of hypervisor are they most likely using?
   A. Type 1
   B. Enterprise hypervisor
   C. Type 2
   D. Open source

Virtualization Host

6. You are deploying two virtual servers. One of the virtual servers is a heavily used database server and the other is a lightly used print server. What virtual CPU configuration would you recommend?

  A. One virtual CPU for the database server and two virtual CPUs for the print server

  B. Two virtual CPUs for the database server and two virtual CPUs for the print server

  C. Two virtual CPUs for the database server and one virtual CPU for the print server

  D. Three virtual CPUs for the print server and two virtual CPUs for the database server

7. An administrator is trying to enable hardware-assisted virtualization in the BIOS of a computer and notices it is not an option. He checks the specification on the manufacturer's website and finds that the system should support hardware-assisted virtualization. What is most likely the reason why he can't enable it?

  A. The BIOS needs a firmware update.

  B. The BIOS is corrupt.

  C. Hardware-assisted virtualization is enabled in the operating system, not the BIOS.

  D. The firmware is corrupt.

8. You have been tasked with planning the purchase of a new virtualization host computer. When it comes time to recommend the processor type, which processor capability is more important?

  A. CPUs are more important than CPU cores and cache.

  B. CPU cores and cache are more important than CPUs.

  C. CPU speed is more important than CPU cores and cache.

  D. CPU cores and cache are more important than CPU speed.

9. True or False. When purchasing a NIC for a host computer, it is important to purchase one that supports advanced features such as jumbo frames and TCP Off-loads.

  A. True

  B. False

10. Which of the following would be a requirement when planning the compute resources for a host computer?

  A. The host computer does not need to have enough compute resources to support the virtual machine workload.

  B. The host computer must have enough compute resources to support the virtual machine workload.

  C. The host computer must be running a support operating system.

  D. The number of virtual machines running Microsoft Windows must be known.

Virtual Machine

11. In a virtual machine, which component appears as an Ethernet adapter?

- **A.** Virtual HBA
- **B.** Virtual NIC
- **C.** Virtual switch
- **D.** Virtual router

12. An administrator deploys a new virtual machine. After logging on to the virtual machine, he notices that it has a different time setting than the host. What is most likely the cause of this issue?

- **A.** The virtual machine cannot communicate with the network.
- **B.** The guest tools are not installed.
- **C.** The virtual NIC is not configured correctly.
- **D.** The VLAN tag is incorrect.

13. Which of the following groups multiple network storage devices into a single storage unit that can be managed from a central console and used by a virtual machine or host computer?

- **A.** Virtual switch
- **B.** Virtual HBA
- **C.** Virtual NIC
- **D.** Storage virtualization

14. Which type of memory allows a virtual machine to start with a smaller amount of memory and increase it based on the workload of the virtual machine?

- **A.** Startup RAM
- **B.** Static memory
- **C.** Virtual memory
- **D.** Dynamic memory

15. Which component controls how the network traffic flows between the virtual machines and the host computer and also how network traffic flows between the virtual machine and other network devices in the organization?

- **A.** Virtual NIC
- **B.** Virtual storage
- **C.** Virtual HBA
- **D.** Virtual switch

SELF TEST ANSWERS

Hypervisor

1. Which of the following hypervisors would provide the best performance for a host machine?
    A. Type 1
    B. Type 2
    C. Open source
    D. Proprietary

    ☑ **A.** A type 1 hypervisor is one that is created and deployed on a bare metal installation. The hypervisor communicates directly with the physical server hardware and boots before the operating system. Due to the way the hypervisor interacts with the host computer, a type 1 hypervisor will provide improved performance versus the other answer choices.
    ☒ **B, C,** and **D** are incorrect. A type 2 hypervisor is loaded on top of an already existing operating system installation, and the underlying operating system is what impacts performance. While it could be argued that open source might perform better than proprietary, the open-source hypervisor would still be considered a type 1 hypervisor.

2. You are investigating which technology is best suited for virtualizing a server operating system for personal use on a desktop computer. Which of the following technologies would you recommend?
    A. Type 1
    B. Type 2
    C. SAN
    D. RAID 6

    ☑ **B.** A type 2 hypervisor is more suited for personal use because it can be installed directly on top of an existing operating system. Most desktop manufacturers support hardware virtualization on their desktops, which would allow you to run a type 2 hypervisor on your existing operating system.
    ☒ **A, C,** and **D** are incorrect. A type 1 hypervisor is more suited for an enterprise environment where the host computer is designed and configured to do nothing but virtualization. A SAN and RAID 6 would not be a required consideration when running a personal virtualization solution.

3. Which of the following hypervisors runs on a bare metal system?
   A. Open source
   B. Proprietary
   C. Type 1
   D. Type 2

   ☑ **C.** A type 1 hypervisor is one that is created and deployed on a bare metal installation.
   ☒ **A, B,** and **D** are incorrect. A type 2 hypervisor is loaded on top of an already existing operating system installation. Type 1 or type 2 hypervisors can be either open source or proprietary hypervisors.

4. What type of hypervisor is provided to an enterprise to use without cost?
   A. Proprietary
   B. Open source
   C. Type 1
   D. Type 2

   ☑ **B.** An open-source hypervisor is provided at no cost and delivers the same ability to run multiple guest virtual machines on a single host as a proprietary hypervisor.
   ☒ **A, C,** and **D** are incorrect. A proprietary hypervisor is one that is developed and licensed under an exclusive legal right of the copyright holder and must be purchased by the customer. Type 1 or type 2 hypervisors can be either open source or proprietary hypervisors.

5. An administrator is testing a variety of operating systems while performing other functions like surfing the Internet and word processing. What type of hypervisor are they most likely using?
   A. Type 1
   B. Enterprise hypervisor
   C. Type 2
   D. Open source

   ☑ **C.** A type 2 hypervisor allows an administrator to run virtual machines on top of an existing operating system while surfing the Internet and running word processing on the host computer.
   ☒ **A, B,** and **D** are incorrect. A type 1 hypervisor could be used to run virtual machines and at the same time surf the Internet and do word processing, but it would not be best practice. It is not advised to run additional applications on the host computer other than the type 1 hypervisor software due to security risks and resource utilization. An enterprise hypervisor is not a valid hypervisor. An open-source hypervisor can be either a type 1 or type 2 hypervisor.

Virtualization Host

6. You are deploying two virtual servers. One of the virtual servers is a heavily used database server and the other is a lightly used print server. What virtual CPU configuration would you recommend?

   A. One virtual CPU for the database server and two virtual CPUs for the print server

   B. Two virtual CPUs for the database server and two virtual CPUs for the print server

   C. Two virtual CPUs for the database server and one virtual CPU for the print server

   D. Three virtual CPUs for the print server and two virtual CPUs for the database server

   ☑ **C.** When assigning virtual CPUs, you want to assign as many as possible to the heavily used application. If an application is not going to be heavily utilized, you should assign the minimum amount of virtual CPUs. In this case the database server is heavily utilized so it should get more CPUs than the lightly used print server.

   ☒ **A, B,** and **D** are incorrect. You would not need to assign the print server more than one virtual CPU, and you would want to assign the database server more virtual CPUs than the print server.

7. An administrator is trying to enable hardware-assisted virtualization in the BIOS of a computer and notices it is not an option. He checks the specification on the manufacturer's website and finds that the system should support hardware-assisted virtualization. What is most likely the reason why he can't enable it?

   A. The BIOS needs a firmware update.

   B. The BIOS is corrupt.

   C. Hardware-assisted virtualization is enabled in the operating system, not the BIOS.

   D. The firmware is corrupt.

   ☑ **A.** If the manufacturer states that the hardware should support hardware-assisted virtualization and the option is unavailable in the BIOS, the most likely cause is that the BIOS needs a firmware update to add the additional feature.

   ☒ **B, C,** and **D** are incorrect. While there could be additional reasons that the feature is not available in the BIOS, the first thing to consider would be to update the BIOS firmware.

8. You have been tasked with planning the purchase of a new virtualization host computer. When it comes time to recommend the processor type, which processor capability is more important?

   A. CPUs are more important than CPU cores and cache.

   B. CPU cores and cache are more important than CPUs.

C. CPU speed is more important than CPU cores and cache.

D. CPU cores and cache are more important than CPU speed.

☑ **D.** You are better off spending money on more cores with more cache rather than on faster CPU speed. When it comes to virtualization, you want as many CPU cores as possible to assign to the virtual machine.

☒ **A, B,** and **C** are incorrect. While CPU speed is important, CPU cores and cache are more important. When determining where to spend the extra budget, you want to spend it on cores and cache over speed.

9. True or False. When purchasing a NIC for a host computer, it is important to purchase one that supports advanced features such as jumbo frames and TCP Off-loads.

A. True

B. False

☑ **A.** You should use only server-class NICs in a virtualization host, and the NIC should support advanced features such as jumbo frames to help minimize network latency.

☒ **B** is incorrect. You should not purchase NICs that do not support the advanced features listed in the question for a host computer.

10. Which of the following would be a requirement when planning the compute resources for a host computer?

A. The host computer does not need to have enough compute resources to support the virtual machine workload.

B. The host computer must have enough compute resources to support the virtual machine workload.

C. The host computer must be running a support operating system.

D. The number of virtual machines running Microsoft Windows must be known.

☑ **B.** When you are planning for and determining the compute resources for a host computer, you need to make sure there are enough resources to handle the virtual machine workload that the host computer is expected to support.

☒ **A, C,** and **D** are incorrect. The most important thing for planning compute resources on a host computer is to have enough resources to cover the virtual machine load.

Virtual Machine

11. In a virtual machine, which component appears as an Ethernet adapter?
A. Virtual HBA
B. Virtual NIC
C. Virtual switch
D. Virtual router

☑ **B.** A virtual network interface card does not have any physical components; it is a software component made up of software drivers that mimic a physical NIC and appears as an Ethernet adapter on a virtual machine.

☒ **A, C,** and **D** are incorrect. None of these options would be shown as an Ethernet adapter on a virtual machine when they are added to a virtual machine.

12. An administrator deploys a new virtual machine. After logging on to the virtual machine, he notices that it has a different time setting than the host. What is most likely the cause of this issue?
A. The virtual machine cannot communicate with the network.
B. The guest tools are not installed.
C. The virtual NIC is not configured correctly.
D. The VLAN tag is incorrect.

☑ **B.** Guest tools are software additions that are added to a virtual machine after the operating system has been installed. Among other things, the guest tools allow a virtual machine to synchronize its time with a host computer.

☒ **A, C,** and **D** are incorrect. The guest tools allow the virtual machine to use the host computer as a time source. Without the guest tools the virtual machine might not have the correct time.

13. Which of the following groups multiple network storage devices into a single storage unit that can be managed from a central console and used by a virtual machine or host computer?
A. Virtual switch
B. Virtual HBA
C. Virtual NIC
D. Storage virtualization

☑ **D.** Storage virtualization consolidates multiple storage devices into a single unit and simplifies the administration of common storage tasks.

☒ **A, B,** and **C** are incorrect. Virtual switch, virtual HBA, and a virtual NIC can all be used to access shared storage over the network, but they would not be used to create shared storage.

14. Which type of memory allows a virtual machine to start with a smaller amount of memory and increase it based on the workload of the virtual machine?
    A. Startup RAM
    B. Static memory
    C. Virtual memory
    D. Dynamic memory

    ☑ **D.** Dynamic memory allows you to assign a minimum and maximum amount of memory to a virtual machine. This allows a virtual machine to consume memory dynamically based on its current workload.

    ☒ **A, B,** and **C** are incorrect. The other memory options in the question do not allow the virtual machine to increase its memory as needed since they are statically assigned.

15. Which component controls how the network traffic flows between the virtual machines and the host computer and also how network traffic flows between the virtual machine and other network devices in the organization?
    A. Virtual NIC
    B. Virtual storage
    C. Virtual HBA
    D. Virtual switch

    ☑ **D.** The virtual switch is responsible for how the network traffic flows between virtual machines and the host and between virtual machines and other network devices.

    ☒ **A, B,** and **C** are incorrect. A virtual NIC allows you to connect to a virtual switch. A virtual HBA would allow you to connect to a storage device. Virtual storage does not allow you to control how the virtual machine connects with the network.

6

Virtualization and the Cloud

Virtualization is the key building block to cloud computing. While it is not a requirement for cloud computing, it is the component that makes it possible to provide a scalable, elastic, and on-demand environment. Virtualization allows an organization to easily scale their computing environment both up and down to meet their needs. When combined with cloud computing, virtualization allows an organization to take advantage of unlimited computing resources provided externally by a cloud provider. Virtualization will continue to play a big role in cloud computing, as it is the technology that allows a cloud provider to deliver low-cost hosting environments to organizations no matter what the size of the enterprise.

CERTIFICATION OBJECTIVE 6.01

Benefits of Virtualization in a Cloud Environment

Cloud computing and virtualization go hand in hand. Virtualization makes cloud computing more efficient and easier to manage. It allows an organization to consolidate their servers by running multiple applications instead of a single application on each server, thus reducing the number of servers they need to purchase and in turn lessening rack space, power consumption, and administration. What this means for a cloud environment is that an organization is now able to look at compute resources as a centralized resource that allows them to allocate business units on demand while still maintaining control of resources and applications.

Shared Resources

Cloud computing can provide compute resources as a centralized resource by using shared resources. Shared resources give a cloud provider the ability to distribute resources on an as-needed basis to the cloud consumer, which improves efficiency and reduces costs for an organization. Virtualization helps to simplify the process of sharing compute resources. As we discussed in Chapter 5, virtualization also increases the efficiency of hardware utilization. The cloud, on the other hand, adds a layer of management that allows a virtual machine to be created quickly and scaled to meet the demands of the organization. While virtualization is not a requirement of cloud computing, the majority of cloud deployments are built upon virtualization to provide the elasticity and scalability a cloud consumer needs. Figure 6-1 shows an example of how shared resources are configured.

Elasticity

Elastic computing allows compute resources to vary dynamically to meet a variable workload. This is a primary reason organizations implement a cloud computing model. The organization needs the ability to dynamically increase or decrease the compute resources of their virtual environment. A cloud provider can support elasticity by using resource pooling. Resource pooling allows compute resources to be pooled to serve multiple consumers by using a multitenant model, with different physical and virtual resources dynamically assigned and reassigned based on cloud consumer demands. With cloud computing and elasticity, the time to service and the time it takes to implement an application can both be drastically reduced. When an organization implements cloud computing and virtualization, they can quickly provision a new server to host an application and then provision that application, which in turn reduces the time it takes to implement new applications and services.

FIGURE 6-1

An illustration of shared resources in a cloud environment.

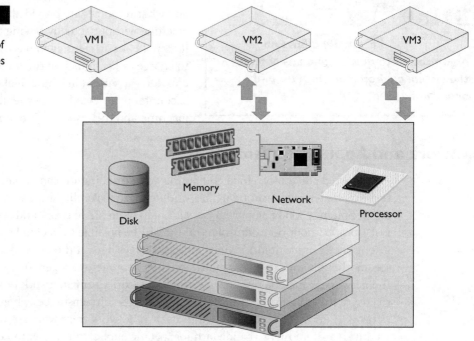

Elasticity allows an organization to scale resources up and down as an application or service requires. In this scenario the organization becomes a cloud consumer and the resources in the cloud appear to the consumer to be infinite, allowing the organization to consume as much or as few resources as they require. With this new scalable and elastic computing model, an organization can respond to compute resource demands in a quick and efficient manner, saving them time and money. Not only can an organization as a cloud consumer dynamically scale the resources it needs, it can also migrate its applications and data between cloud providers, making the applications portable. With the cloud an organization has the ability to deploy applications to any cloud provider, making all of the applications portable and scalable.

While virtualization alone could provide many of these same benefits of elasticity and scalability, it would rely on compute resources being purchased and owned by the organization rather than leased from a seemingly infinite resource like a cloud provider. Another benefit of combining cloud computing and virtualization is the ability to self-provision virtual systems. An IT department in a cloud computing model can grant permissions that give users in other departments the ability to self-provision virtual machines. The IT department still controls how the virtual machine is created and what resources are provided to that virtual machine without actually having to create it. The IT department even has the ability to charge or keep track of the users who are creating the virtual machine, making the users accountable for whether they really need the machine and the resources it requires.

<table>
<tr><td>

e x a m

ⓦatch

</td><td>

Elasticity allows an organization to quickly and easily scale the virtual environment both up and down, as needed.

</td></tr>
</table>

Network and Application Isolation

As discussed previously, cloud computing and virtualization can enhance network security, increase application agility, and improve scalability and availability of the environment. Cloud computing can also help to create network and application isolation. Without network isolation it might be possible for a cloud consumer to intentionally or unintentionally consume a large share of the network fabric or see another tenant's data in a multitenant environment. Proper configuration of the network to include resource control and security using network isolation helps to ensure these issues are mitigated. There are also circumstances where certain network traffic needs to be isolated to its own network to provide an initial layer of security, to afford higher bandwidth for specific applications, to enforce chargeback policies, or for use in tiered networks.

Virtualization and cloud computing now provide organizations with a means to isolate an application without having to deploy a single application to a single physical server. By combining virtualization and network isolation, it is possible to isolate an application just by correctly configuring a virtual network. Organizations now have the ability to install multiple applications on one physical server and then isolate a given application so that it can communicate only with the network devices it is configured to. For example, you can install an application on a virtual machine that is the same version or a newer version of an existing application yet have that install be completely isolated to its own network for testing. The ability for an organization to isolate an application without having to purchase additional hardware is a key factor in the decision to move to virtualization and cloud computing.

Infrastructure Consolidation

Virtualization allows an organization to consolidate its servers and infrastructure by allowing multiple virtual machines to run on a single host computer and even providing a way to isolate a given application from other applications that are installed on other virtual machines on the same host computer. Cloud computing can take it a step further by allowing an organization not only to take advantage of virtualization but also to purchase compute resources from a cloud provider. If an organization purchases their compute resources from a cloud provider, they would require fewer hardware resources internally. Consolidating the infrastructure means lower costs to an organization since it no longer needs to provide the same power, cooling, administration, and hardware that would be required without virtualization and cloud computing. The network environment becomes easier to manage and maintain as an organization moves to a consolidated infrastructure.

Virtual Data Center Creation

Another option an organization has in terms of infrastructure consolidation is a virtual data center. A virtual data center offers data center infrastructure as a service and is the same concept as a physical data center with the advantages of cloud computing mixed in. A virtual data center offers compute resources, network infrastructure, external storage, backups, and security just like a physical data center. A virtual data center also offers virtualization, pay-as-you-grow billing, elasticity, and scalability. An administrator can control the virtual resources by using quotas and security profiles. A cloud user would then have the ability to create virtual servers and host applications on those virtual servers based on the security permissions assigned to the user's account. It is also possible to create multiple virtual data centers based on either geographic or application isolation requirements.

CERTIFICATION OBJECTIVE 6.02

Virtual Resource Migrations

Now that you understand how cloud computing benefits from virtualization, you need to know how to migrate an organization's current resources into either a virtual environment or a cloud environment. Migrating servers to a virtual or cloud environment is one of the first steps in adopting a cloud computing model. Organizations do not want to start from scratch when building a virtual or cloud environment; they want the ability to migrate what is in their current data center to a cloud environment. With the advancements in virtualization and consolidated infrastructures, organizations now see IT resources as a pool of resources that can be managed centrally, not as a single resource. IT administrators now have the ability to easily move resources across the network from server to server, from data center to data center, or into a private or public cloud, giving them the ability to balance resource and compute loads more efficiently across multiple, even global, environments. This section explains the different options for migrating an organization's current infrastructure to a virtual or cloud environment.

Virtual Machine Templates

When an organization is migrating their environment to the cloud, it is important for them to have a standardized installation policy or profile for their virtual servers. The virtual machines need to have a very similar base installation of the operating system so all the machines have the same security patches, service packs, and base applications installed. Virtual machine templates provide a streamlined approach to deploying a fully configured base server image or even a fully configured application server. Virtual machine templates help decrease the installation and configuration costs when deploying virtual machines and lower ongoing maintenance costs, allowing for faster deploy times and lower operational costs. A virtual machine template can be exported from one virtualization host, and then imported on another virtualization host and be used as a master virtual machine template for all virtualization hosts.

Virtual machine templates provide a standardized group of hardware and software settings that can be reused repeatedly to create new virtual machines that are configured with those specified settings. For example, a virtual machine template can be defined to create a virtual machine with 1024 MB of memory, one vCPU, and three virtual hard disks. Or a virtual machine template can be created based on an existing, fully configured virtual machine. In essence a virtual machine template acts as a master image that an organization can use to quickly and efficiently deploy similar virtual machine instances in their environment. They can then maintain the virtual machine templates by applying operating system updates and application patches so that any new virtual machine instances that are created with the template are updated and ready to use instantly. Figure 6-2 displays a graphical representation of how virtual machine templates work.

FIGURE 6-2

Representation of a virtual machine template.

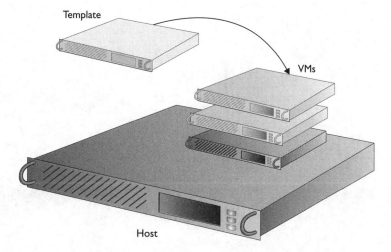

Physical to Virtual (P2V)

Along with creating new virtual machines and provisioning those virtual machines quickly and efficiently using virtual machine templates, there will be occasions when an organization needs to convert a physical server to a virtual server. The process of creating a virtual machine from a physical server is called physical to virtual (P2V). P2V enables the migration of a physical server's operating system, applications, and data to a newly created guest virtual machine on a host computer. Figure 6-3 illustrates how a P2V migration works.

There are a few different ways to convert a physical server to a virtual server. You can manually create a new virtual machine on a host computer and copy all the files from the OS, applications, and data from the source physical server. The manual

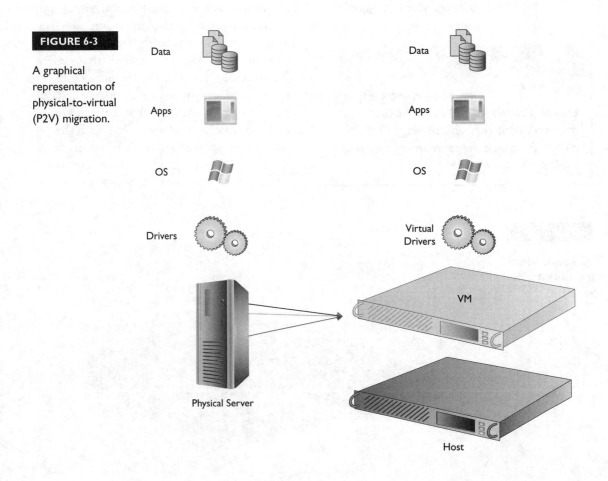

FIGURE 6-3

A graphical representation of physical-to-virtual (P2V) migration.

Data

Apps

OS

Drivers

Physical Server

Data

Apps

OS

Virtual Drivers

VM

Host

process is time consuming and not very effective. Then there is a semi-automated P2V approach that uses a software tool to assist in the migration from a physical server to a virtual server. This simplifies the process and gives the administrator some guidance when migrating the physical server. There are also free software tools that help migrate a physical server from a virtual server. The last option, and the option that requires the least amount of work for an administrator, is the fully automated P2V migration. The fully automated version uses a software utility that can migrate a physical server over the network without any assistance from an administrator.

EXAM AT WORK

Migrating a Physical Environment to a Virtual Environment

A while back we were brought in to an organization to explain the benefits of virtualization and the cloud and why this particular organization should look at virtualizing their data center. After many discussions and planning sessions, the organization decided that virtualization was the right step for them. We as the consultants were responsible for building and configuring the host computer along with the network and storage solution. After all of that was set up and configured, the next task was to migrate their systems from their current physical environment to a virtual environment. We went over the options they had of using a manual approach or automating the P2V conversion process. We ended up using a combination of manual and fully automated. Some physical servers were easier to migrate manually or were not supported for migration using the fully automated piece.

We helped them migrate their physical server to the virtual server using P2V on the noncritical servers first; then we worked toward the more critical application servers. The automated process is driven by a wizard and was run from the physical server. We loaded the P2V software on the physical server; stopped any services that might cause an issue during the migration; and answered the prompts of the wizard, telling it what host computer to migrate the server to, the name of the virtual machine, virtual hard disk, and so on. After successfully completing that process, the next step was to shut down the physical server and start the virtual server. Once the virtual server loaded, we had to install the guest tools and configure a few minor settings, with the final step to test the application that the server was running. After all the tests ran smoothly, our conversion of the physical server to a virtual server was complete.

Migrating a virtual machine from a physical server can be done either online or offline. With an online migration the physical computer or source computer remains running and operational during the migration. One of the advantages of the online option is that the source computer is still available during the migration process. This may not be a big advantage, however, depending on the application that is running on the source computer. When doing an offline P2V, the source computer is taken offline during the migration process. An offline migration provides for a more reliable transition since the source computer is not being utilized. For example, if you are doing a migration of a database server or a domain controller, it would be better to do the migration offline since the system is constantly being utilized.

Before migrating a physical machine to a virtual machine, it is always advisable to check with the application vendor to make sure they support their application in a virtual environment.

Virtual to Virtual (V2V)

Similar to P2V, virtual to virtual (V2V) is the process of migrating an operating system, applications, and data, but instead of migrating them from a physical server you are migrating them from a virtual server. Just like for P2V, software tools are available to fully automate a V2V migration. V2Vcan be used to copy or restore files and programs from one virtual machine to another. It can also be used to convert a VMware virtual machine to a Hyper-V-supported virtual machine or vice versa. If the conversion is from VMware to Hyper-V, the process creates a .vhd file and copies the contents of the .vmdk to the new .vhd file so that the virtual machine can be supported in Hyper-V. There is also the open virtualization format (OVF), which is a platform-independent extensible open packaging and distribution format for virtual machines. OVF allows for efficient and flexible distribution of applications, making virtual machines mobile between vendors because the application is vendor and platform neutral. An OVF virtual machine can be deployed on any virtualization platform.

on the
job

Recently we were brought into an organization to help them convert their entire virtual environment from VMware to Hyper-V. After building the new Hyper-V host computers and configuring all the settings necessary to support a highly available Hyper-V environment, we used System Center Virtual Machine Manager to do a V2V migration of all the VMware virtual machines to Hyper-V, again starting with the server running the least critical application and working toward the most critical.

Virtual to Physical (V2P)

The virtual-to-physical (V2P) migration process is not as simple as a P2V. A variety of tools are needed to convert a virtual machine back to a physical machine. First, Microsoft Sysprep would need to be installed on the virtual machine to prepare the image for transfer and allow for hardware configuration changes. Next, all the drivers for the target physical server need to be installed before doing the migration. Finally, a software tool such as Symantec Ghost is needed to facilitate the virtual-to-physical migration.. Unlike the P2V process, which requires only the software tool to do the migration, the V2P process involves more planning and utilities and is much more complex.

While a V2P conversion is not something that is done often, it is sometimes required for a couple of different reasons. One of the reasons is to test how the application performs on physical hardware. Some applications may perform better on physical hardware than on virtual hardware. This is not a common circumstance, however, and it is fairly easy to increase the compute resources for a virtual machine to improve the performance of an application that is hosted there. The more common reason to perform a V2P is that some application vendors do not support their product running a virtual environment. Today almost all vendors do support their application in a virtual environment, but there are still a few who do not.

on the
job *We were called into an organization to help troubleshoot a specific application that was not functioning correctly following a P2V conversion. We determined that an application error was causing the issue. We called the vendor to get support, and they told us they do not support their application in a virtual environment. We were required to do a V2P before the vendor would support it because they wanted to rule out that the virtualization layer was causing the application issue.*

Virtual Machine Cloning

Whether an organization creates a virtual machine from scratch or uses one of the migration methods we just discussed, at some point they might want to make a copy of that virtual machine. Installing a guest operating system and all of the applications is a time-consuming process, so virtual machine cloning makes it possible to create one or multiple copies of a virtual machine or a virtual machine template. When a company creates a virtual machine clone, they are creating an exact copy of an existing virtual machine. The existing virtual machine then becomes the parent virtual machine of the virtual machine clone. After the clone is created, it is a separate virtual machine that has the ability to share virtual disks with the parent virtual machine or create its own separate virtual disks.

Once the virtual machine clone is created, any changes made to the clone do not impact the parent virtual machine and vice versa. A virtual machine clone's MAC address and universally unique identifier (UUID) are different from those of the parent virtual machine. An organization would use virtual machine cloning if they want to make a separate copy of a virtual machine for either testing or separate use. If they are looking to save the current state of a virtual machine so that they can revert back to that state in case of a software installation failure or an administrative mistake, they should create a snapshot, not a virtual machine clone.

Virtual machine cloning allows for deploying multiple identical virtual machines to a group. This is useful in a variety of situations. For example, the IT department might create a clone of a virtual machine for each employee, and that clone would contain a group of preconfigured applications. Or they might want to use virtual machine cloning to create a development environment. A virtual machine could be configured with a complete development environment and cloned multiple times to create a baseline configuration for testing new software and applications.

Storage Migration

Storage migration is the process of transferring data between storage devices. Storage migration can be automated or done manually. Storage migration makes it possible to migrate a virtual machine's storage or disks to a new location and across storage arrays while maintaining continuous availability and service to the virtual machine. It also allows for migrating a virtual machine to a different storage array without any downtime to the virtual machine.

Storage migration eliminates service disruptions to a virtual machine and provides a live and automated way to migrate the virtual machine's disk files from the existing storage location to a new storage destination. Migrating virtual machine storage to different classes of storage is a cost-effective way to manage virtual machine disks based on usage, priority, and need. It also provides a way to take advantage of tiered storage, which we discussed in Chapter 2.

Storage migration allows a virtual machine to be moved from SAN-based storage to NAS- or DAS-based storage according to the current needs of the virtual machine.

FIGURE 6-4

Using storage
migration
in a virtual
environment.

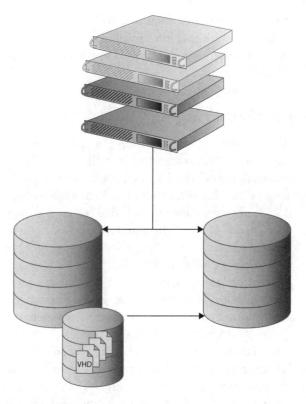

Storage migration helps an organization prioritize its storage and the virtual machines that access and utilize that storage. Figure 6-4 displays how storage is migrated between storage devices.

CERTIFICATION OBJECTIVE 6.03

Migration Considerations

Before an organization can migrate a virtual machine using one of the migration methods discussed in the previous section, there are a few things they need to consider. Among the most important of those considerations are the compute resources: the CPU, memory, disk I/O, and storage requirements. Migrating a physical server to a virtual machine takes careful planning for it to be successful.

It is the job of the IT administrator to plan the migration of physical servers to the virtual environment. It is critical that they perform their due diligence and discover all the necessary information about both the server and the application that the server is hosting.

Requirements Gathering

When looking to migrate their physical servers to a virtual environment, it is important that an organization gather as much information as possible. This information will help them define which servers to migrate first and which servers are good candidates for migration. When evaluating a physical server to determine if it is a good candidate for a virtual server, it is important to monitor that server over a period of time. The monitoring period helps to produce an accurate profile of the physical server and its workload. To monitor the physical server performance, a monitoring tool such as the Microsoft Performance Monitor or other comparable tools in the Linux environment can be used to get an accurate assessment of the resource usage for that particular server. The longer the trends of the physical server are monitored, the more accurate the assessment of resource usage will be. The time spent monitoring the system also varies depending on the applications the physical server is hosting. For example, it would make sense to monitor a database server for a longer period of time than a print server. In the end the organization needs to have an accurate picture of memory and CPU usage under various conditions so they can use that information to plan the resources the physical server might need after it is converted to a virtual machine.

Another consideration to make when determining if a physical server is a good candidate for virtualization is the status of the file system. When converting a physical server to a virtual server, all the data from the physical server is copied to the virtual server as part of the P2V process. Files and data are sometimes kept on a server that are not required, and those files do not need to be migrated as part of the P2V process, nor should they be. It is important, then, to examine the hard drive of the physical server before performing a migration and to remove all files and data that are not required for the server to function and provide the application it is hosting. Examples of these files might be WiFi files, or other files meant to be used only by a physical machine.

Maintenance Scheduling

After gathering the proper information to perform a successful physical-to-virtual migration, the organization then needs to plan when the project should be completed. When migrating a physical server to a virtual server, they should expect some downtime as part of the migration. They will at least have to take the time to start the new virtual machine and shut down the old physical server. DNS changes may also need to be made and replicated to support the new virtual instance of the physical server. Maintenance schedules should also be implemented or taken into consideration when planning the migration of a physical-to-virtual server. Most organizations have some type of maintenance schedule set up for routing maintenance on their server infrastructure, and all P2V migrations should take place during that planned maintenance.

So before an IT administrator embarks on the P2V migration process, they should provide the business case for some downtime of the systems to the change management team. Part of that downtime goes back to the resource provisioning discussion earlier in this chapter. The IT department does not want to under-provision the new virtual servers from the beginning and cause additional and unnecessary downtime of the virtual server and the application the virtual server is hosting. On the other hand, they don't want to overprovision the virtual server either, reserving too many resources to the virtual machine and consuming precious host resources where they are not required or are sometimes detrimental.

Upgrading

In addition to P2V, V2P, and V2V, an organization also has the option to upgrade an existing virtual machine to the latest virtual hardware or latest host operating system. Virtual machine hardware corresponds to the physical hardware available on the host computer where the virtual machine is created. In order for a virtual machine to take advantage of some of the features that the host computer provides, it might be necessary to upgrade the virtual machine hardware or guest tools. The host file system or hypervisor may also need to be upgraded to support these upgrades. Virtual machine hardware features might include BIOS enhancements, virtual PCI slots, maximum number of CPUs, and maximum memory configuration.

Another scenario that might require upgrading a virtual machine is when a new version of the host operating system is released (e.g., when Microsoft releases a new version of Hyper-V or VMware releases a new version of ESXi). In this instance an organization would need to upgrade or migrate their virtual machines to the new host server. This can be accomplished with a V2V migration of the virtual machines or by exporting the virtual machines from the previous version and importing them into the new version of the host operating system software. The import and export process of a virtual machine is covered in more detail in Chapter 12. Upgrading to a new host operating system and migrating the virtual machines to that new host requires the same planning that would be needed to perform a P2V migration. The IT administrator needs to understand the benefits of the new host operating system and how those benefits will impact the virtual machines and, specifically, their compute resources. Once again, careful planning is key before the upgrading process starts.

Testing

The process of P2V, or V2V for that matter, generally leaves the system in complete working and functional order and the entire system is migrated and left intact. With that said, any system that is being migrated should be tested both before and after the migration process. The IT administrator needs to define a series of checks that should be performed after the migration and before the virtual server takes over for the physical server. Some of the tests that should be completed on the virtual server after migration are as follows:

- Remove all unnecessary hardware from the virtual machine. (If you are migrating from a physical server to a virtual server, you might have some hardware devices that were migrated as part of the P2V process.)
- When first booting the virtual machine, disconnect it from the network. This allows the boot to occur without having to worry about duplicate IP addresses or DNS names on the network.
- Reboot the virtual machine several times to clear the logs and verify that it is functioning as expected during the startup phase.
- Verify network configurations on the virtual server while it is disconnected from the network. Make sure the IP address configuration is correct so that the virtual machine does not have any issues connecting to the network once network connectivity is restored.

Performing these post-migration tests will help to ensure a successful migration process and to minimize any errors that might arise after the migration is complete. As with anything there could still be issues once the virtual machine is booted on the network, but performing these post-conversion tests will lessen the likelihood of problems.

CERTIFICATION SUMMARY

There are many benefits to adopting a virtualized environment, including shared resources, elasticity, and network isolation for testing applications. Migrating to a virtual environment takes careful planning and consideration to define proper compute resources for the newly created virtual machine. Understanding how to properly perform a physical-to-virtual (P2V) migration is a key concept for the test and the real world, as you will be required to migrate physical servers to a virtual environment if you are working with virtualization or the cloud.

KEY TERMS

Use the list below to review the key terms that were discussed in this chapter. The definitions can be found within this chapter and in the glossary.

Shared resources   Allows a cloud provider to provide compute resources as a centralized resource and distribute those resources on an as-needed basis to the cloud consumer

Elasticity   Allows an organization to dynamically provision and de-provision processing, memory, and storage resources to meet the demands of the network

Network isolation   Allows for a section of the network to be isolated from another section so that multiple identical copies of the environment are executed at the same time

Virtual data center   Provides compute resources, network infrastructure, external storage, backups, and security similar to a physical data center

Virtual machine templates   Provides a standardized group of hardware and software settings that can be reused multiple times to create a new virtual machine that is configured with those specified settings

Resource pooling   Allows compute resources to be pooled to serve multiple consumers by using a multitenant model

Physical to virtual (P2V)   Process of migrating a physical server's operating system, applications, and data from the physical server to a newly created guest virtual machine on a virtualization host

Virtual to virtual (V2V)   Migrates an operating system, applications, and data from one virtual machine to another virtual machine

Virtual to physical (V2P)   Migrates a virtual machine to a physical computer

Online migration   Migrates a physical server to a virtual machine while the source computer remains available during the migration process

Offline migration   Migrates a physical server to a virtual machine by taking the source computer offline so that it is not available during the migration process

Virtual machine cloning   Allows a virtual machine to be copied either once or multiple times for testing

Storage migration   Process of transferring data between storage devices allowing data from a virtual machine to be migrated to a new location and across storage arrays while maintaining continuous availability and service to the virtual machine

✓ TWO-MINUTE DRILL

Benefits of Virtualization in a Cloud Environment

❑ Virtualization allows an organization to consolidate their infrastructure by running multiple applications on each server instead of one application per server.

❑ Cloud computing enables an organization to evaluate compute resources as a centralized resource and allocate them on demand while maintaining control of those resources. Shared resources allow a cloud provider to distribute compute resources on an as-needed basis to a cloud consumer.

❑ Elastic computing allows compute resources to vary dynamically to meet a variable workload and scale resources up and down as an application requires.

❑ Virtualization allows for segmenting an application's network access and isolating that virtual machine to a specific network segment.

❑ Virtualization allows an organization to consolidate its servers and infrastructures by having multiple virtual machines run on a single host computer.

❑ Virtual data centers offer data center infrastructure as a service; they have the same capabilities as a physical data center but with the advantages of cloud computing.

Virtual Resource Migrations

❑ Virtual machine templates provide a standardized group of hardware and software settings that can be deployed quickly and efficiently to multiple virtual machines.

❑ The process of migrating a physical server to a virtual server is called physical to virtual (P2V).

❑ P2V allows you to convert a physical server's operating system, applications, and data to a virtual server.

❑ Virtual-to-virtual (V2V) migrations allow you to migrate a virtual machine to another virtual machine by copying the files, operating system, and applications from one virtual machine to another.

❑ An online migration of a physical server to a virtual server leaves the physical server running and operational during the migration process.

❏ If an application does not support installation on a virtual server, virtual-to-physical (V2P) migration can be used to copy the virtual machine to a physical server.

❏ Virtual machine cloning creates an exact copy of a virtual machine for use in a development or test environment.

❏ A virtual machine's virtual hard disk can be migrated from one storage device to another using storage migration. This allows you to take advantage of tiered storage.

Migration Considerations

❏ Migrating a physical server to a virtual server takes careful planning in order for it to be successful.

❏ It is very important for an organization to gather all the hardware and application requirements of a physical server before migrating it to a virtual server.

❏ It is advisable to migrate a physical server to a virtual server during scheduled and planned maintenance hours.

❏ Proper testing of a virtual machine after the P2V migration process is required to verify that the virtual server is operating at peak performance.

SELF TEST

The following questions will help you measure your understanding of the material presented in this chapter.

Benefits of Virtualization in a Cloud Environment

1. Which of the following allows you to scale resources up and down dynamically as required for a given application?
   A. Subnetting
   B. Resource pooling
   C. Elasticity
   D. VLAN

2. Which of the following data centers offers the same concepts as a physical data center with the benefits of cloud computing?
   A. Private data center
   B. Public data center
   C. Hybrid data center
   D. Virtual data center

3. How does virtualization help to consolidate an organization's infrastructure?
   A. It allows a single application to be run on a single computer.
   B. It allows multiple applications to run on a single computer.
   C. It requires more operating system licenses.
   D. It does not allow for infrastructure consolidation and actually requires more compute resources.

4. Which of the following gives a cloud provider the ability to distribute resources on an as-needed basis to the cloud consumer and in turn helps to improve efficiency and reduce costs?
   A. Elasticity
   B. Shared resources
   C. Infrastructure consolidation
   D. Network isolation

Virtual Resource Migrations

5. Your organization is planning on migrating their data center, and you as the administrator have been tasked with reducing the footprint of the new data center by virtualizing as many servers as possible. A physical server running a legacy application has been identified as a candidate for virtualization. Which of the following methods would be used to migrate the server to the new data center?

   A. V2V

   B. V2P

   C. P2P

   D. P2V

6. You have been tasked with migrating a virtual machine to a new host computer. Which migration process would be required?

   A. V2V

   B. V2P

   C. P2P

   D. P2V

7. An application was installed on a virtual machine and is now having issues. The application provider has asked you to install the application on a physical server. Which migration process would you use to test the application on a physical server?

   A. V2V

   B. V2P

   C. P2P

   D. P2V

8. You have been tasked with deploying a group of virtual machines quickly and efficiently with the same standard configurations. What process would you use?

   A. V2P

   B. P2V

   C. Virtual machine templates

   D. Virtual machine cloning

9. Which of the following allows you to migrate a virtual machine's storage to a different storage device while the virtual machine remains operational?

   A. Network isolation

   B. P2V

   C. V2V

   D. Storage migration

10. You need to create an exact copy of a virtual machine to deploy in a development environment. Which of the following processes is the best option?

    A. Storage migration

    B. Virtual machine templates

    C. Virtual machine cloning

    D. P2V

11. You are migrating a physical server to a virtual server. The server needs to remain available during the migration process. What type of migration would you use?

    A. Offline

    B. Online

    C. Hybrid

    D. V2P

Migration Considerations

12. You notice that one of your virtual machines will not successfully complete an online migration to a hypervisor host. Which of the following is most likely preventing the migration process from completing?

    A. The virtual machine needs more memory than the host has available.

    B. The virtual machine has exceeded the allowed CPU count.

    C. The virtual machine does not have the proper network configuration.

    D. The virtual machine license has expired.

13. After a successful P2V migration, which of the following tests should be completed on the new virtual machine?

    A. Testing is not required.

    B. Remove all unnecessary software.

    C. Verify the IP address, DNS, and other network configurations.

    D. Run a monitoring program to verify compute resources.

14. True or False. A physical-to-virtual migration should not be done during scheduled maintenance windows.

    A. True

    B. False

15. You are planning your migration to a virtual environment. Which of the following physical servers should be migrated first? Choose two.

A. A development server

B. A server that is running a non-mission-critical application and is not heavily utilized day to day

C. A highly utilized database server

D. A server running a mission-critical application

SELF TEST ANSWERS

Benefits of Virtualization in a Cloud Environment

1. Which of the following allows you to scale resources up and down dynamically as required for a given application?
   A. Subnetting
   B. Resource pooling
   C. Elasticity
   D. VLAN

   ☑ **C.** Elasticity allows an organization to scale resources up and down as an application or service requires.
   ☒ **A, B,** and **D** are incorrect. Subnetting is the practice of creating subnetworks, or subnets, which are logical subdivisions of an IP network. A virtual local area network or VLAN is the concept of partitioning a physical network to create separate independent broadcast domains that are part of the same physical network.

2. Which of the following data centers offers the same concepts as a physical data center with the benefits of cloud computing?
   A. Private data center
   B. Public data center
   C. Hybrid data center
   D. Virtual data center

   ☑ **D.** A virtual data center offers compute resources, network infrastructure, external storage, backups, and security, just like a physical data center. A virtual data center also offers virtualization, pay-as-you-grow billing, elasticity, and scalability.
   ☒ **A, B,** and **C** are incorrect. The other options are definitions of cloud deployment and service models.

3. How does virtualization help to consolidate an organization's infrastructure?
   A. It allows a single application to be run on a single computer.
   B. It allows multiple applications to run on a single computer.
   C. It requires more operating system licenses.
   D. It does not allow for infrastructure consolidation and actually requires more compute resources.

☑ **B.** Virtualization allows an organization to consolidate its servers and infrastructure by allowing multiple virtual machines to run on a single host computer.

☒ **A, C,** and **D** are incorrect. These options would not help to consolidate an organization's infrastructure.

4. Which of the following gives a cloud provider the ability to distribute resources on an as-needed basis to the cloud consumer and in turn helps to improve efficiency and reduce costs?

   A. Elasticity
   B. Shared resources
   C. Infrastructure consolidation
   D. Network isolation

☑ **B.** Shared resources give a cloud provider the ability to distribute resources on an as-needed basis to the cloud consumer which helps to improve efficiency and reduce costs for an organization. Virtualization helps to simplify the process of sharing compute resources.

☒ **A, C,** and **D** are incorrect. Elasticity allows an organization to scale resources up and down as an application or service requires but does not allow the cloud provider the ability to distribute resources as needed. Infrastructure consolidation allows an organization to consolidate their physical servers into a smaller virtualized data center but is not used to distribute resources automatically. Network isolation allows you to isolate the network the virtual machine is connected to but has nothing to do with distributing resources.

Virtual Resource Migrations

5. Your organization is planning on migrating their data center, and you as the administrator have been tasked with reducing the footprint of the new data center by virtualizing as many servers as possible. A physical server running a legacy application has been identified as a candidate for virtualization. Which of the following methods would be used to migrate the server to the new data center?

   A. V2V
   B. V2P
   C. P2P
   D. P2V

☑ **D.** P2V would allow you to migrate the physical server running the legacy application to a new virtual machine in the new virtualized data center.

☒ **A, B,** and **C** are incorrect. These options do not allow you to migrate the physical server running the legacy application to a new virtual server.

6. You have been tasked with migrating a virtual machine to a new host computer. Which migration process would be required?

   A. V2V

   B. V2P

   C. P2P

   D. P2V

   ☑ **A.** V2V would allow you to migrate the virtual machine to a new virtual machine on the new host computer.

   ☒ **B, C,** and **D** are incorrect. These options would not be the most efficient way to migrate a virtual machine to a new host computer.

7. An application was installed on a virtual machine and is now having issues. The application provider has asked you to install the application on a physical server. Which migration process would you use to test the application on a physical server?

   A. V2V

   B. V2P

   C. P2P

   D. P2V

   ☑ **B.** One of the primary reasons for using the V2P process is to migrate a virtual machine to a physical machine to test an application on a physical server if requested by the application manufacturer.

   ☒ **A, C,** and **D** are incorrect. These options do not allow you to migrate a virtual machine to a physical server.

8. You have been tasked with deploying a group of virtual machines quickly and efficiently with the same standard configurations. What process would you use?

   A. V2P

   B. P2V

   C. Virtual machine templates

   D. Virtual machine cloning

   ☑ **C.** Virtual machine templates would allow you to deploy multiple virtual machines and those virtual machines would have identical configurations, which streamlines the process.

   ☒ **A, B,** and **D** are incorrect. When you create a virtual machine clone, you are creating an exact copy of an existing virtual machine. P2V and V2P do not allow you to deploy multiple standardized virtual machines.

9. Which of the following allows you to migrate a virtual machine's storage to a different storage device while the virtual machine remains operational?
   A. Network isolation
   B. P2V
   C. V2V
   D. Storage migration

   ☑ **D.** Storage migration is the process of transferring data between storage devices and can be automated or done manually and allows the storage to be migrated while the virtual machine continues to be accessible.

   ☒ **A, B,** and **C** are incorrect. Network isolation allows you to isolate the network the virtual machine is connected to. P2V and V2V migrate the entire virtual machine or physical server, not just the virtual machine's storage.

10. You need to create an exact copy of a virtual machine to deploy in a development environment. Which of the following processes is the best option?
    A. Storage migration
    B. Virtual machine templates
    C. Virtual machine cloning
    D. P2V

    ☑ **C.** When you create a virtual machine clone, you are creating an exact copy of an existing virtual machine.

    ☒ **A, B,** and **D** are incorrect. Virtual machine templates provide a streamlined approach to deploying a fully configured base server image or even a fully configured application server but do not create an exact copy of a virtual machine. Storage migration migrates the virtual machine's storage to another storage device; it does not create an exact copy of the virtual machine. P2V would allow you to create a copy of a physical machine as a virtual machine, not an exact copy of a virtual machine.

11. You are migrating a physical server to a virtual server. The server needs to remain available during the migration process. What type of migration would you use?
    A. Offline
    B. Online
    C. Hybrid
    D. V2P

☑ **B.** With an online migration the physical computer or source computer remains running and operational during the migration.

☒ **A, C,** and **D** are incorrect. An offline migration requires the server to be shut down before the migration process can take place.

Migration Considerations

12. You notice that one of your virtual machines will not successfully complete an online migration to a hypervisor host. Which of the following is most likely preventing the migration process from completing?

    A. The virtual machine needs more memory than the host has available.
    B. The virtual machine has exceeded the allowed CPU count.
    C. The virtual machine does not have the proper network configuration.
    D. The virtual machine license has expired.

    ☑ **A.** During a P2V migration the host computer must support the source computer's memory. More than likely the host does not have enough available memory to support the import of the virtual machine in a migration scenario.

    ☒ **B, C,** and **D** are incorrect. These settings would need to be planned and thought out, but they would not prevent a virtual machine from being migrated to a host computer.

13. After a successful P2V migration, which of the following tests should be completed on the new virtual machine?

    A. Testing is not required.
    B. Remove all unnecessary software.
    C. Verify the IP address, DNS, and other network configurations.
    D. Run a monitoring program to verify compute resources.

    ☑ **C.** After a successful migration, the network settings should be checked and verified before bringing the virtual machine online.

    ☒ **A, B,** and **D** are incorrect. Testing the virtual machine after a successful migration is something that should always be done. Testing the performance of the virtual machine should be done after the network settings have been configured and verified.

14. True or False. A physical-to-virtual migration should not be done during scheduled maintenance windows.
    A. True
    B. False

    ☑ **B.** Migrating a physical server to a virtual machine should be done during planned and scheduled maintenance hours.
    ☒ **A** is incorrect. A migration of a physical-to-virtual server should not be done outside of scheduled maintenance windows.

15. You are planning your migration to a virtual environment. Which of the following physical servers should be migrated first? Choose two.
    A. A development server
    B. A server that is running a non-mission-critical application and is not heavily utilized day to day
    C. A highly utilized database server
    D. A server running a mission-critical application

    ☑ **A** and **B.** When planning a migration from a physical data center to a virtual data center, the first servers that should be migrated are noncritical servers that are not heavily utilized. A development server would be a good candidate since it is most likely not a mission-critical server.
    ☒ **C** and **D** are incorrect. You would not want to migrate mission-critical or highly utilized servers before migrating noncritical servers. This helps to prevent downtime of critical applications and provides a means of testing the migration process and the virtual environment before migrating critical servers to the virtual environment.

7
Network Management

Monitoring the cloud environment is a key component of a successful cloud computing environment. Proper monitoring leads to increased availability for servers, services, and applications and helps uncover any problems early on. Monitoring the environment also helps an organization detect network outages quickly and efficiently. Understanding how to properly monitor the cloud computing environment allows an organization to plan for future resource utilization and to become proactive instead of reactive.

An organization needs to be able to monitor and manage the cloud environment quickly and efficiently. The ability to remotely manage the virtualization environment allows for a flexible way to manage the environment and respond to any issues or alerts that might arise. There are a variety of options for managing the cloud environment securely and remotely.

CERTIFICATION OBJECTIVE 7.01

Resource Monitoring Techniques

Cloud computing provides an efficient way of load balancing, task scheduling, and allocating compute resources. Monitoring those resources is an important part of maintaining a cloud environment. Monitoring is a key metric when providing chargeback and resource provisioning. Monitoring the environment allows an organization to plan for future growth and to be proactive when it comes to distributing compute resources. Without a proper monitoring solution, it becomes difficult to respond quickly to a constantly changing environment.

Effective monitoring techniques provide an efficient means of monitoring all aspects of a cloud environment without placing a major performance burden on the environment itself. Monitoring techniques should be able to manage the performance of the enterprise and give detailed information on the current usage of the cloud environment.

Protocols and Methods

When defining a monitoring solution, it is important to understand the different protocols that are available for monitoring and the different options an administrator has for being alerted to problems that might arise in the cloud environment.

An administrator can use a variety of protocols to monitor an environment, and there are different ways in which an administrator can be notified of potential problems. One of the goals of monitoring the environment is to ensure the overall health of the environment. An administrator can even publish this information on a corporate Intranet site, allowing the entire organization access to the health data. For example, an administrator might publish a dashboard on the company Intranet site that shows the current service level agreements (SLAs) of the organization and whether or not the IT department has met those SLAs. Another place to use monitoring is in a chargeback situation. An IT department can monitor the environment and get a report on who consumed which compute resources and for how long, allowing the organization to charge the proper department or show the proper individual the use of those compute resources.

One of the common protocols used to manage and monitor an environment is simple network management protocol (SNMP). SNMP is commonly supported on devices such as routers, switches, printers, and servers and is used to monitor these devices for any issues or conditions that might arise on the devices that would require administrative attention. A monitoring solution that uses SNMP has an administrative computer, commonly referred to as a manager, that monitors or manages a group of network devices. Each managed device constantly executes a software component called an agent, which reports information, using the SNMP protocol, back to the manager. For example, an SNMP agent on a router can provide information about the router's network configuration and operations (such as network interface configurations and routing tables) and transmit that information back to the manager. There are a variety of vendors that use SNMP to monitor devices on the network; they use the information from SNMP to give an administrator a means of monitoring and managing network performance, reporting and troubleshooting network issues, and better understanding and preparing for network growth. An administrator can also use SNMP to modify and apply new configurations to network devices and be alerted when certain issues arise on a network device. In addition to monitoring and managing an environment, SNMP allows for alerts to be generated and notifications known as SNMP traps to be sent. SNMP traps are network packets that contain data relating to a particular component of the network device running the SNMP agent; they have the ability to notify the management stations, by way of an unsolicited SNMP message, that a particular event has occurred.

Another option for monitoring an environment is Windows Management Instrumentation (WMI), which is Microsoft's version of Web-Based Enterprise Management (WBEM). WBEM is an industry initiative to develop a standardized way of accessing management information in an enterprise environment. WMI allows you to write scripts to automate certain administrative tasks and run those scripts against remote computers. WMI also allows an administrator to query and set information on a workstation, server, or application. WMI provides a way to gather hardware information from multiple physical servers or virtual servers and put that information into a centralized database, allowing an administrator to quickly view a variety of information, including CPU, memory, operating system, and hard drive space. Using this information the administrator can determine if a system is close to maximizing compute resources and is in need of an upgrade to meet demands. For example, Microsoft System Center Configuration Manager uses WMI to gather hardware information from its clients and allows an administrator to manage and report on those systems based on the information gathered from the WMI queries.

e x a m

w a t c h

The WMI protocol can be used to gather information about the installed software and the operating system version on a computer, along with hardware information. Out-of-band management allows for remotely monitoring BIOS settings.

Out-of-band management allows an administrator to remotely manage and monitor a device even if that device is not powered on. If an organization wants to perform out-of-band management, they would use the intelligent platform management interface (IPMI) protocol to monitor their environment. The IPMI protocol operates independently of the operating system, which allows BIOS settings to be remotely monitored or configured.

One of the most common ways to gather event messages is with the use of syslog. Syslog provides a mechanism for a network device to send event messages to a logging server or syslog server using UDP port 514 or TCP 514. One of the benefits to a syslog server is that the syslog protocol is supported by a wide range of devices and has the capability to log different types of events. Syslog does not have the ability to poll devices to gather information like SNMP does; it simply gathers messages sent by various devices to a central syslog server when a specific event has triggered. Syslog gives an administrator the ability to consolidate logs from multiple devices into a single location. Figure 7-1 shows an example of a common syslog server.

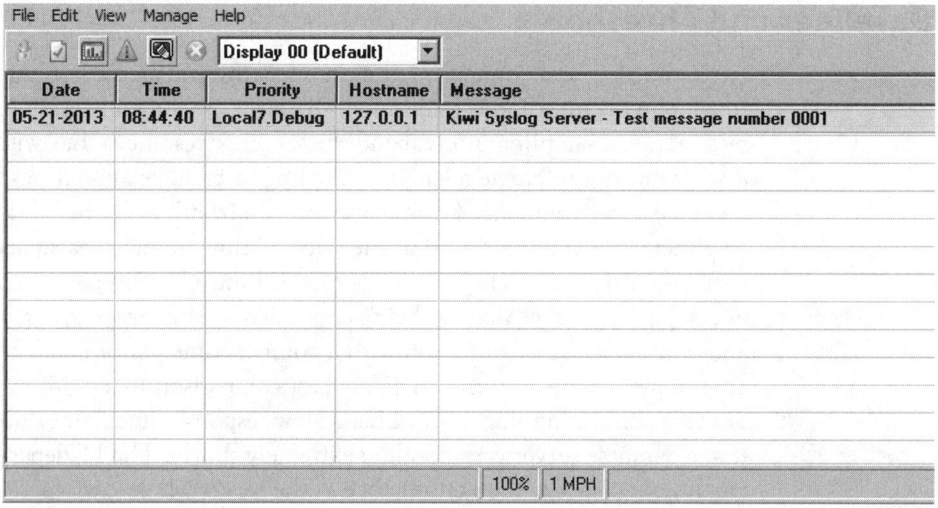

FIGURE 7-1

A sample syslog
entry.

FIGURE 7-1 A sample syslog entry.

Regardless of the protocol selected to monitor an environment, an organization still needs a way to be alerted when certain events occur. For example, if the company is monitoring a server and that server loses network connectivity, they need to be notified of that occurrence so they can fix the issue that is causing the problem. Many vendors offer network monitoring and alerting solutions both for on-premises and cloud-based deployments. Most vendors provide a website or some form of web service to centrally monitor an organization's cloud environment, whether the cloud is private or public. The web service provides a dashboard that gives the administrator a quick and easy view of the entire environment.

One of the most common alerting methods used is the simple mail transfer protocol (SMTP), discussed in Chapter 4. When configured by a device, SMTP sends an e-mail when a monitored event occurs. The alert can be configured to e-mail a single user or a group of users so that more than one person receives the alert. SMTP is a quick and easy way of sending alerts from the monitoring software when certain events occur on the network. Another option for receiving alerts is the short message service (SMS). SMS is a text messaging service that allows an alert to be sent to a mobile device. The use of SMS is a great way to notify an on-call technician when an alert has been generated after hours. Monitoring an environment is normally a 24-hour job because the network needs to be available 24 hours a day.

Baselines and Thresholds

After choosing and configuring their monitoring and alerting solution, the next step for an organization is to develop a baseline. A company establishes a baseline by selecting a sampling interval and the server or resources they wish to monitor. It is advisable not to create a lengthy sampling interval because it has the potential to consume a large amount of disk space and bandwidth if the network is gathering the baseline; but it is important that the selected time frame gives an accurate analysis to use going forward. The purpose of establishing a baseline is to create a sample of compute resources that are being consumed by the server over a period of time and to provide the organization with a point-in-time performance chart of their environment. This in turn can be used for comparison to a point in time when the server is performing sluggishly or has a slow response time. For example, a user says that a database server is responding extremely slowly. The IT department can use a baseline to compare the performance of the server when it was performing well to when the user reported the slow performance. An organization should run a baseline every month to get a chart of how the server is consuming resources. Some software (e.g., VCOPs) builds the baseline on its own over time. The baseline may also reveal patterns on other software. For example, an IT administrator may notice over a 12-month period that the average memory usage has increased 10 percent, which helps in planning additional resources for the server in the near future.

In addition to establishing a baseline, an organization also needs to configure thresholds. When it comes to monitoring a cloud environment, thresholds are a key piece of the process. Thresholds can be set so that if a virtualization host consumes more than 95% of its CPU for more than 10 minutes, it sends an alert via either SMTP or SMS to the appropriate party. Setting a threshold allows for a more robust alerting system. Thresholds can also be used to automatically and dynamically create and orchestrate resources in the cloud computing environment. ("Orchestration" refers to automated tasks that could be scripted to happen based on a particular threshold being met or exceeded.)

Cloud computing allows a cloud consumer to define a threshold policy to check and manage resources when workload demands require. This allows the cloud provider to create instances of resources depending on how much the workload exceeds the threshold level. For example, a defined threshold could state that if CPU utilization for a particular virtual machine reaches 95 percent for 5 minutes, utilizing orchestration APIs, an additional processor should be added dynamically.

Automated Event Responses

While monitoring and alerting are great ways to minimize problems in the cloud environment, there are some issues that arise with using these features. When an organization is monitoring and alerting on all their devices, the amount of alerts that might arise could be staggering. If an administrator gets too many alerts, they may not have enough time to respond to those alerts and some issues may go unnoticed or may not be given the attention they deserve. This is where automated event responses can help. For example, let's say an administrator gets an alert that a hard drive is at 99 percent capacity. Instead of having to manually log in to the server and delete files or run a disk cleanup program, why not automate that task? The administrator can respond to that event with a program or script that automatically starts when the alert is generated (i.e., orchestration, mentioned previously). Automating minor tasks can save administrators considerable time and allow them to focus on more pressing issues.

on the
⦿ o b

Recently we were brought in to help an organization manage their monitoring environment. We recommended the organization buy monitoring software that allows for automated responses. We configured thresholds and alerts based on the organization's needs. We then configured the most common alerts with an automated response that would run a script to fix the issue and resolve the alert in the monitoring software.

CERTIFICATION OBJECTIVE 7.02

Remote-Access Tools

As we have discussed, monitoring the environment is an integral piece of successfully implementing a cloud computing model, and so is responding to the alerts that are generated by the monitoring process. Being able to remotely access and troubleshoot a virtualization host or virtual machine requires less time and makes fixing and maintaining the environment easier to accomplish. Remotely accessing a server does not always have to mean accessing the server from an offsite location. There are times when simply connecting to a host computer or virtual machine from a workstation is more convenient than physically walking over to the server and logging in. When a quick fix or change needs to be made to a virtual machine or host computer, being able to access that server from a local workstation saves time and prevents the need to walk or drive to the data center and physically sit at the machine that requires the change.

Remote Hypervisor Access

There are a variety of ways to remotely connect to a hypervisor. Most vendors allow a console to be installed on a workstation or server that is not the hypervisor. This allows a user to connect to a hypervisor server from their workstation. A console or client can be installed on a workstation, and that console allows the user to remotely connect to the hypervisor from the workstation. This is oftentimes referred to as a jump or step machine. It is also possible to add multiple hypervisors into a single console on a workstation. The ability to manage a hypervisor from a local workstation allows for managing all the hypervisor hosts from a single console, giving a single-pane-of-glass approach to hypervisor management.

With the hypervisor console installed on a client workstation, the administrator can perform most of the tasks for the hypervisor as if they were connecting directly to the actual hypervisor host. The client console gives them the ability to create or modify virtual machines or virtual hard disks, configure virtual machine settings, and so on. This allows them to do all the administrative tasks that are required on a day-to-day basis from a single workstation. The administrator still requires the correct administrative permissions on the hypervisor to modify any of the settings for the host computer or the virtual machines. Using a console from a workstation is a great way to connect to a hypervisor host because it looks and acts just as it would if the user were locally logged in to the hypervisor host.

Remote Desktop Protocol (RDP)

Remote desktop protocol (RDP) differs from installing the hypervisor console on a workstation in that RDP allows for remotely connecting and logging in directly to the hypervisor host. RDP provides remote display and input capabilities over the network. In order to use RDP for connecting to a remote server, RDP client software is required. Figure 7-2 shows an example of RDP client software that is used to remotely connect to a hypervisor host. RDP is a multichannel protocol that provides separate virtual channels for transmitting device communication and presentation data from the server.

EXAM AT WORK

Employing a Console to Connect to a Remote Hypervisor Host

Recently we were brought into an organization that had deployed multiple hypervisor hosts in their environment. They had a total of 20 hypervisor hosts and 250 virtual machines. The data center that the hypervisor hosts were installed on was in an adjacent building, and the time it took to walk to the data center was time that could have been spent doing other tasks. The organization needed a way to centrally manage the hosts from their workstation computers without having to individually log in to each one.

The solution was to install the console on each of the administrators' workstations and add the hypervisor hosts into the single console. This allowed each administrator to not only see all 20 of the hypervisor host computers but manage those hosts as well. It was a great solution that satisfied all of the organization's needs by saving them time and effort and allowing them to manage all 20 hypervisor hosts from a single console. The console that is installed on each workstation looks and responds just like the console that is installed on the hypervisor host computer.

FIGURE 7-2

Remote Desktop Connection: An example of RDP software.

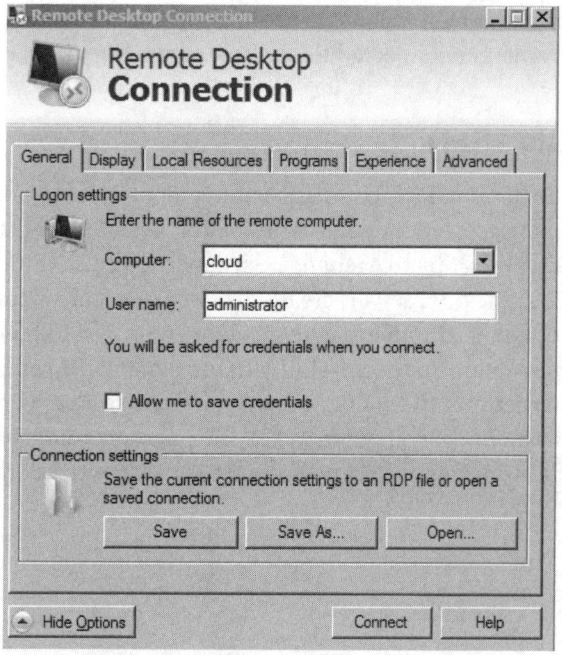

The advantage of using RDP to connect to a hypervisor is that the user has direct access to the hypervisor server without having to be physically sitting at the hypervisor host. RDP allows a user to interact with the server just as if they were sitting in front of it. So instead of just having access to the hypervisor console, RDP enables access to the entire server. The user can launch other applications on the server as well as change system settings on the hypervisor host computer itself. RDP allows for complete control of the server operating system, not just the hypervisor settings, without having to physically be at the hypervisor host computer.

One of the disadvantages of using RDP for managing a virtualization environment is that an administrator cannot manage multiple hypervisor hosts in a single RDP session like they can with a remote hypervisor client console. The option to use RDP is currently only available for the Microsoft hypervisor. Connections made to other popular hypervisors such as VMware, Citrix, and Oracle require the use of a software client installed on a jump machine.

Console Port

A console port allows an administrator to use a cable to connect directly to a hypervisor host computer or a virtual machine. The administrator can use a parallel or serial port to connect peripherals to a virtual machine and can add parallel and serial ports and change the serial port configuration. The virtual serial port can connect to a physical serial port or to a file on the host computer. Using a console port allows for managing a virtualization host computer directly from another computer connected to the host computer with a console cable.

Secure Shell (SSH)

Secure shell (SSH), discussed in Chapter 4, provides a secure way to remotely manage network devices, including hypervisor hosts. SSH uses public key cryptography to exchange a symmetric key covertly between the SSH client and the SSH server, creating a fast and secure channel and then using that channel to authenticate a remote computer and user if required. SSH also gives an administrator the ability to use a manually generated public-private key pair to perform the encryption and authentication. They can also use SSH to log in to a remote computer and execute certain command strings against a hypervisor host machine. SSH provides strong authentication if using the latest version and secure communication over an unsecure channel. It was designed to replace remote shell (RSH) because RSH sends unencrypted traffic over the network, making it an unsecure transmission. When designing a virtualization environment, it is not recommended to have the hypervisor host directly exposed to the Internet.

Normally the hypervisor host is installed behind a firewall or some other form of protection, which makes it difficult to access the hypervisor host off-site. SSH allows for the creation of a secure management tunnel to the hypervisor host computer and provides a secure way to manage those devices since all the traffic is sent through an encrypted tunnel.

e x a m

Ⓦatch *SSH provides a way to securely access a hypervisor host from an off-site location.*

HTTP

Another option for remotely accessing a hypervisor host machine is through a web console that is using the HTTP or HTTPS protocol. Most hypervisor vendors have a web console that allows an administrator to access a hypervisor host from virtually anywhere. The administrator may have to install an additional component when doing the initial hypervisor host installation in order to provide web access to a host computer. The hypervisor host web service should be configured to use HTTPS to ensure a secure way to connect to it. Some hypervisors (like Microsoft IIS) may require additional software on the host computer as well. Connecting to a hypervisor host computer using a web console is a quick and easy way to perform simple configuration on a virtual machine.

CERTIFICATION SUMMARY

Monitoring the network is a key component to cloud computing. Monitoring allows an organization to plan for future resource utilization and respond to issues that arise with the cloud environment. Combining monitoring and alerting gives an administrator a way to be proactive instead of reactive when it comes to the cloud environment. Remotely managing the virtualization environment provides flexibility and ease of administration. Being able to control multiple virtualization host computers from a single console saves time and makes managing the cloud environment an easier task.

KEY TERMS

Use the list below to review the key terms that were discussed in this chapter.

Simple network management protocol (SNMP)   Commonly supported protocol on devices such as routers, switches, printers, and servers and can be used to monitor those devices for any issues

Windows Management Instrumentation (WMI)   Protocol used to gather information about installed hardware, software, and operating system of a computer

Web-Based Enterprise Management (WBEM)   Standardized way of accessing management information in an enterprise environment

Intelligent platform management interface (IPMI)   Used for out-of-band management of a computer allowing an administrator to manage a system remotely without an operating system

Out-of-band management   Allows for remote management and monitoring of a computer system without the need for an operating system

Syslog   Provides a mechanism for a network device to send event messages to a logging server or a syslog server

Syslog server   Computer used as a centralized repository for syslog messages

Simple mail transfer protocol (SMTP)   Protocol used to send electronic messages (e-mail) over the Internet

Short message service (SMS)   Text messaging service that allows an alert to be sent to a mobile device

Performance baselines   Performance chart displaying current performance of the environment

Thresholds   Used to set the amount of resources that can be consumed before an alert is generated

Automated event responses   Automation of minute tasks that continuously generate alerts on a computer system

Orchestration   Process of automating tasks based upon specific thresholds or events

Remote hypervisor access   The ability to manage a hypervisor from another computer across a network

Remote desktop protocol (RDP)   Provides remote display and input capabilities over a computer network

Console port   Allows an administrator to use a cable to directly connect to a hypervisor host computer or virtual machine

Secure shell (SSH)   Used to secure logins, file transfers, and port forwarding

Remote shell (RSH)   Command-line program that executes shell commands across a network in an unsecured manner

✓ # TWO-MINUTE DRILL

Resource Monitoring Techniques

❑ Monitoring a cloud environment can ensure the overall health of the environment and gives an IT department the ability to measure the cloud service against its SLAs.

❑ Simple network management protocol gives an administrator the ability to monitor and manage network performance, report and troubleshoot network issues, and understand and plan for network growth.

❑ Windows Management Instrumentation (WMI) allows an administrator to create scripts that can be run against a remote computer to perform administrative tasks. WMI also allows an administrator to gather information about installed software and the operating system version of a computer.

❑ Intelligent platform management interface (IPMI) provides an administrator with the ability to perform out-of-band management to remotely manage and monitor a device even if the device is powered off.

❑ Syslog provides a mechanism for a network device to send event messages to a central logging server or syslog server over UDP port 514 or TCP 514 and is supported by a wide range of devices.

❑ Creating a baseline for a server can help an administrator troubleshoot performance issues for that server and plan for additional resources simply by looking for an increase in resource utilization compared to the baseline.

❑ Setting thresholds allows an administrator to be alerted when system resources are being overutilized and to respond to that alert.

Remote-Access Tools

❑ The ability to remotely manage a hypervisor host saves administration time.

❑ Multiple hypervisor hosts can be managed from a single console installed on a local workstation.

❑ Remote desktop protocol (RDP) allows for remotely connecting directly to a hypervisor host by providing remote display and input capabilities over the network.

❑ Secure shell (SSH) provides a secure way to remotely manage network devices.

❑ A web console can be used over HTTP or HTTPS to connect to a hypervisor host computer or management device that controls that host.

SELF TEST

The following questions will help you measure your understanding of the material presented in this chapter.

Resource Monitoring Techniques

1. Which of the following protocols can be used to identify which operating system version is installed on a virtual machine?
   A. WMI
   B. SMTP
   C. SMS
   D. IMAP

2. Which of these can be used by both a cloud consumer and a cloud provider to give a visual picture of performance metrics?
   A. API
   B. SNMP
   C. Dashboard
   D. SMTP

3. Which of the following utilizes UDP port 514 when collecting events?
   A. SNMP
   B. Syslog
   C. WMI
   D. Web services

4. Which of the following protocols can be used to create scripts that can be run against target computers to perform simple administrative tasks?
   A. WMI
   B. SMTP
   C. SMS
   D. IMAP

5. Which of the following protocols constantly executes a software component called an agent, which reports information using the protocol back to a manager?
   A. WMI
   B. SMTP
   C. SMS
   D. SNMP

6. Which of the following alerting methods allows a technician to receive an alert on a mobile device such as a cell phone?
   A. SMTP
   B. SMS
   C. SNMP
   D. Syslog

7. Which of the following alerting methods can be configured to send an e-mail when a certain alert is triggered?
   A. SMTP
   B. SMS
   C. SNMP
   D. Syslog

8. Which of the following protocols allows for out-of-band management of a computer?
   A. WMI
   B. SMS
   C. SNMP
   D. IPMI

Remote-Access Tools

9. You receive an alert that a virtual machine is down. The server does not respond to a ping. What tool should be used to troubleshoot the server if you were off-site?
   A. Console port
   B. SSH
   C. Hypervisor console
   D. SMTP

10. Which of the following would you use to remotely access a virtualization host in a secure fashion?
    A. Telnet
    B. Ping
    C. HTTPS
    D. Console port

11. You have been tasked with gathering a list of software installed on all the computers in your environment. You want to gather this information remotely. Which of the following would you use to gather this information?

    A. WMI

    B. SNMP

    C. HTTP

    D. Syslog

12. Which of the following protocols would be used to directly connect to a hypervisor host remotely to modify operating system settings on the hypervisor host?

    A. RDP

    B. Console port

    C. SMTP

    D. HTTPS

13. Which of the following is a benefit of remote hypervisor administration?

    A. Only being able to modify one hypervisor host at a time

    B. Being able to remotely manage multiple hypervisor hosts from a single console

    C. Not having access to a hypervisor host

    D. Remotely accessing a hypervisor host has no benefit

SELF TEST ANSWERS

Resource Monitoring Techniques

1. Which of the following protocols can be used to identify which operating system version is installed on a virtual machine?
   A. WMI
   B. SMTP
   C. SMS
   D. IMAP

   ☑ **A.** WMI provides an administrator a way to gather hardware information from multiple physical servers or virtual servers and put that information into a centralized database.
   ☒ **B, C,** and **D** are incorrect. Simple mail transfer protocol (SMTP) can send an e-mail when a certain monitored event occurs. SMS is a text messaging service that allows an alert to be sent to a mobile device. Internet message access protocol (IMAP) allows an e-mail client to access e-mail on a remote mail server.

2. Which of these can be used by both a cloud consumer and a cloud provider to give a visual picture of performance metrics?
   A. API
   B. SNMP
   C. Dashboard
   D. SMTP

   ☑ **C.** A dashboard is a great way for both the cloud consumer and cloud provider to access key metrics when it comes to monitoring cloud resources. A dashboard can give a summary of the current usage of the cloud resources in an easy-to-view format of charts and graphs.
   ☒ **A, B,** and **D** are incorrect. An application programming interface (API) is a protocol that can be used as an interface into a software component. SNMP is commonly supported on devices such as routers, switches, printers, and servers and is used to monitor these devices for any issues or conditions that might arise, but it does not provide performance metrics. Nor does SMTP, which is used to send e-mail alerts when certain monitored events occur.

3. Which of the following utilizes UDP port 514 when collecting events?
- A. SNMP
- B. Syslog
- C. WMI
- D. Web services

☑ **B.** Syslog provides a mechanism for a network device to send event messages to a logging server or syslog server using UDP port 514 or TCP 514.

☒ **A, C,** and **D** are incorrect. Simple network management protocol (SNMP) is one of the common protocols used to manage and monitor an environment, but it does not utilize UDP port 514. WMI allows an administrator to query and set information on a workstation, server, or application, but it does not use UDP port 514. Web services provide a centralized console to view events but again would not use UDP port 514.

4. Which of the following protocols can be used to create scripts that can be run against target computers to perform simple administrative tasks?
- A. WMI
- B. SMTP
- C. SMS
- D. IMAP

☑ **A.** WMI allows you to write scripts to automate certain administrative tasks and run those scripts against remote computers.

☒ **B, C,** and **D** are incorrect. None of these options allow you to create scripts to automate specific administrative tasks.

5. Which of the following protocols constantly executes a software component called an agent, which reports information using the protocol back to a manager?
- A. WMI
- B. SMTP
- C. SMS
- D. SNMP

☑ **D.** A monitoring solution that uses SNMP has an administrative computer, commonly referred to as a manager, that monitors or manages a group of network devices. Each managed device constantly executes a software component called an agent, that reports back to the manager.

☒ **A, B,** and **C** are incorrect. WMI allows you to write scripts to automate certain administrative tasks and run the scripts against remote computers. SMTP sends an e-mail alert when a certain monitored event occurs. SMS allows you to send short text messages to alert about issues and does not report back to a manager.

6. Which of the following alerting methods allows a technician to receive an alert on a mobile device such as a cell phone?

   A. SMTP
   B. SMS
   C. SNMP
   D. Syslog

☑ **B.** SMS is a text messaging service that allows an alert to be sent to a mobile device.

☒ **A, C,** and **D** are incorrect. SMTP can send an e-mail when a certain monitored event occurs, but it cannot transmit to a cell phone or other mobile device. Syslog provides a mechanism for a network device to send event messages to a logging server or syslog server using UDP port 514.

7. Which of the following alerting methods can be configured to send an e-mail when a certain alert is triggered?

   A. SMTP
   B. SMS
   C. SNMP
   D. Syslog

☑ **A.** Simple mail transfer protocol (SMTP) sends an e-mail alert when a certain monitored event occurs.

☒ **B, C,** and **D** are incorrect. SMS is a text messaging service that allows an alert to be sent to a mobile device. Syslog provides a mechanism for a network device to send event messages to a logging server or syslog server using UDP port 514. SNMP does not allow an administrator to receive messages on a cell phone.

8. Which of the following protocols allows for out-of-band management of a computer?
   A. WMI
   B. SMS
   C. SNMP
   D. IPMI

> ☑ **D.** IPMI operates independently of the operating system. It provides out-of-band management and monitoring of a system before the operating system is loaded, which allows BIOS settings to be remotely monitored or configured.
> ☒ **A, B,** and **C** are incorrect. WMI, SMS, and SNMP do not allow you to perform out-of-band management of a device.

Remote-Access Tools

9. You receive an alert that a virtual machine is down. The server does not respond to a ping. What tool should be used to troubleshoot the server if you were off-site?
   A. Console port
   B. SSH
   C. Hypervisor console
   D. SMTP

> ☑ **B.** Secure shell (SSH) provides a secure way to remotely manage network devices, including hypervisor hosts.
> ☒ **A, C,** and **D** are incorrect. A console port would not allow management of the hypervisor host from an off-site location. SMTP sends e-mail alerts in response to monitored events; it does not remotely manage network devices. A hypervisor console would not be available since you are accessing the hypervisor host from an off-site location.

10. Which of the following would you use to remotely access a virtualization host in a secure fashion?
   A. Telnet
   B. Ping
   C. HTTPS
   D. Console port

☑ **C.** HTTPS gives you a way to access a virtualization host remotely in a secure fashion.

☒ **A, B,** and **D** are incorrect. Telnet and Ping do not allow you to access a virtualization host remotely in a secure fashion. A console port doesn't allow you to access the host remotely.

11. You have been tasked with gathering a list of software installed on all the computers in your environment. You want to gather this information remotely. Which of the following would you use to gather this information?

A. WMI

B. SNMP

C. HTTP

D. Syslog

☑ **A.** With WMI it is possible to query workstations remotely and gather a list of all the software installed on those workstations.

☒ **B, C,** and **D** are incorrect. HTTP does not allow you to remotely gather all the software installed on a computer. Syslog provides a mechanism for a network device to send event messages to a logging server or syslog server using UDP port 514 but will not allow you to query for installed software. SNMP collects event messages from SNMP-enabled devices but does not query for installed software.

12. Which of the following protocols would be used to directly connect to a hypervisor host remotely to modify operating system settings on the hypervisor host?

A. RDP

B. Console port

C. SMTP

D. HTTPS

☑ **A.** The remote desktop protocol (RDP) lets you establish a remote connection directly to a hypervisor host. It allows you to change system settings on the hypervisor host computer itself.

☒ **B, C,** and **D** are incorrect. The console port gives you direct access to a hypervisor host but not remotely. SMTP does not allow you to remotely connect to the hypervisor host to modify settings. HTTPS gives you a web console that could access some management features of the hypervisor software but not the hypervisor host machine.

13. Which of the following is a benefit of remote hypervisor administration?
   A. Only being able to modify one hypervisor host at a time
   B. Being able to remotely manage multiple hypervisor hosts from a single console
   C. Not having access to a hypervisor host
   D. Remotely accessing a hypervisor host has no benefit

☑ **B.** The ability to remotely manage multiple hypervisor hosts from a single console from your workstation allows for a quick and easy way to make changes to multiple hosts and is an important benefit of remote hypervisor administration.

☒ **A, C,** and **D** are incorrect. Modifying a single host remotely is not as big of an advantage as modifying multiple hosts remotely, as it would require more administration to connect to each individual host computer remotely to modify the same settings.

8

Performance
Tuning

CERTIFICATION OBJECTIVES

P roperly distributing compute resources is one of the most important aspects of a virtualized IT environment. Planning for future growth and the ability to adjust compute resources on demand is one of the many benefits of a virtualized environment. This chapter explains how to configure compute resources on a host computer and a virtual machine and how to optimize the performance of a virtualized environment.

CERTIFICATION OBJECTIVE 8.01

Host Resource Allocation

Building a virtualization host computer requires careful consideration and planning. First, the amount of resources required for the host and the distribution of those resources to a virtual machine must be well thought out and defined. Along with planning for the host resources, it is also necessary to plan for the virtual machine configuration that the host computer will serve. Then configuring of the compute resources and licensing of the host and virtual machines must be attended to in the process of moving to a virtualized environment.

Compute Resources

When configuring a virtualization host computer, the compute resources are the key to success. Proper planning of the compute resources for the host computer ensures that the host can deliver the performance needed to support the virtualization environment. Compute resources can best be defined as the resources that are required for the delivery of virtual machines. They are the disk, processor, memory, and networking resources that are shared across pools of virtual machines and underpin their ability to deliver the value of the cloud models as covered in Chapter 1. As a host is a physical entity, the compute resources that the host utilizes are naturally physical, too. These compute resources are displayed in Figure 8-1. For disk resources, physical rotational disks and solid state hard drives are utilized, as well as their controller cards, disk arrays, host bus adapters, and networked storage transmission media. For network resources, network interface cards (NICs) and physical transmission media such as Ethernet cables are employed. Central processing units are employed for the processor, and physical banks of RAM are used to supply memory.

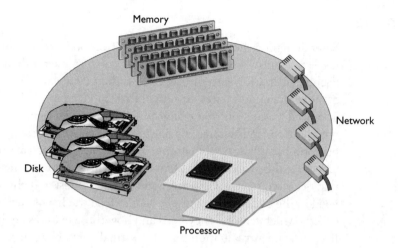

FIGURE 8-1

Host compute resources: processor, disk, memory, and network.

Quotas and Limits

Because compute resources are limited, cloud providers must protect them and make certain that their customers only have access to the amount that they are contracted to provide. Two methods used to deliver no more than the contracted amount of resources are quotas and limits. Limits are a defined floor or ceiling on the amount of resources that can be used, and quotas are limits that are defined for a system on the total amount of resources that can be utilized. When defining limits on host resources, you have the option of setting a hard or soft limit. A hard limit is the maximum amount of resources that can be utilized. For example, a hard limit of 100 Gigabytes (GB) for a storage partition will not allow anything to be added to that partition once it reaches 100 GB and will log an event or notify the user. A soft limit, on the other hand, will allow the user to save a file even if the drive reaches 100 GB but will still log an alert and notify the user. The quotas that are typically defined for host systems have to do with allocation of the host compute resources to its guest machines. These quotas are established according to service level agreements (SLAs) that are created between the provider and their customers to indicate a specific level of capacity. Capacity management is explored in more detail in Chapter 9, but it is essentially the practice of allocating the correct amount of resources in order to deliver a business service. The resources that these quotas enforce limits upon may be physical disks, disk arrays, host bus adapters, RAM chips, physical processors, and network adapters. They are allocated from the total pool of resources available to individual guests based on their SLA. Quotas and limits on hosts can be compared to speed limits on the highway; very often there are both minimum and maximum speeds defined for all traffic on the roads. A quota can be defined as the maximum speed, and a limit can be defined as the minimum speed for all vehicles using that road's resources.

Licensing

After designing the host computer's resources and storage limits, an organization needs to identify which vendor they are going to use for their virtualization software. Each virtualization software vendor has their own way of licensing their products. Some of them have a free version of their product and only require a license for advanced feature sets that enable functionality, like high availability, performance optimization, and systems management. Others offer a completely free virtualization platform but might not offer some of the more advanced features with their product. Choosing the virtualization platform is a critical step, and licensing is a factor in that decision. Before deploying a virtualization host and choosing a virtualization vendor, the organization must be sure to read the license agreements and determine exactly which features they need and how those features are licensed. In addition to licensing the virtualization host, the virtual machine requires a software license as well.

Reservations

Reservations work similarly to quotas. Whereas quotas are designed to ensure the correct capacity gets delivered to customers by defining an upper limit for resource usage, reservations are designed to operate at the other end of the capacity spectrum by ensuring that a lower limit is enforced for the amount of resources guaranteed to a cloud consumer for their virtual machine or machines. The importance of a reservation for host resources is that it ensures certain virtual machines always have a defined baseline level of resources available to them regardless of the demands placed on them by other virtual machines. The reason these guest reservations are so important is that they enable cloud service providers to deliver against their SLAs.

Resource Pools

Resource pools are slices or portions of compute resources, namely, CPU, memory, and storage, from a single host or a cluster of hosts. They can be partitioned off in order to provide different levels of resources to specific groups or organization, and they can be nested within a hierarchy for organizational alignment. Resource pools provide a flexible mechanism with which to organize the sum total of the compute resources in a virtual environment and link them back to their underlying physical resources.

CERTIFICATION OBJECTIVE 8.02

Virtual Machine Resource Allocation

Before creating a guest virtual machine, there are several factors that need to be considered. A guest virtual machine should be configured based on the intended application or task that the virtual machine is going to support. For example, a virtual machine running a database server may require special performance considerations, such as more CPUs or memory based on the designated role of the machine and the system load. In addition to CPUs and memory, a virtual machine may require higher-priority access to certain storage or disk types. An organization must consider not only the role of the virtual machine, the load of the machine, and the number of clients it is intended to support, but also the performance of ongoing monitoring and assessment based on these factors. The amount of disk space the virtual machine is using should be monitored and considered when deploying and maintaining storage.

Compute Resources

The compute resources for virtual machines enable service delivery in the same way that compute resources for hosts do, but the resources themselves are different in that they are virtualized components instead of physical components that can be held in your hand or plugged into a motherboard. Virtual machine compute resources are still made up of disk, network, processor, and memory components, but these components are made available to virtual machines not as physical resources but as abstractions of physical components presented by a hypervisor that emulates those physical resources for the virtual machine. Physical hosts have a basic input/ output system (BIOS) that presents physical compute resources to a host so they can be utilized to provide computing services, such as running an operating system and its component software applications. With virtual machines, the BIOS is emulated by the hypervisor to provide the same functions. When the BIOS is emulated and these physical resources are abstracted, administrators have the ability to divide the virtual compute resources from their physical providers and distribute those subdivided resources across multiple virtual machines. This ability to subdivide physical resources is one of the key elements that make cloud computing and virtualization so powerful.

When splitting resources among multiple virtual machines, there are vendor-specific algorithms that help the hypervisor make decisions about which resources are available for each request from its specific virtual machine. There are requirements of the host resources for performing these activities, including small amounts of processor, memory, and disk. These resources are utilized by the hypervisor for carrying out the algorithmic calculations to determine which resources will be granted to which virtual machines. These determinations are based on many factors, including defined quotas and limits, which resource is requested by which virtual machine, the business logic that may be applied by a management system for either a virtual machine or a pool of virtual machines, and the resources that are available at the time of the request. It is possible for the processing power required to make these decisions to outweigh the benefit of the resource allocations, and in those situations administrators can configure their systems to allocate specific resources or blocks of resources to specific hosts to shortcut that logic and designate which resources to use for a specific virtual machine or pool on all requests. CPU affinity is one such application, in which processes or threads from a specific virtual machine are tied to a specific processor or core, and all subsequent requests from that process or thread are executed by that same processor or core. Organizations can utilize reservations for virtual machines to guarantee an amount of compute resources for that virtual machine.

Quotas and Limits

As with host resources, virtual machines utilize quotas and limits to constrain the ability of users to consume compute resources and thereby prevent users from either completely depleting or monopolizing those resources. Quotas can be defined either as hard or soft. Hard quotas set limits that users and applications are barred from exceeding. If an attempt to use resources beyond the set limit is registered, the request is rejected, and an alert is logged that can be acted upon by a user, administrator, or management system. The difference with a soft quota is that the request is granted instead of rejected, and the resources are made available to service the request. The same alert, however, is still logged so that action can be taken to either address the issue with the requester for noncompliance with the quota or charge the appropriate party for the extra usage of the materials.

Licensing

Managing hardware resources can be less of a challenge than managing license agreements. Successfully managing software license agreements in a virtual environment is a tricky proposition. The software application must support licensing a virtual

EXAM AT WORK

A painful example that most people can relate to in terms of soft quotas is cell phone minutes usage. With most carriers, if a customer goes over the limit of their allotted cell phone minutes on their plan, they are charged an additional nominal amount per minute over. They will receive a warning when they go over the limit if their account is configured for such alerts, or they will receive an alert in the form of their bill that lets them know just how many minutes over quota they have gone and what they owe because of their overage. They are not, however, restricted from using more minutes once they have gone over their quota. If their cell phone minutes were configured as a hard quota, customers would be cut off in the middle of a phone call as soon as they eclipsed their quota. This usage of soft quotas is a great example of engineering cellular phone service by the phone companies, and it can be utilized across many other cloud services by their providers.

instance of the application. Some software vendors still require the use of a dongle or a hardware key when licensing their software. Others have adopted their licensing agreements to coexist with a virtual environment. A virtual machine requires a license to operate just as a physical server does. Some vendors have moved to a per-CPU-core type of license agreement to adapt to virtualization. No matter if the application is installed on a physical server or a virtual server, it still requires a license.

Physical Resource Redirection

Parallel and serial ports are interfaces that allow for the connection of peripherals to computers. There are times when it is useful to have a virtual machine connect its virtual serial port to a physical serial port on the host computer. For example, a user might want to install an external modem or another form of a handheld device on the virtual machine, and this would require the virtual machine to use a physical serial port on the host computer. It might also be useful to connect a virtual serial port to a file on a host computer and then have the virtual machine send output to a file on the host computer. An example of this would be to send data that was captured from a program running on the virtual machine via the virtual serial port and transfer the information from the guest to the host computer.

In addition to using a virtual serial port, it is also helpful in certain instances to connect to a virtual parallel port. Parallel ports are used for a variety of devices, including printers, scanners, and dongles. Much like the virtual serial port, a virtual parallel port allows for connecting the virtual machine to a physical parallel port on the host computer.

In addition to supporting serial and parallel port emulation for virtual machines, some virtualization vendors support USB device pass-through from a host computer to a virtual machine. USB pass-through allows a USB device plugged directly into a host computer to be passed through to a virtual machine. USB pass-through allows for multiple USB devices (such as security dongles and storage devices) that are physically attached to a host computer to be added to a virtual machine. When a USB device is attached to a host computer, that device is available only to the virtual machines that are running on that host computer and only to one virtual machine at a time.

Resource Pools

A resource pool is a hierarchical abstraction of compute resources that can give relative importance, or weight, to a defined set of virtualized resources. Pools at the higher level in the hierarchy are called parent pools; these parents can contain either child pools or individual virtual machines. Each pool can have a defined weight assigned to it based on either the business rules of the organization or the SLAs of a customer. These pools also allow administrators to define a flexible hierarchy that can be adapted at each pool level as required by the business. This hierarchical structure makes it possible to maintain access control and delegation of the administration of each pool and its resources; to ensure isolation between the pools, as well as sharing within the pools; and finally to separate the compute resources from discrete host hardware. This last feature frees administrators from the typical constraints of managing the available resources from the host they originated from. Those resources are bubbled up to a higher level for management and administration when utilizing pools.

Dynamic Resource Allocation

Just because administrators have the ability to manage their compute resources at a higher level with resource pools, it doesn't mean they want to spend their precious time doing it. Enter dynamic resource allocation. Instead of relying on administrators to evaluate resource utilization and apply changes to the environment that result in the best performance, availability, and capacity arrangements, a computer can do it for them based on business logic that has been predefined by either the management software's default values or the administrator's modification to those values. Management platforms have the ability to manage compute resources not only for performance, availability, and capacity reasons but also to realize more cost-effective implementation of those resources in a data center, employing only the hosts required at the given time and shutting down any resources that are not needed. By employing dynamic resource allocation, providers are able to both reduce power costs and go greener by shrinking their power footprint and waste.

CERTIFICATION OBJECTIVE 8.03

Optimizing Performance

Utilization of the allocation mechanisms we have talked about thus far in this chapter allows administrators to achieve the configuration states that they seek within their environment. The best practices for these configurations are the focus for the remainder of this chapter: those allocation mechanisms that allow for the greatest value to be realized by service providers.

Configuration Best Practices

There are a number of best practices for the configuration of each of the compute resources within a cloud environment. To best understand their use cases and potential impact, we investigate common configuration options for memory, processor, and disk.

Memory

Memory may be the most critical of all computer resources, as it is usually the limiting factor on the number of guests that can be run on a given host, and performance issues appear when too many guests are fighting for enough memory to perform their functions. Two configuration options available for addressing shared memory concerns are memory ballooning and swap disk space.

Memory Ballooning   Hypervisors have device drivers that they build into the host virtualization layer from within the guest operating system. Part of this installed tool set is a balloon driver, which can be observed inside the guest. The balloon driver communicates to the hypervisor to reclaim memory inside the guest when it is no longer valuable to the operating system. If the host begins to run low on memory, it will grow the balloon driver to reclaim memory from the guest. This reduces the chance that the physical host will begin to utilize virtualized memory from a defined paging file on its available disk resource, which causes performance degradation. An illustration of the way this ballooning works can be found in Figure 8-2.

Swap Disk Space   Swap space is disk space that is allocated to service memory requests when the physical memory capacity limit has been reached. When virtualizing and overcommitting memory resources to virtual machines, administrators must make certain to reserve enough swap space for the host to balloon memory in addition to reserving disk space within the guest operating system for it to perform its own swap operations.

Processor

CPU time is the amount of time a process or thread spends executing on a processor core. For multiple threads, the CPU time of the threads is additive. The application

FIGURE 8-2

How memory
ballooning works.

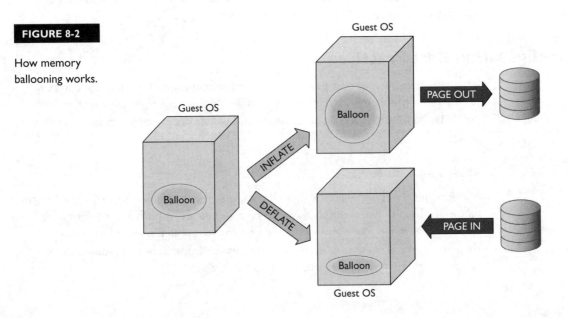

CPU time is the sum of the CPU time of all the threads that run the application. Wait time is the amount of time that a given thread waits to be processed; it could be processed but must wait on other factors such as synchronization waits and I/O waits. High CPU wait times signal that there are too many requests for a given queue on a core to handle, and performance degradation will occur. While high CPU wait time can be alleviated in some situations by adding processors, these additions sometimes hurt performance as well. Caution must be exercised when adding processors as there is a potential for causing even further performance degradation if the applications using them are not designed to be run on multiple CPUs. Another solution for alleviating CPU wait times is to scale out instead of scaling up, two concepts that we explore in more detail later in this chapter.

Disk

Poor disk performance, or poorly designed disk solutions, can have performance ramifications in traditional infrastructures, slowing users down as they wait to read or write data for the server they are accessing. In a cloud model, however, disk performance issues can limit access to all organization resources because multiple virtualized servers in a networked storage environment might be competing for the same storage resources, thereby crippling their entire deployment of virtualized servers or desktops. Listed below are some common configurations and measurements that assist in designing a high-performance storage solution.

Disk Performance   Disk performance can be configured with several different configuration options. Media type can affect performance, and administrators can choose between the most standard types of traditional rotational media or chip-based solid state drives. Solid state drives are much faster than their rotational counterparts as they are not limited by the physical seek arm speed that reads the rotational platters. Solid state drives, while becoming more economical in the last few years, are still much more expensive than rotational media and are not utilized except where only the highest performance standards are required.

The next consideration for disk performance is the speed of the rotational media, should that be the media of choice. Server-class disks start at 7,200 rpm and go up to 15,000 rpm, with seek times for the physical arm reading the platters being considerably lower on the high-end drives. In enterprise configurations, price point per gigabyte is largely driven on the rotation speed and only marginally by storage space per gigabyte. When considering enterprise storage, the adage is that you pay for performance, not space.

Once the media type and speed have been determined, the next consideration is the type of RAID array that the disks are placed in to meet the service needs. Different levels of RAID can be employed based on the deployment purpose. These RAID levels should be evaluated and configured based on the type of I/O and on the need to read, write, or a combination of both.

Disk Tuning   Disk tuning is the activity of analyzing what type of I/O traffic is taking place across the defined disk resources and moving it to the most appropriate set of resources. Virtualization management platforms enable the movement of storage, without interrupting current operations, to other disk resources within their control. This allows either administrators or dynamic resource allocation programs to move applications, storage, databases, and even entire virtual machines among disk arrays with no downtime to make sure that those virtualized entities get the performance they require based on either business rules or SLAs.

Disk Latency   Disk latency is a counter that provides administrators with the best indicator of when a resource is experiencing degradation due to a disk bottleneck and needs to have action taken against it. If high latency counters are experienced, a move to either another disk array with quicker response times or a different configuration, such as higher rotational speeds or a different array configuration, is warranted. Another option is to configure I/O throttling.

I/O Throttling   I/O throttling does not eliminate disk I/O as a bottleneck for performance, but it can alleviate performance problems for specific virtual machines based on a priority assigned by the administrator. I/O throttling defines limits that can be utilized specifically for disk resources assigned to virtual machines to ensure that they are not performance or availability constrained when working in an environment that has more demand than availability of disk resources. This may be a valuable option when an environment contains both development and production resources. The production I/O can be given a higher priority than the development resources, allowing the production environment to perform better for its users. It does not eliminate the bottleneck; it just passes it on to the development environment, which becomes even further degraded in performance as it waits for all production I/O requests when the disk is overallocated. We can then assign a priority or pecking order for the essential components that need higher priority.

I/O Tuning   When designing systems, administrators need to analyze input and output (I/O) needs from the top down, determining which resources are needed in order to achieve the required performance levels. In order to perform this top-down evaluation, first the application I/O requirements need to be evaluated to understand how many reads and writes are required by each transaction and how many transactions take place each second. Once those application requirements are understood, the disk configuration (specifically, which types of media, what array configuration, the number of disks, and the access methods) can be built to support that number.

Common Issues

There are a number of failures that can occur within a cloud environment, and the system must be configured to be tolerant of those failures and provide availability in line with the organization's SLA. Any mechanical environment will experience failures; it is just a matter of when and the quality of the equipment the company has purchased. Failures occur mainly on each of the four primary compute resources: disk, memory, network, and processor. This section examines each of these resources in turn.

Common Disk Failures

Disk failures can happen for a variety of reasons, but they fail more frequently than the other compute resources because they are the only compute resource that has a mechanical component. Due to the moving parts, failure rates are typically quite high. Some common disk failures are listed below.

Physical Hard Disk Failures   Physical hard disks fail frequently because they are mechanical, moving devices. In enterprise configurations they are deployed as components of drive arrays, and single failures do not affect array availability.

Controller Card Failures   Controller cards are the components that control arrays and their configurations. Like all components, they fail from time to time. Redundant controllers are very expensive to run in parallel as they require double the amount of drives to become operational, and that capacity is lost as it is never in use until failure. Therefore, an organization should do a return-on-investment analysis to determine the feasibility of making such devices redundant.

Disk Corruption   Disk corruption occurs when the structured data on the disk is no longer accessible. This can happen as a result of malicious acts or programs, skewing of the mechanics of the drive, or even a lack of proper maintenance.

Disk corruption is difficult to repair, as the full contents of the disks need to be reindexed or restored from backups. Backups can also be unreliable for these failures if the corruption began prior to its identification, as the available backup sets may also be corrupted.

Host Bus Adapter (HBA) Failures   HBA failures, while not as common as physical disk failures, need to be expected and storage solutions need to be designed with them in mind. HBAs have the option of being multipathed, which prevents a loss of availability in the event of a failure.

Fabric/Network Failures   Similar to arrays, fabric or network failures can be fairly expensive to design around, as they happen when a storage networking switch or switch port fails. The design principles to protect against such a failure are similar to those for HBAs, as multipathing needs to be in place to make certain all hosts that depend on the fabric or network have access to their disk resources through another channel.

Common Memory Failures

Memory failures, while not as common as disk failures, can be just as disruptive. Good system design in cloud environments will take RAM failure into account as a risk and ensure that there is always some RAM available to run mission-critical systems in case of memory failure on one of their hosts. Listed below are some types of memory failures.

RAM Failures   Memory chip failures happen less frequently than physical device failures since they have no moving parts and mechanical wear does not play a part. They will, however, break from time to time and need to be replaced.

Motherboard Failures   Similar to memory chip failures, motherboards have no moving parts and because of this they fail less frequently than mechanical devices. When they do fail, however, virtual machines are unable to operate as they have no processor, memory, or networking resources that they can access. In this situation, they must be moved immediately to another host or go offline.

Swap Files Out of Space   Swap space failures often occur in conjunction with a disk failure, when disks run out of available space to allocate to swap files for memory overallocation. They do, however, result in out-of-memory errors for virtual machines and hosts alike.

Network Failures

Similar to memory failures, network components are fairly reliable because they do not have moving parts. Unlike memory, network resources are highly configurable and prone to errors based on human mistakes during implementation. Some common types of network failures are described below.

Physical NIC Failures   Network interface cards can fail in a similar fashion to other printed circuit board components like motherboards, controller cards, and memory chips. Because they fail from time to time, redundancy needs to be built into the host through multiple physical NICs and into the virtualization through designing multiple network paths using virtual NICs for the virtual machines.

Speed/Duplex Mismatches   Mismatch failures happen only on physical NICs and switches, as virtual networks negotiate these automatically. Speed and duplex mismatches result in dropped packets between the two connected devices, and can be identified through getting many cyclical redundancy check (CRC) errors on the devices.

Switch Failures   Similar to fabric and network failures, network switch failures are expensive to plan for as they require duplicate hardware and cabling. Switches fail wholesale only a small percentage of the time, but more frequently have individual ports fail. When these individual ports do fail, the resources that are connected to them need to have another path available or their service will be interrupted.

Physical Transmission Media Failures   Cables break from time to time when their wires inside are crimped or cut. This can happen either when they are moved, when they are stretched too far, or when they become old and the connector breaks loose from its associated wires. As with other types of network failures, multiple paths to the resource using that cable is the way to prevent a failure from interrupting operations.

Physical Processor Failures

Processors fail for one of three main reasons: they get broken while getting installed, they are damaged by voltage spikes, or they are damaged due to overheating from failed or ineffective fans. Damaged processors either take hosts completely off-line or degrade performance based on the damage and the availability of a standby or alternative processor in some models.

Performance Concepts

There are a number of performance concepts that underlie each of the failure types and the allocation mechanisms discussed in this chapter. As we did with the failure mechanisms, let's look at each of these according to their associated compute resources.

Disk

Configuration of disk resources is an important part of a well-designed cloud system. Based on the user and application requirements and usage patterns, there are numerous design choices that need to be made to implement a storage system that meets an organization's needs in a cost-effective fashion. Some of the considerations for disk performance are described below.

IOPS IOPS, or input/output operations per second, are the standard measurement for disk performance. They are usually gathered as read IOPS, write IOPS, and total IOPS to distinguish between the types of requests that are being received.

Read Versus Write As we just mentioned in IOPS, there are two types of operations that can take place: reading and writing. As their names suggest, reads take place when a resource requests data from a disk resource, and writes take place when a resource requests new data be recorded on a disk resource. Based on which type of operation takes place, different configuration options exist both for troubleshooting and performance tuning.

File System Performance File system performance is debated as a selling point among different technology providers. File systems can be formatted and cataloged differently based on the proprietary technologies of their associated vendors. There is little to do in configuration of file systems performance outside of evaluating the properties of each that is planned for operation in the environment.

Metadata Performance Metadata performance refers to how quickly files and directories can be created, removed, or checked. Applications exist now that produce millions of files in a single directory and create very deep and wide directory structures, and this rapid growth of items within a file system can have a huge impact on performance. The ability to create, remove, and check their status efficiently grows in direct proportion to the number of items in use on any file system.

Caching   In order to improve performance, hard drives are architected with a mechanism called a disk cache that reduces both read and write times. On a physical hard disk, the disk cache is usually a RAM chip that is built in and holds data that is likely to be accessed again soon. On virtual hard disks, the same caching mechanism can be employed by using a specified portion of a memory resource.

Network

Similar to disk resources, the configuration of network resources is critical.

Bandwidth   Bandwidth is the measurement of available or consumed data communication resources on a network. Performance of all networks is dependent on having available bandwidth.

Throughput   Throughput is the amount of data that can be realized between two network resources. Throughput can be greatly increased through the use of bonding or teaming of network adapters, which allows resources to see multiple interfaces as one single interface with aggregated resources.

Jumbo Frames   Jumbo frames are Ethernet frames with more than 1500 bytes of payload. These frames can carry up to 9000 bytes of payload, but depending on the vendor and the environment they are deployed in, there may be some deviation. Jumbo frames are utilized because they are much less processor intensive to consume than a large number of smaller frames, therefore freeing up expensive processor cycles for more business-related functions.

Network Latency   Network latency refers to any performance delays experienced during the processing of any network data. A low-latency network connection is one that generally experiences small delay times, such as a dedicated T-1, while a high-latency connection generally suffers from long delays, like DSL or a cable modem.

Hop Counts   A hop count represents the total number of devices a packet passes through in order to reach its intended network target. The more hops data must pass through to reach their destination, the greater the delay will be for the transmission. Network utilities like ping can be used to determine the hop count to an intended destination. Ping generates packets that include a field reserved for the hop count (typically referred to as a TTL, or time-to-live), and each time a capable device (typically a router) along the path to the target receives one of these packets, that device modifies the packet, decrementing the TTL by one. Each packet is sent out with a particular time-to-live value, ranging from 1 to 254; for every router (hop) that it traverses, that TTL count is decremented. In addition, for every one second that the packet resides in the memory of the router, it is also decremented by one. The device then compares the hop count against a predetermined limit and discards the packet if its hop count is too high. If the TTL is decremented to zero at any point during its transmission, an ICMP port unreachable message is generated, with the IP of the source router or device included, and sent back to the originator. The finite TTL is used as it counts down to zero in order to prevent packets from endlessly bouncing around the network due to routing errors.

Quality of Service (QoS)   QoS is a set of technologies that can identify the type of data in data packets and divide those packets into specific traffic classes that can be prioritized according to defined service levels. QoS technologies enable administrators to meet their service requirements for a workload or an application by measuring network bandwidth, detecting changing network conditions, and prioritizing the network traffic accordingly. QoS can be targeted at a network interface, toward a given server or router's performance, or in terms of specific applications. A network monitoring system is typically deployed as part of a QoS solution to ensure that networks are performing at the desired level.

Multipathing   Multipathing is the practice of defining and controlling redundant physical paths to I/O devices, so that when an active path to a device becomes unavailable, the multipathing configuration can automatically switch to an alternate path in order to maintain service availability. The capability of performing this operation without intervention from an administrator is known as automatic failover. A prerequisite for taking advantage of multipathing capabilities is to design and configure the multipathed resource with redundant hardware, such as redundant network interfaces or host bus adapters.

Load Balancing   A load balancer is a networking solution that distributes incoming traffic among multiple servers hosting the same application content. Load balancers improve overall application availability and performance by preventing any application server from becoming a single point of failure. If deployed alone, however, the load balancer becomes a single point of failure by itself. Therefore, it is always recommended to deploy multiple load balancers in parallel. In addition to improving availability and performance, load balancers add to the security profile of a configuration by the typical usage of network address translation, which obfuscates the IP address of the back-end application servers.

Scalability   Scalability is the ability of a system or network to manage a growing workload in a proficient manner or its ability to be expanded to accommodate the workload growth. All cloud environments need to be scalable, as one of the chief tenets of cloud computing is elasticity, or the ability to adapt to growing workload quickly. Scalability can be handled either vertically or horizontally, more commonly referred to as "scaling up" or "scaling out," respectively. To scale vertically means to add resources to a single node, thereby making that node capable of handling more of a load within itself. This type of scaling is most often seen in virtualization environments where individual hosts add more processors or more memory with the objective of adding more virtual machines to each host. To scale horizontally, more nodes are added to a configuration instead of increasing the resources for any one node. Horizontal scaling is often used in application farms, where more web servers are added to a farm to better handle distributed application delivery. A third type of scaling, diagonal scaling, is a combination of both, increasing resources for individual nodes and adding more of those nodes to the system. Diagonal scaling allows for the best configuration to be achieved for a quickly growing, elastic solution.

e x a m

W a t c h   *Know the difference between scaling up and scaling out.*

CERTIFICATION SUMMARY

When building a virtualization host, special consideration needs to be given to adequately planning the resources to ensure that the host is capable of supporting the virtualized environment. Creating a virtual machine requires thorough planning regarding the role the virtual machine will play in the environment and the resources needed for the virtual machine to accomplish that role. Planning carefully for the virtual machine and the primary resources of memory, processor, disk, and network can help prevent common failures.

KEY TERMS

Use the list below to review the key terms that were discussed in this chapter.

Compute resources   The resources that are required for the delivery of virtual machines: disk, processor, memory, and networking

Limit   A floor or ceiling on the amount of resources that can be utilized for a given entity

Quota   The total amount of resources that can be utilized for a system

Reservation   A mechanism that ensures a lower limit is enforced for the amount of resources guaranteed to an entity

Resource pools   Partitions of compute resources from a single host or a cluster of hosts

Memory ballooning   A device driver loaded inside a guest operating system that identifies underutilized memory and allows the host to reclaim memory for redistribution.

I/O throttling   Defined limits utilized specifically for disk resources assigned to virtual machines to ensure they are not performance or availability constrained when working in an environment that has more demand than availability of disk resources

CPU wait time   The delay that results when the CPU can't perform computations because it is waiting on I/O operations

IOPS   Input/output operations per second

Read operations   Operations in which a resource requests data from a disk resource

Write operations   Operations in which a resource requests that new data be recorded on a disk resource

Metadata performance   A measure of how quickly files and directories can be created, removed, or checked on a disk resource

Caching   A mechanism for improving the time it takes to read from or write to a disk resource

Bandwidth   A measurement of available or consumed data communication resources on a network

Throughput   The amount of data that can be realized between two network resources

Jumbo frames   Large frames that are used with large data transfers to lessen the burden on processors

Network latency   Any delays typically incurred during the processing of any network data

Hop count   The total number of devices a packet passes through in order to reach its intended network target

Quality of Service (QoS)   A set of technologies that provide the ability to manage network traffic and prioritize workloads in order to accommodate defined service levels as part of a cost-effective solution

Multipathing   The practice of defining and controlling redundant physical paths to I/O devices

Load balancing   Networking solution that distributes incoming traffic among multiple resources

Scalability   Ability of a system or network to manage a growing workload in a proficient manner or its ability to be expanded to accommodate the workload growth

✓ TWO-MINUTE DRILL

Host Resource Allocation

❑ Proper planning of the compute resources for a host computer ensures that the host can deliver the performance needed in order to support its virtualized environment.

❑ Quotas and limits allow cloud providers to control the amount of resources a cloud consumer has access to.

❑ A reservation helps to ensure that a host computer receives a guaranteed amount of resources to support their virtual machine.

❑ Resource pools allow an organization to organize the sum total of compute resources in the virtual environment and link them back to their underlying physical resources.

Virtual Machine Resource Allocation

❑ Virtual machines utilize quotas and limits to constrain the ability of users to consume compute resources, and can prevent users from either completely depleting or monopolizing those resources.

❑ Software applications and operating systems must support the ability to be licensed in a virtual environment, and the licensing needs to be taken into consideration before a physical server becomes a virtual server.

❑ A virtual machine can support the emulation of a parallel and serial port; some can support the emulation of a USB port.

❑ Dynamic resource allocation can be used to automatically assign compute resources to a virtual machine based on utilization.

Optimizing Performance

❑ There are a number of best practices for configuration of compute resources within a cloud environment.

❑ There are multiple failures that can occur within a cloud environment, including hard disk failure, controller card failures, disk corruption, HBA failure, network failure, RAM failure, motherboard failure, network switch failure, and processor failure.

SELF TEST

The following questions will help you measure your understanding of the material presented in this chapter.

Host Resource Allocation

1. Which of the following would be considered a host compute resource?
   A. Cores
   B. Power supply
   C. Processor
   D. Bandwidth

2. Quotas are a mechanism for enforcing what?
   A. Limits
   B. Rules
   C. Access restrictions
   D. Virtualization

3. How are quotas defined?
   A. By management systems
   B. According to service level agreements that are defined between providers and their customers
   C. Through trend analysis and its results
   D. With spreadsheets and reports

4. When would a reservation be used?
   A. When a maximum amount of resources needs to be allocated to a specific resource
   B. When a minimum amount of capacity needs to be available at all times to a specific resource
   C. When capacity needs to be measured and controlled
   D. When planning a dinner date

Virtual Machine Resource Allocation

5. How does the hypervisor enable access for virtual machines to the physical hardware resources on a host?
   A. Over Ethernet cables
   B. By using USB 3.0
   C. Through the system bus
   D. By emulating a BIOS that abstracts the hardware

6. What mechanism allows one core to handle all requests from a specific thread on a specific processor core?

A. V2V

B. CPU affinity

C. V2P

D. P2V

7. In a scenario where an entity exceeds its defined quota, but is granted access to the resources anyway, what must be in place?

A. Penalty

B. Hard quota

C. Soft quota

D. Alerts

8. Which of the following must be licensed when running a virtualized infrastructure?

A. Hosts

B. Virtual machines

C. Both

D. Neither

9. What do you need to employ if you have a serial device that needs to be utilized by a virtual machine?

A. Network isolation

B. Physical resource redirection

C. V2V

D. Storage migration

10. You need to divide your virtualized environment into groups that can be managed by separate groups of administrators. Which of these tools can you use?

A. Quotas

B. CPU affinity

C. Resource pools

D. Licensing

Optimizing Performance

11. Which tool allows guest operating systems to share noncritical memory pages with the host?
   A. CPU affinity
   B. Memory ballooning
   C. Swap file configuration
   D. Network attached storage

12. Which of these options is not a valid mechanism for improving disk performance?
   A. Replacing rotational media with solid state media
   B. Replacing rotational media with higher-speed rotational media
   C. Decreasing disk quotas
   D. Employing a different configuration for the RAID array

SELF TEST ANSWERS

Host Resource Allocation

1. Which of the following would be considered a host compute resource?
   A. Cores
   B. Power supply
   C. Processor
   D. Bandwidth

> ☑ **C.** The four compute resources used in virtualization are disk, memory, processor, and network. On a host, these are available as the physical entities of hard disks, memory chips, processors, and network interface cards (NICs).
>
> ☒ **A, B,** and **D** are incorrect. Cores are a virtual compute resource. Power supplies, while utilized by hosts, are not compute resources because they do not contribute resources toward the creation of virtual machines. Bandwidth is a measurement of network throughput capability, not a resource itself.

2. Quotas are a mechanism for enforcing what?
   A. Limits
   B. Rules
   C. Access restrictions
   D. Virtualization

> ☑ **A.** Quotas are rules that enforce limits on the resources that can be utilized for a specific entity on a system.
>
> ☒ **B, C,** and **D** are incorrect. Quotas cannot be used to enforce rules or setup virtualization. Access restrictions are security entities, not quantities that can be limited, and virtualization is the abstraction of hardware resources, which has nothing to do with quotas.

3. How are quotas defined?
   A. By management systems
   B. According to service level agreements that are defined between providers and their customers
   C. Through trend analysis and its results
   D. With spreadsheets and reports

☑ **B.** Quotas are defined according to service level agreements that are negotiated between a provider and its customers.

☒ **A, C,** and **D** are incorrect. Management systems and trend analysis provide measurement of levels of capacity, and those levels are reported on using spreadsheets and reports, but these are all practices and tools that are used once the quotas have already been negotiated.

4. When would a reservation be used?
   A. When a maximum amount of resources needs to be allocated to a specific resource
   B. When a minimum amount of capacity needs to be available at all times to a specific resource
   C. When capacity needs to be measured and controlled
   D. When planning a dinner date

☑ **B.** Reservations should be utilized when there is a minimum amount of resources that needs to have guaranteed capacity.

☒ **A, C,** and **D** are incorrect. Dealing with maximum capacity instead of minimums is the opposite of a reservation. Capacity should always be measured and controlled, but not all measurement and control of capacity deals with reservations. Obviously, if you are planning for a dinner date you will want to make reservations, but that has nothing to do with cloud computing.

Virtual Machine Resource Allocation

5. How does the hypervisor enable access for virtual machines to the physical hardware resources on a host?
   A. Over Ethernet cables
   B. By using USB 3.0
   C. Through the system bus
   D. By emulating a BIOS that abstracts the hardware

☑ **D.** The host computer BIOS is emulated by the hypervisor to provide compute resources for a virtual machine.

☒ **A, B,** and **C** are incorrect. These options do not allow a host computer to emulate compute resources and distribute them among virtual machines.

6. What mechanism allows one core to handle all requests from a specific thread on a specific processor core?
   A. V2V
   B. CPU affinity
   C. V2P
   D. P2V

   ☑ **B.** CPU affinity allows all requests from a specific thread or process to be handled by the same processor core.
   ☒ **A, C,** and **D** are incorrect. You can use a V2V to copy or restore files and program from one virtual machine to another. V2P allows you to migrate a virtual machine to a physical server. P2V allows you to migrate a physical server's operating system, applications, and data from the physical server to a newly created guest virtual machine on a host computer.

7. In a scenario where an entity exceeds its defined quota, but is granted access to the resources anyway, what must be in place?
   A. Penalty
   B. Hard quota
   C. Soft quota
   D. Alerts

   ☑ **C.** Soft quotas enforce limits on resources, but do not restrict access to the requested resources when the quota has been exceeded.
   ☒ **A, B,** and **D** are incorrect. Penalties may be incurred if soft quotas are exceeded, but the quota must first be in place. A hard quota denies access to resources after it has been exceeded. Alerts should be configured, regardless of the quota type, to be triggered when the quota has been breached.

8. Which of the following must be licensed when running a virtualized infrastructure?
   A. Hosts
   B. Virtual machines
   C. Both
   D. Neither

   ☑ **C.** Both hosts and guests must be licensed in a virtual environment.
   ☒ **A, B,** and **D** are incorrect. Both hosts and guests must be licensed in a virtual environment.

9. What do you need to employ if you have a serial device that needs to be utilized by a virtual machine?

A. Network isolation

B. Physical resource redirection

C. V2V

D. Storage migration

☑ **B.** Physical resource redirection enables virtual machines to utilize physical hardware as if they were physical hosts that could connect to the hardware directly.

☒ **A, C,** and **D** are incorrect. These options do not allow you to redirect a virtual machine to a physical port on a host computer.

10. You need to divide your virtualized environment into groups that can be managed by separate groups of administrators. Which of these tools can you use?

A. Quotas

B. CPU affinity

C. Resource pools

D. Licensing

☑ **C.** Resource pools allow the creation of a hierarchy of virtual machine groups that can have different administrative privileges assigned to them.

☒ **A, B,** and **D** are incorrect. Quotas are employed to limit the capacity of a resource, CPU affinity is used to isolate specific threads or processes to one processor core, and licensing has to do with the acceptable use of software or hardware resources.

Optimizing Performance

11. Which tool allows guest operating systems to share noncritical memory pages with the host?

A. CPU affinity

B. Memory ballooning

C. Swap file configuration

D. Network attached storage

☑ **B.** Memory ballooning allows guest operating systems to share noncritical memory pages with the host.

☒ **A, C,** and **D** are incorrect. CPU affinity is used to isolate specific threads or processes to one processor core. Swap file configuration is the configuration of a specific file to emulate memory pages as an overflow for physical RAM. Network attached storage is a disk resource that is accessed across a network.

12. Which of these options is not a valid mechanism for improving disk performance?
    A. Replacing rotational media with solid state media
    B. Replacing rotational media with higher-speed rotational media
    C. Decreasing disk quotas
    D. Employing a different configuration for the RAID array

☑ **C.** Decreasing disk quotas helps with capacity issues, but not with performance.

☒ **A, B,** and **D** are incorrect. Changing from rotational to solid state media increases performance since it eliminates the dependency on the mechanical seek arm to read or write. Upgrading rotational media to higher rotational speed also speeds up both read and write operations. Changing the configuration of the array to a different RAID level can also have a dramatic effect on performance.

9

Systems Management

U p until this point, this book has primarily focused on the technologies required to deliver cloud services. This chapter explores the nontechnical aspects of cloud service delivery in policies, procedures, and best practices. These components are critical to the efficient and effective execution of cloud solutions.

CERTIFICATION OBJECTIVE 9.01

Policies and Procedures

Policies and procedures are the backbone of any IT organization. While the hardware, software, and their associated configurations are the products that enable the functionality businesses desire from their IT services, it is policy and procedure that enable its implementation, maintenance, and ongoing support. Policies define the rule sets by which users and administrators must abide, and procedures are the prescribed methodologies by which activities are carried out in the IT environment according to those defined policies. While most administrators focus on the technical aspects of IT, a growing percentage of all IT organizations are placing an emphasis on policy and procedure development to ensure that they get the most out of their technology investment. These nontechnical areas greatly impact not only the operational efficiency and effectiveness of the businesses they serve, but also protect them from risk by making sure they stay compliant with industry regulation as well.

Change Management

The process of making changes to the IT environment from its design phase to its operations phase in the least impactful way possible is known as change management. Change management is a collection of policies and procedures that are designed to mitigate risk by evaluating change, ensuring thorough testing, providing proper communication, and training both administrators and end users. In IT nomenclature, a change is defined as the addition, modification, or removal of anything that could have an effect on IT services. It is important to note that this definition is not restricted to IT infrastructure components; it should also be applied to documentation, people, procedures, and other nontechnical items that are critical to a well-run IT environment.

Change management has several objectives:

- To maximize business value through modification of the IT environment while reducing disruption to the business and unnecessary IT expense due to rework
- To ensure that all proposed changes are both evaluated and recorded
- To prioritize, plan, test, implement, document, and review all changes in a controlled fashion according to defined policies and procedures
- To optimize overall business risk (by optimizing, we mean both the risks and the benefits of a proposed change are evaluated, and contribute to the decision to either approve or reject the change)
- To act as a control mechanism for the configuration management process by ensuring that all changes to configuration item baselines in the IT environment are updated in the configuration management system (CMS)

A change management process can be broken down into several constituent concepts that work together to meet these objectives.

- A request for change (RFC) is a formal request for a change that can be submitted by anyone that is involved with, or has a stake in, that particular item or service. IT leadership may submit changes focused on increasing the profitability of an IT service; a systems administrator may submit a change to improve system stability; and an end user may submit a change that requests additional functionality for their job role. All are valid requests for change.
- Change proposals are similar to RFCs but are reserved for changes that have the potential for major organizational impact or serious financial implications. The reason for a separate designation for RFCs and change proposals is to make sure that the decision making for very strategic changes is handled by the right level of leadership within the organization. Change proposals are generally handled by the CIO or higher position in an organization. They are not as detailed as an RFC, and are a high-level description of the change requiring the approval of those responsible for the strategic direction associated with the change. Change proposals help IT organizations stay efficient by not wasting resources on the intensive process required by an RFC to analyze and plan the proposed change if it is not in the strategic best interest of the organization to begin with.

- Change types are used to categorize both the amount of risk and the amount of urgency each request carries. There are three types of changes: normal changes, standard changes, and emergency changes. Normal changes are changes that are evaluated by the defined change management process to understand the benefits and risks of any given request. Standard changes request a type of change that has been evaluated previously and now poses little risk to the health of the IT services. Because it is well understood, low risk, and the organization does not stand to benefit from another review, a standard change is preauthorized. Emergency changes, as the name suggests, are used in case of an emergency and designate a higher level of urgency to move into operation. Although the urgency is greater, all steps of the process for implementing the change must still be followed. The review and approval of emergency changes, however, is usually executed by a smaller group of people than is used for a normal change, to facilitate moving the requested change into operation.

- The change manager is the individual who is directly responsible for all the activities within the change management process. They are ultimately responsible for the approval or rejection of each RFC and for making sure that all RFCs follow the defined policies and procedures as a part of their submission. The change manager is also responsible for assembling the right collection of stakeholders to help advise on the risks and benefits of a given change and to provide the input that will allow the change manager to make the right decision when it comes to approval or rejection of a request.

- The body of stakeholders that provides input to the change manager about RFCs is known as the change advisory board (CAB). This group of stakeholders should be composed of members from all representative areas of the business as well as customers who might be affected by the change (see Figure 9-1). As part of their evaluation process for each request, the board needs to consider the following:
  - The reason for the change
  - The benefit of implementing the change
  - The risks associated with implementing the change
  - The risks associated with not implementing the change
  - The resources required to implement the change
  - The scheduling of the implementation

- The impact of the projected service outage to agreed upon service levels
- The planned backout strategy in case of a failed change

While this may seem like a lot of people involved in and a lot of time spent on the consideration of each change to the environment, these policies and procedures pay off in the long run by limiting the impact of unknown or unstable configurations going into a production environment and limiting the value of the IT services to its business community and/or customers.

FIGURE 9-1

The entities represented by a change advisory board (CAB).

Another consideration about organizing CABs is that they take a good deal of planning to get all the stakeholders together. In the case of an emergency change, there may not be time to assemble the full CAB. For such situations an emergency change advisory board (ECAB) should be formed. This emergency CAB should follow the same procedures as the standard CAB; it is just a subset of the stakeholders who would usually convene for the review. Often the ECAB is defined as a certain percentage of a standard CAB that would be required by the change manager to make sure they have all the input required to make an informed decision about the request.

- After every change has been completed, it must go through a defined procedure for both change review and closure. This review process is intended to evaluate whether the objectives of the change were accomplished, the users and customers were satisfied, and any new side effects were produced. It is also intended to evaluate the resources expended in the implementation of the change, the time it took to implement, and the overall cost.

Configuration Management

Change management offers value to both information technology organizations and its customers. One problem when implementing change management, however, lies in how the objects that are being modified are classified and controlled. To this end we introduce configuration management, which deals with IT assets and their relationships to one another.

The purpose of the configuration management process is to ensure that the assets required to deliver services are properly controlled, and that accurate and reliable information about those assets is available when and where it is needed. This information includes details of how the assets have been configured and the relationships between assets.

The objectives of configuration management are as follows:

- Identifying configuration items (CIs)
- Controlling CIs
- Protecting the integrity of CIs
- Maintaining an accurate and complete configuration management system (CMS)
- Maintaining information about the state of all CIs
- Providing accurate configuration information

The implementation of a configuration management process results in improved overall service performance. It is also important for optimization of both the costs and risks that can be caused by poorly managed assets, such as extended service outages, fines, incorrect license fees, and failed compliance audits. Some of the specific benefits to be achieved through its implementation are the following:

- A better understanding on the part of IT staffs of the configurations of the resources they support and the relationships they have with other resources, resulting in the ability to pinpoint issues and resolve incidents and problems much faster
- A much richer set of detailed information for change management from which to make decisions about the implementation of planned changes
- Greater success in the planning and delivery of scheduled releases
- Improved compliance with legal, financial, and regulatory obligations with less administration required to report on those obligations
- Better visibility to the true, fully loaded cost of delivering a specific service
- Ability to track both baselined configuration deviation and deviation from requirements
- Reduced cost and time to discover configuration information when required

Although configuration management may appear to be a simple enough process of just tracking assets and defining the relationships among them, you will find that it has the potential to become very tricky as we explore each of the activities associated with it.

At the very start of the process implementation, configuration management is responsible for defining and documenting which assets of their IT environments should be managed as configuration items (CIs). This is an extremely important decision, and careful selection at this stage of the implementation is a critical factor in its success or failure. Once the items that will be tracked as CIs have been defined, the configuration management process has many CI-associated activities that must be executed. For each CI, it must be possible to do the following:

- Identify the instance of that CI in the environment. A CI should have a consistent naming convention and a unique identifier associated with it to distinguish it from other CIs.
- Control changes to that CI through the use of a change management process.
- Record all the attributes of the CI in a configuration management database (CMDB). A CMDB is the authority for tracking all attributes of a CI. An environment may have multiple CMDBs that are maintained under disparate authorities, and all CMDBs should be tied together as part of a larger configuration management system (CMS). One of the key attributes that all CIs must contain is ownership. By defining an owner for each CI, organizations are able to achieve asset accountability. This accountability imposes responsibility for keeping all attributes current, inventorying, financial reporting, safeguarding, and other controls necessary for optimal maintenance, use, and disposal of the CI. The defined owner for each asset should be a key stakeholder in any CAB that deals with a change that affects the configuration of that CI, thus providing them configuration control.
- Report on, periodically audit, and verify the attributes, statuses, and relationships of any and all CIs at any requested time.

If any one of these activities is not achievable, the entire process fails for all CIs. Much of the value derived from configuration management comes from a trust that the configuration information presented by the CMS is accurate and does not need to be investigated. Any activity that undermines that trust and requires a stakeholder to investigate CI attributes, statuses, or relationships eliminates the value the service is intended to provide.

on the **!** **()** o b *An enterprise IT organization at a large manufacturing company recognized the need to implement an improved configuration management process and invested large amounts of time and money into the effort. With the assistance of a well-respected professional services company leading the way and an investment in best-of-breed tools, they believed they were positioned for success. After the pilot phase of the implementation, when they believed they had a good system in place to manage a subset of the IT environment, one failure in the ability to audit their CIs led to outdated data. That outdated data was used to make a decision about a planned implementation by the CAB. When the change failed because the expected configuration was different than the configuration running in their production environment, all support for configuration management eroded and stakeholders began demanding configuration reviews prior to any change planning, thus crippling the value of configuration management in that environment.*

Capacity Management

Capacity management is the process of ensuring that both the current and future capacity and performance demands of an IT organization's customers regarding service provision are delivered according to justifiable costs. Capacity management has overall responsibility for ensuring that there is adequate IT capacity (as the name suggests) to meet required service levels, that the appropriate stakeholders are correctly advised on how to match capacity and demand, and that existing capacity is optimized.

In order to enable capacity management in an environment for success, great attention needs to be paid to the design of the configuration. The design phase must ensure that all service levels are understood and that the capacity to fulfill them is incorporated into its configurations. Once those configurations have been adequately designed and documented, operations can establish a baseline, as discussed in Chapter 7. This baseline is a measuring stick against which capacity can be monitored to understand both the current demand and trend for future needs.

The capacity management process includes producing and maintaining an appropriate capacity plan that reflects the current and future requirements of its customers. The plan is designed to accomplish the following objectives:

- Provide advice and guidance to all other areas of the business and IT on all capacity- and performance-related issues.
- Ensure that service performance achievements meet or exceed all of their agreed upon performance targets by managing the performance and capacity of both services and resources.

■ Ensure the current and future capacity and performance demands of the customer regarding IT service provision are delivered within justifiable costs.

■ Assist with the diagnosis and resolution of both performance- and capacity-related incidents and problems.

■ Assess the impact of any changes to the capacity plan and the performance and capacity of all IT services and resources.

■ Ensure that proactive measures to improve the performance of services are implemented.

When building this capacity plan, its architects must factor in all IT resources, including both human and technical resources. Keep in mind that people are resources as well.

on the **Job** *There was a systems administrator who was in charge of a major corporate website back in the 1990s whose story serves as a great object lesson both for capacity and change management. His company had recently hired him to work on the ramp-up for a new website, and he worked closely with the marketing group to make sure his team designed the site for all the functionality to be captured in the capacity requirements. Subsequently, the marketing team decided to run an advertisement during the Super Bowl that was intended to drive users to their redesigned website. However, they failed to involve IT in the discussion. Since the expected capacity requirements had changed and IT had not been informed, the website, which had been designed for a far smaller load, crashed within seconds of the ad running. The IT department hadn't staffed administrators for support and monitoring during the costly advertisement, so they were unable to recover quickly. Because of this capacity planning failure, what had started out as a great marketing idea turned into a colossal marketing nightmare.*

Life Cycle Management

Life cycle management is the process or processes put in place by an organization to assist in the management, coordination, control, delivery, and support of their configuration items from requirement to retirement. The two most prevalent frameworks for implementing life cycle management are the Information Technology Infrastructure Library (ITIL) and Microsoft Operations Framework (MOF), which is based on ITIL. What ITIL utilizes as its model for life cycle management is a continuum consisting of the following five phases:

1. Service strategy
2. Service design
3. Service transition
4. Service operation
5. Continual service improvement

Each phase has inputs and outputs that connect the phases to one another, and continual improvement is recognized via multiple trips through the life cycle. Each time through, improvements are documented and then implemented based on feedback from each of the life cycle phases. These improvements enable the organization to execute each of its service offerings as efficiently and effectively as possible, and ensure that each of those services provides as much value to its users as possible.

MOF has shortened the life cycle to four phases:

1. Plan
2. Deliver
3. Operate
4. Manage

These phases are usually depicted graphically in a continuum, as we see in Figure 9-2. This continuum represents the cyclical nature of process improvement, with a structured system of inputs and outputs that lead to continual improvement.

FIGURE 9-2

A representation of the MOF life cycle continuum.

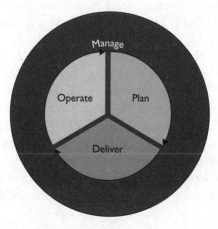

CERTIFICATION OBJECTIVE 9.02

Systems Management Best Practices

The processes and procedures that IT organizations implement in order to achieve results more effectively and efficiently are the result of careful design, standardized environments, and thorough documentation.

Documentation

In order to build supportable technical solutions that consistently deliver their intended value, documentation must be maintained at every step of the life cycle. Documentation of the business requirements for any proposed IT service additions or changes should be the first step in the life cycle, followed by documentation for the proposed technical design, continuing into implementation planning documents and support documentation, and coming full circle in the life cycle through documented service improvement plans. Let's examine each phase in a bit more detail using the ITIL life cycle model.

During the service strategy phase of ITIL, business requirements are documented as the entry point for all IT services. After all, if there isn't a business reason to justify the existence of an IT service, what would be the point of expending the resources to implement and support it? The key piece of documentation in this stage is the service portfolio. The service portfolio is a full list of quantified services that will enable the business to achieve positive return on its investment in the service.

During the service design phase, the IT organization develops technical solutions to fulfill the business requirements that were defined and documented in the service strategy phase. The technical solutions, such as routers, switches, servers, and storage, are documented, along with the support processes for maintaining the service. The service level agreements (SLAs) with the customer as to the mutually agreed upon levels of capacity, availability, and performance are documented as well. All of these considerations—technical solutions, support processes, and SLAs—are included in the most important piece of documentation produced in this phase, which is the service design package (SDP). The service design package is utilized as the primary input for the service transition phase, which is when those services begin to produce value for the customer.

The service transition phase is focused on delivering the service design package and all of its detail into a living, breathing operational environment.

The documentation in this phase supports the processes that were covered earlier in this chapter: change and configuration management. All change requests and configuration items need to be documented to make certain that the requirements documented as part of the strategy phase are fulfilled by its corresponding design. An example of this is the documentation of the IP addresses of all configuration items on a specific subnet.

For the service operation phase of the life cycle, documentation is the key to being able to effectively and efficiently support an environment. Along with standardization, which we discuss in the next section, documentation is the most important factor in the supportability of an IT environment. The goal of successful support engineers in service operation is to maintain a defined level of performance, availability, and capacity for their operational IT services. If those service levels are not documented, or if the technical design that has been baselined and tested to support those service levels is not documented, the support engineer has no point of reference from which to gauge whether or not the environment is running as expected. The documentation utilized by support engineers includes configuration documentation, implementation documentation, and knowledge management systems that contain known errors and either solutions or work-arounds for those errors.

Lastly, continual service improvement relies on a very important set of documentation known as the service improvement register. This key document is the authoritative record of identified opportunities for improving any given IT service. Within this register, opportunities are sorted into short-, medium-, and long-term options; they are evaluated as part of the service strategy phase once the life cycle restarts to see what services need to either be added or modified in order to provide the greatest value to their customers.

Standardization

Documentation is one vehicle that drives effective systems administration, as it allows administrators to expand their ability to comprehend very complex environments without having to keep all the information in their heads. Another very effective way to accomplish this goal is through standardization. Standardization of configurations allows systems administrators to learn one set of complexities and have that same set be applicable across many systems. Standardization can take the form of naming conventions, configuration options, vendor escalation procedures, and known errors, as well as baselines of performance, availability, and capacity. The importance of baselines cannot be overemphasized, because in order to fulfill the service level agreement and show proof of compliance, appropriate tools and procedures need to be in place to evaluate performance and ensure user satisfaction. The inability to prove compliance may put a company at risk financially, as many contracts specify penalties if they are unable to demonstrate their fulfillment of the stated requirements.

The methodology for producing proof of compliance is to first establish a baseline measurement of the environment for each of those areas that have defined service levels and to share those baselines with the customer. Once the baselines have been established, documented, and contractually agreed upon, it is then the goal of service operations to do whatever is needed to maintain those baseline states. This maintenance requires a proper tool set as well as procedures to regularly and consistently monitor and measure the baseline and to understand the pattern of varying measurements over the course of time, known as trending. Administrators also need to be alerted to significant deviations from the baseline so that they can restore service to the previously defined baseline state.

Planning

Once the baseline states are documented, agreed upon in writing, and put in place, what happens when maintenance needs to occur or system upgrades take place? Such events almost certainly disrupt a baseline. These events must be planned for under controlled circumstances by the systems administrator, and cannot happen at random times without the consent of the customer. Maintenance windows need to be established as part of any IT environment for all of its configuration items. These windows should be scheduled at periods of least potential disruption to the customer, and the customer should be involved in the maintenance scheduling process. After all, the customer knows their patterns of business activity better than the systems administrators ever could.

All technology upgrades and patches should utilize these maintenance windows whenever possible, and the timing of their implementation should always be reviewed as part of the standard change management process by the CAB.

CERTIFICATION SUMMARY

Successful delivery of a cloud solution is driven not just by the technical components that make up that solution but by the systems management life cycle and well-defined policies and procedures. The successful design, documentation, and methodical implementation and support of those technical resources results in an effective solution that is profitable for the IT provider and valuable to their customers.

Processes and procedures allow for control of the environment through change, configuration, capacity, and life cycle management. These control mechanisms make certain that the environments are designed to meet business requirements and are deployed and supported according to that design. Such best practices are realized through planning, standardization, and documentation.

KEY TERMS

Use the list below to review the key terms that were discussed in this chapter. The definitions can be found within this chapter and in the glossary.

Change management   The process of making changes to the IT environment from its design phase to its operations phase in the least impactful way possible

Configuration standardization   Documented baseline configuration for similar configuration items (CIs)

Documentation   Written copy of a procedure, policy, or configuration

Configuration control   The ability to maintain updated, accurate documentation of all CIs

Asset accountability   The documented assignment of a CI to a human resource

Approval process   Set of activities that presents all relevant information to stakeholders and allows an informed decision to be made about a request for change

Backout plan   Action plan that allows a change to be reverted to its previous baseline state

Configuration management   The process that ensures all assets required to deliver IT services are controlled, and that accurate and reliable information about them is available when and where it is needed, including details of how the assets have been configured and the relationships between assets

Configuration management database (CMDB)   Database used to store configuration records throughout their life cycle. The configuration management system maintains one or more CMDBs, and each database stores attributes of configuration items and relationships with other configuration items.

Capacity management   A process to ensure that the capacity of IT services and the IT infrastructure is able to meet agreed capacity- and performance-related requirements in a cost-effective and timely manner

Monitoring for changes   Process of watching the production environment for any unplanned configuration changes

Trending   The pattern of measurements over the course of multiple time periods

Systems life cycle management   The process or processes put in place by an organization to assist in the management, coordination, control, delivery, and support of their configuration items from requirement to retirement

Maintenance windows   An agreed upon, predefined time period during which service interruptions are least impactful to the business. This could fall at any time, and depends on the patterns of business activity for that particular entity.

Server upgrades and patches   Updates to the software running on servers that can either provide fixes for known errors or add functionality

Policies   Rule sets by which users and administrators must abide

Procedures   Prescribed methodologies by which activities are carried out in the IT environment according to defined policies

✓ TWO-MINUTE DRILL

Policies and Procedures

❑ Policies define the rule sets by which users and administrators must abide.

❑ Procedures are the prescribed methodologies by which activities are carried out in the IT environment according to defined policies.

❑ Change management is the process of making changes to the IT environment from its design phase to its operations phase in the least impactful way.

❑ Configuration management ensures that the assets required to deliver services are properly controlled, and that accurate and reliable information about those assets is available when and where it is needed.

❑ Capacity management is the process of ensuring that both the current and future capacity and performance demands of an IT organization's customers regarding service provision are delivered according to justifiable costs.

❑ Life cycle management is the process or processes put in place by an organization to assist in the management, coordination, control, delivery, and support of their configuration items (CIs) from requirement to retirement.

Systems Management Best Practices

❑ In order to build supportable technical solutions that consistently deliver their intended value, documentation must be maintained at every step of the life cycle.

❑ Standardization of configurations allows systems administrators to learn one set of complexities and have that same set be applicable across many systems.

❑ Maintenance windows need to be established as part of any IT environment for all of its configuration items. These windows should be scheduled at periods of least potential disruption to the customer, and the customer should be involved in the maintenance scheduling process.

SELF TEST

The following questions will help you measure your understanding of the material presented in this chapter.

Policies and Procedures

1. Which of the following defines the rule sets by which users and administrators must abide?
   A. Procedures
   B. Change management
   C. Policies
   D. Trending

2. Which of the following are objectives of change management? Choose all that apply.
   A. Maximize business value
   B. Ensure that all proposed changes are both evaluated and recorded
   C. Identify configuration items (CIs)
   D. Optimize overall business risk

3. Which of the following are objectives of configuration management? Choose all that apply.
   A. Protect the integrity of CIs
   B. Evaluate performance of all CIs
   C. Maintain information about the state of all CIs
   D. Maintain an accurate and complete CMS

4. Which of the following terms best describes life cycle management?
   A. Baseline
   B. Finite
   C. Linear
   D. Continuum

5. Capacity management has responsibility for ensuring that the capacity of the IT service is optimally matched to what?
   A. Demand
   B. Future trends
   C. Procedures
   D. Availability

6. What is the desired end result of life cycle management?
   A. CAB
   B. Continual service improvement
   C. Service strategy
   D. Service operation

7. Dieter is a systems administrator in an enterprise IT organization. The servers he is responsible for have recently been the target of a malicious exploit, and the vendor has released a patch to protect against this threat. If Dieter would like to deploy this patch to his servers right away without waiting for the weekly change approval board meeting, what should he request to be convened?
   A. ECAB
   B. Maintenance window
   C. Service improvement opportunity
   D. CAB

Systems Management Best Practices

8. What is the most important output from the service design phase?
   A. CMDB
   B. Service design package
   C. CMS
   D. Service portfolio

9. Which three items should be baselined for any IT service?
   A. Performance
   B. Maintenance
   C. Availability
   D. Capacity

10. When should maintenance windows be scheduled?
   A. In the morning
   B. In the evening
   C. On weekends
   D. When they will least impact their customers

SELF TEST ANSWERS

Policies and Procedures

1. Which of the following defines the rule sets by which users and administrators must abide?
   A. Procedures
   B. Change management
   C. Policies
   D. Trending

   ☑ **C.** Policies are defined as rule sets by which users and administrators must abide.
   ☒ **A, B,** and **D** are incorrect. Procedures are prescribed methodologies by which activities are carried out in the IT environment according to defined policies; change management is the process of making changes to the IT environment from its design phase to its operations phase in the least impactful way; and trending is the pattern of measurements over the course of multiple time periods.

2. Which of the following are objectives of change management?
   A. Maximize business value
   B. Ensure that all proposed changes are both evaluated and recorded
   C. Identify configuration items (CIs)
   D. Optimize overall business risk

   ☑ **A, B,** and **D** are correct. Maximizing business value, ensuring that all changes are evaluated and recorded, and optimizing business risk are all objectives of change management.
   ☒ **C** is incorrect. Identification of configuration items is an objective of the configuration management process.

3. Which of the following are objectives of configuration management?
   A. Protect the integrity of CIs
   B. Evaluate performance of all CIs
   C. Maintain information about the state of all CIs
   D. Maintain an accurate and complete CMS

☑ **A, C,** and **D** are correct. The objectives of configuration management are identifying CIs, controlling CIs, protecting the integrity of CIs, maintaining an accurate and complete CMS, and providing accurate configuration information when needed.

☒ **B** is incorrect. Evaluation of the performance of specific CIs is the responsibility of service operations, not configuration management.

4. Which of the following terms best describes life cycle management?

A. Baseline

B. Finite

C. Linear

D. Continuum

☑ **D.** Life cycle management is a continuum with feedback loops going back into itself to enable better management and continual improvement.

☒ **A, B,** and **C** are incorrect. Baselines are utilized for measurement but are not cyclical. By definition the word "finite" implies that there is an ending, and life cycle management has no ends since it is continually improving. Linear does not fit because there are many feedback loops and it doesn't always progress forward; rather, it frequently circles back.

5. Capacity management has responsibility for ensuring that the capacity of the IT service is optimally matched to what?

A. Demand

B. Future trends

C. Procedures

D. Availability

☑ **A.** Capacity management's primary objective is to ensure that the capacity of an IT service is optimally matched with its demand. Capacity should be planned to meet agreed upon levels, no higher and no lower. Because controlling costs are a component of capacity management, designs that incorporate too much capacity are just as bad as designs that incorporate too little capacity.

☒ **B, C,** and **D** are incorrect. Future trends are extrapolations made from trending data captured in operations. They provide inputs into capacity and availability planning but are not a good description for the entire life cycle. Procedures are predefined sets of activities that resources utilize to carry out defined policies. Availability is the ability of a configuration item to perform its defined functions when required.

6. What is the desired end result of life cycle management?
   A. CAB
   B. Continual service improvement
   C. Service strategy
   D. Service operation

   ☑ **B.** The end result of each cycle within life cycle management is to identify opportunities for improvement that can be incorporated into the service to make it more efficient, effective, and profitable.
   ☒ **A, C,** and **D** are incorrect. CABs are utilized for the evaluation of a proposed change. Service strategy and service operation are both phases in the life cycle.

7. Dieter is a systems administrator in an enterprise IT organization. The servers he is responsible for have recently been the target of a malicious exploit, and the vendor has released a patch to protect against this threat. If Dieter would like to deploy this patch to his servers right away without waiting for the weekly change approval board meeting, what should he request to be convened?
   A. ECAB
   B. Maintenance window
   C. Service improvement opportunity
   D. CAB

   ☑ **A.** Dieter would want to convene an emergency change advisory board (ECAB). The ECAB follows the same procedures that a CAB follows in the evaluation of a change; it is just a subset of the stakeholders that would usually convene for the review. Because of the urgency for implementation, convening a smaller group assists in expediting the process.
   ☒ **B, C** and **D** are incorrect. A maintenance window is an agreed upon, predefined time period during which service interruptions are least impactful to the business. The requested change may or may not take place during that time frame based on the urgency of the issue. Service improvement opportunities are suggested changes that are logged in the service improvement register to be evaluated and implemented during the next iteration of the life cycle. Life cycle iterations do not happen quickly enough for an emergency change to be considered even as a short-term service improvement item. CAB is close to the right answer, but based on the urgency of this request, Dieter likely could not wait for the next scheduled CAB meeting to take place before he needed to take action. The risk of waiting would be greater than the risk of deploying before the CAB convenes.

Systems Management Best Practices

8. What is the most important output from the service design phase?
  A. CMDB
  B. Service design package
  C. CMS
  D. Service portfolio

☑ **B.** The most important piece of documentation produced in the service design phase is the service design package (SDP), which includes documentation of the organization's technical solutions, support processes, and service level agreements (SLAs). The service design package is utilized as the primary input for the service transition phase, which is when those services begin to produce value for the customer.

☒ **A, C,** and **D** are incorrect. The configuration management database (CMDB) and the configuration management (CMS) are both utilized in the service transition phase, not the service design phase. The service portfolio is the key piece of documentation produced in the service strategy phase.

9. Which three items should be baselined for any IT service?
  A. Performance
  B. Maintenance
  C. Availability
  D. Capacity

☑ **A, C,** and **D** are correct. Establishing baselines for performance, availability, and capacity is an important part of standardization practice. These baselines are significant for ensuring proof of compliance and fulfillment of service level agreements.

☒ **B** is incorrect. Maintenance is an activity that is performed in order to prevent changes to the baseline state of a CI. It does not itself need to be baselined.

10. When should maintenance windows be scheduled?
  A. In the morning
  B. In the evening
  C. On weekends
  D. When they will least impact their customers

☑ **D.** A maintenance window is an agreed upon, predefined time period during which service interruptions are least impactful to the business. This could fall at any time, and depends on the patterns of business activity for that particular entity.

☒ **A, B,** and **C** are incorrect. An IT organization should not define mornings, evenings, or weekends as maintenance windows without first validating that time frame with its customers and making certain that it falls during a period when business activity would least be affected by a service outage.

10

Testing and Troubleshooting

Oane of the challenges of a cloud environment is service and maintenance availability. When an organization adopts a cloud model instead of hosting their own infrastructure, it is important for them to know that the services and data they need to access is available whenever and wherever they need it, without experiencing undue delays. Service and maintenance availability must be a priority when choosing a cloud provider. Having the ability to test and troubleshoot the cloud environment is a critical step in providing the service availability an organization requires.

CERTIFICATION OBJECTIVE 10.01

Testing Techniques

Testing the application from the server hosting the application to the end user's device using the application, and everything in between, is a critical piece in monitoring the cloud environment. In addition to this end-to-end testing, an organization needs to be able to test the connectivity to the cloud service. Without connectivity to the cloud that services the organization, the company could experience downtime and costly interruptions to their data. It is the cloud administrator's job to test the network for things such as network latency and replication and to make sure that an application hosted in the cloud can be delivered to the users inside the organization.

Configuration Testing

Configuration testing allows an administrator to test and verify that the cloud environment is running at optimal performance levels. Configuration testing needs to be done on a regular basis and should be part of a weekly or monthly routine. When testing a cloud environment, a variety of aspects need to be verified. The ability to access data that is stored in the cloud and hosted with a cloud provider is one of the most essential aspects of the cloud environment. Accessing that data needs to be tested for efficiency and compliance so that an organization has confidence in the cloud computing model.

One of the first things that needs to be tested is network latency. Testing network latency measures the amount of time between a networked device's request for data and the network's response from the requester. This helps an administrator determine when a network is not performing at an optimal level. In addition to testing network latency, it is also important to test the network's bandwidth or, more simply, speed. A common practice for measuring bandwidth is to transfer a large file from one system to another and measure the amount of time it takes to complete the transfer or to copy the file. The throughput, or the average rate of a successful message delivery over the network, is then determined by dividing the file size by the time it takes to transfer the file and is measured in megabits or kilobits per second. However, this test does not provide a maximum throughput and can be misleading because of overhead factors. When determining bandwidth and throughput, it is important to understand that overheads need to be accounted for, like network latency and system limitations. In order to get a more accurate measure of maximum bandwidth, then, an administrator should use dedicated software to measure the throughput (e.g., NetCPS and Iperf). Testing the bandwidth and latency of a network that is supporting a cloud environment is important since the applications and data that are stored in the cloud would not be accessible without the proper network configurations.

Some situations require an organization to replicate or sync data between their internal data center and a cloud provider. This is typically done for fault tolerance or load balancing reasons. After testing network latency and bandwidth, it is important to test and verify that the data is replicating correctly between the internal data center and the cloud provider. An organization might also opt to use a cloud provider as a backup source instead of using tapes or storing the backup locally. Doing so also meets the needs of an off-site backup, discussed in Chapter 12. Testing the replication between the internal data center and the cloud provider helps to ensure that those backups and all other replication occur with no interruption.

Once the organization and the cloud provider have determined how to test the network, they need to be able to test any applications and application servers that are being migrated to the cloud. Application performance testing is used to test an application's performance and to verify that the application is able to meet the organization's service level agreements. After moving an application or application server to the cloud, testing of that application or server still needs to be performed at regular intervals. There are a variety of different ways to test an application: some can be done manually and some are automated. An IT administrator can create performance counters to establish a baseline and verify that an application and application server are performing at expected levels. They can also write batch files or scripts that run specific commands to test the availability of an application or server. Another option is to migrate an application to the cloud to test it in a development environment. Using the cloud as a "sandbox" of sorts allows an organization to test new applications or new versions of applications without impacting the performance or even the security of their current environment. The cloud also allows an organization to migrate an application and perform extensive application and application server testing before making the cloud-based application available to the organization's users. Testing application and application server performance in the cloud is a critical step to ensuring a successful user experience.

A variety of diagnostic tools can be used to collect information about how an application is performing. To test application performance, an organization needs to collect information about the application, including requests and number of connections. They also need to track how often the application is being utilized as well as overall resource utilization (memory and CPU). They can make use of tools to evaluate which piece of an application or service is taking the most time to process and to measure how long it takes each part of the program to execute and how the program is allocating its memory. They can create reports on how quickly an application loads or spins up and analyze performance data on each aspect of the application as it is being delivered to the end user. Applications need to be delivered seamlessly so that the end user is unaware the application is being hosted in a cloud environment. Tracking this information can help determine just how seamless that delivery process is.

After testing the network and application performance, an organization must also test the performance of the storage system. Identifying how well the storage system is performing is critical in planning for growth and proper storage management. In addition to testing the I/O performance of their storage system, a company can use a variety of tools for conducting a load test to simulate what happens to the storage system as load is increased. Testing the storage system allows the organization to be more proactive than reactive with its storage and helps them plan for when additional storage might be required.

When hosting an application in the cloud, there may be times where an organization uses the cloud as a load balancer. As discussed in Chapter 4, load balancing with dedicated software or hardware allows for the distribution of workloads across multiple computers. Using multiple components can help to improve reliability through redundancy, with multiple devices servicing the workload. If a company uses load balancing to improve availability or responsiveness of cloud-based applications, they need to test the effectiveness of a variety of characteristics, including TCP connections per second, HTTP/HTTPS connections per second, and traffic loads simulated to validate performance under a high-traffic scenario. Testing all aspects of load balancing helps to ensure that the computers can handle the workload and that they can respond in the event of a single server outage.

Security Testing

In addition to comprehensive testing of all areas affecting service and performance, it is incumbent on an organization to test for vulnerability as well. Security testing in the cloud is a critical part of having an optimal cloud environment. It is very similar to security testing in a traditional environment in that testing involves components like login security and the security layer in general. Before doing any security tests, the organization should review the contract that is in place with the cloud provider and inform the cloud provider of any planned security testing prior to actually performing it.

Another thing for an organization to consider is that with a public cloud model, they do not own the infrastructure; therefore, the environment the resources are hosted in may not be all that familiar. For example, if you have an application that is hosted in a public cloud environment, that application might make some application programming interface (API) calls back into your data center via a firewall, or the application might be entirely hosted outside of your firewall. Another primary security concern when using a cloud model is who has access to the organization's data in the cloud and what are the concerns and consequences if that data is lost or stolen. Being able to monitor and test access to that data is a primary responsibility of the cloud administrator and should be taken seriously, as a hosted account may not have all the proper security implemented. For example, a hosted resource might be running an older version of system software that has known security issues; so keeping up with the security for the hosted resource and the products that are running on those resources is vital.

The two basic types of security testing on a cloud environment are known as white-box testing and black-box testing. When performing a black-box test, the tester knows as little as possible about the system, similar to a real-world hacker. This is a good method, as it simulates a real-world attack and uncovers vulnerabilities without prior knowledge of the environment. White-box testing is done with an insider's view and can be much faster than black-box testing. White-box testing makes it possible to focus on specific security concerns the organization may have. Oftentimes a black-box test is performed first to garner as much information as possible. Then a white-box test is run, and comparisons are made between the two sets of results. These concepts and other security considerations are discussed in more detail in Chapter 11.

Roles and Responsibilities

Configuration testing can be a complex procedure and involves testing a variety of components, including applications, storage, network connectivity, and server configuration. With so many different aspects of the environment being involved, it is important to separate the duties and responsibilities of those testing procedures among various administrators. There are a number of benefits to having a different administrator in charge of each facet of the cloud environment. Having different people running different configuration tests creates a system of checks and balances since not just one person has ultimate control. For example, a programmer would be responsible for verifying all of the code within their application and for making sure there are no security risks in the code itself, but the programmer would not be responsible for the web server or database server that is hosting or supporting the application.

Separation of duties is a process that needs to be carefully planned and thought out. If implemented correctly, it can act as an internal control to help reduce potential damage caused by the actions of a single administrator. This is known as the principle of least privilege. By limiting permissions and influence over key parts of the cloud environment, no one individual can knowingly or unknowingly exercise full power over the system. For example, in an e-commerce organization with multiple layers of security in place, separation of duties would ensure that a single person would not be responsible for every layer of that security. Therefore, if that person were to leave or become disgruntled, they would not have the ability to take down the entire network; they would only have the ability to access their layer of the security model.

CERTIFICATION OBJECTIVE 10.02

Troubleshooting and Tools

In addition to testing the cloud environment, an organization needs to be able to troubleshoot that environment when there are issues or connectivity problems. A variety of tools are available to troubleshoot the cloud environment. Understanding how to use those tools makes it easier for a company to maintain their service level agreements. This section explains the common usage for those tools.

Tools

There are many tools to choose from when troubleshooting a cloud environment. Sometimes a single tool is all that is required to troubleshoot the issue; other times a combination of tools might be needed. Knowing when to use a particular tool makes the troubleshooting process easier and faster. As with anything, the more you use a particular troubleshooting tool, the more familiar you become with the tool and its capabilities and limitations.

One of the most common and previously most utilized troubleshooting tools is the ping utility. The ping is used to troubleshoot the reachability of a host on an Internet protocol (IP) network. Ping sends an Internet control message protocol (ICMP) echo request packet to a specified IP address or host and waits for an ICMP reply. Ping can also be used to measure the round-trip time for messages sent from the originating workstation to the destination and to record packet loss. Ping generates a summary of the information it has gathered, including packets sent, packets received and lost, and the amount of time taken to receive the responses. Starting with Microsoft Windows XP Service Pack 2, the Windows Firewall was enabled by default and blocks ICMP traffic and ping requests. Figure 10-1 shows an example of the output received when you use the ping utility to ping www.coursewareexperts.com.

<table>
<tr><td>e x a m
⒲ a t c h   Ping allows an administrator to test the availability of a single host.</td></tr>
</table>

Traceroute is a network troubleshooting tool that is used to determine the path that an IP packet has to take to reach a destination. Unlike the ping utility, traceroute displays the path and measures the transit delays of packets across the network to reach a target host. Traceroute sends packets with gradually increasing time-to-live (TTL) values, starting with a TTL value of 1. The first router receives

Screenshot
of ping data.

```
Administrator: Command Prompt                                        _ □ ×

Microsoft Windows [Version 6.2.9200]
(c) 2012 Microsoft Corporation. All rights reserved.

C:\Windows\system32>ping www.coursewareexperts.com

Pinging coursewareexperts.com [173.254.28.136] with 32 bytes of data:
Reply from 173.254.28.136: bytes=32 time=77ms TTL=52
Reply from 173.254.28.136: bytes=32 time=78ms TTL=52
Reply from 173.254.28.136: bytes=32 time=74ms TTL=52
Reply from 173.254.28.136: bytes=32 time=76ms TTL=52

Ping statistics for 173.254.28.136:
    Packets: Sent = 4, Received = 4, Lost = 0 (0% loss),
Approximate round trip times in milli-seconds:
    Minimum = 74ms, Maximum = 78ms, Average = 76ms

C:\Windows\system32>
```

the packet, decreases the TTL value, and drops the packet because it now has a value of zero. The router then sends an ICMP "time exceeded" message back to the source, and the next set of packets is given a TTL value of 2, which means the first router forwards the packets and the second router drops them and replies with its own ICMP "time exceeded" message. Traceroute then uses the returned ICMP "time exceeded" messages with the source IP address of the expired intermediate device to create a list of routers until the destination device is reached and returns an ICMP echo reply. Most modern operating systems support some form of the traceroute tool: on a Microsoft Windows operating system it is named tracert; Linux has a version named trace; on Internet protocol version 6 (IPv6), the tool is called traceroute6. Figure 10-2 displays an example of the tracert command being used to trace the path to www.google.com.

In addition to using the traceroute command to determine the path that an IP packet has to take to reach a destination, the route command can be used to view and manipulate the TCP/IP routing tables of Windows operating systems. When using earlier versions of Linux, the route command and the ifconfig command can be used together to connect a computer to a network and define the routes between the networks; later versions of Linux have replaced the ifconfig and route commands with the iproute2 command, which adds functionality such as traffic shaping. Ifconfig is used to configure the TCP/IP network interface from the command line, which allows for setting the interface's IP address and netmask or even disabling the interface. Microsoft Windows has a similar command to ifconfig in the ipconfig command, which displays the current TCP/IP network configuration settings for

FIGURE 10-2

FIGURE 10-2

Screenshot of
data using the
tracert command.

```
Command Prompt                                                          _ □ ×
Microsoft Windows [Version 6.1.7601]
Copyright (c) 2009 Microsoft Corporation.  All rights reserved.

C:\Users\student>tracert www.google.com

Tracing route to www.google.com [74.125.225.242]
over a maximum of 30 hops:

  1     1 ms     1 ms     1 ms  10.0.102.254
  2     *        *        *     Request timed out.
  3     1 ms     1 ms     1 ms  wsip-72-214-232-97.om.om.cox.net [72.214.232.97]

  4    11 ms    14 ms     8 ms  10.102.32.1
  5     9 ms    17 ms    12 ms  68.13.10.113
  6    11 ms    10 ms    11 ms  68.13.8.253
  7     9 ms     8 ms    10 ms  mtc1dsrj01-ae4.0.rd.om.cox.net [68.13.14.5]
  8    33 ms     *       26 ms  68.1.2.109
  9    31 ms    26 ms    23 ms  72.14.212.233
 10    24 ms    33 ms    28 ms  72.14.233.65
 11    26 ms    27 ms    28 ms  209.85.240.77
 12    28 ms    27 ms    37 ms  dfw06s26-in-f18.1e100.net [74.125.225.242]

Trace complete.

C:\Users\student>
```

a network interface. The ipconfig command can be used to release or renew an IP address that was assigned to the computer via a dynamic host configuration protocol (DHCP) server and can also be used to clear the domain name system (DNS) cache on a workstation. Figure 10-3 shows the command-line switch options available with the ipconfig command.

FIGURE 10-3

Screenshot of
ipconfig options.

```
Administrator: Command Prompt                                          _ □ ×
C:\Windows\system32>ipconfig /?

USAGE:
    ipconfig [/allcompartments] [/? | /all |
                                 /renew [adapter] | /release [adapter] |
                                 /renew6 [adapter] | /release6 [adapter] |
                                 /flushdns | /displaydns | /registerdns |
                                 /showclassid adapter |
                                 /setclassid adapter [classid] |
                                 /showclassid6 adapter |
                                 /setclassid6 adapter [classid] ]

where
    adapter             Connection name
                        (wildcard characters * and ? allowed, see examples)

    Options:
       /?               Display this help message
       /all             Display full configuration information.
       /release         Release the IPv4 address for the specified adapter.
       /release6        Release the IPv6 address for the specified adapter.
       /renew           Renew the IPv4 address for the specified adapter.
       /renew6          Renew the IPv6 address for the specified adapter.
       /flushdns        Purges the DNS Resolver cache.
       /registerdns     Refreshes all DHCP leases and re-registers DNS names
       /displaydns      Display the contents of the DNS Resolver Cache.
       /showclassid     Displays all the dhcp class IDs allowed for adapter.
       /setclassid      Modifies the dhcp class id.
       /showclassid6    Displays all the IPv6 DHCP class IDs allowed for adapter

       /setclassid6     Modifies the IPv6 DHCP class id.
```

e▼**x a m**

ⓦ**a t c h**   *Ipconfig has command-line switches that allow you to perform more advanced tasks, like clearing DNS*

cache and obtaining a new IP address from DHCP, rather than just displaying TCP/IP configuration information.

Another tool that can be used to troubleshoot network connection issues is the nslookup command. With nslookup it is possible to obtain domain name or IP address mappings for a specified DNS record. Nslookup uses the computer's local DNS server to perform the queries. Using the nslookup command requires at least one valid DNS server, which can be verified by using the ipconfig /all command. The domain information groper (dig) command can also be used to query DNS name servers and can operate in interactive command-line mode or be used in batch query mode on Linux-based systems. The host utility can also be used to perform DNS lookups. Figure 10-4 shows an example of the output using nslookup to query www.google.com.

If an organization wants to display all its active network connections, routing tables, and network protocol statistics, they can use the netstat command. Available in most operating systems, the netstat command can be used to detect problems with the network and determine how much network traffic there is. It can also

FIGURE 10-4

Screenshot
of nslookup
addresses.

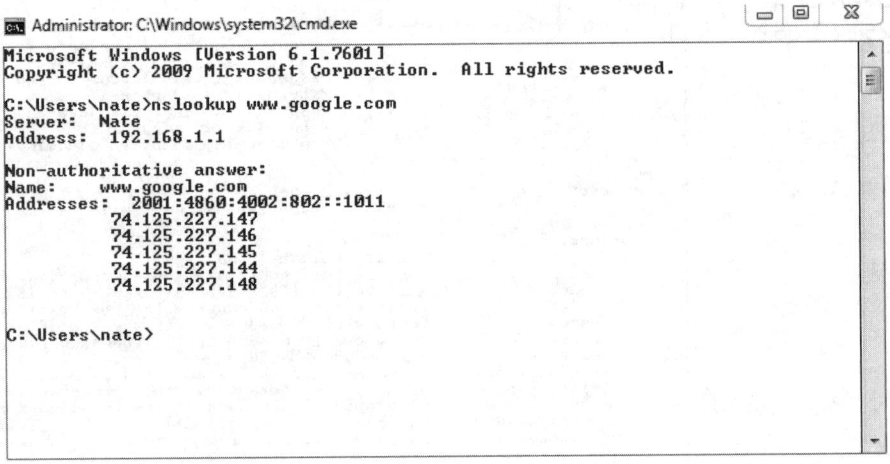

```
Administrator: C:\Windows\system32\cmd.exe

Microsoft Windows [Version 6.1.7601]
Copyright (c) 2009 Microsoft Corporation.  All rights reserved.

C:\Users\nate>nslookup www.google.com
Server:  Nate
Address:  192.168.1.1

Non-authoritative answer:
Name:    www.google.com
Addresses:  2001:4860:4002:802::1011
          74.125.227.147
          74.125.227.146
          74.125.227.145
          74.125.227.144
          74.125.227.148


C:\Users\nate>
```

display protocol and Ethernet statistics and all the currently active TCP/IP network connections. Figure 10-5 shows an example of the netstat command displaying all active connections for a network interface.

Recently while troubleshooting a network connection, we were having issues determining what DNS mapping an IP address had. We used the nslookup tool and entered the IP address that we were trying to map to a DNS name. Nslookup returned the result of the DNS registration for the particular IP address.

Another helpful troubleshooting tool is the address resolution protocol (ARP). The ARP command resolves an IP address to either a physical address or a media access control (MAC) address. The ARP command makes it possible to display the current ARP entries or the ARP table and to add a static entry. Figure 10-6 uses the arp –a command to view the ARP cache of a computer.

FIGURE 10-5

Screenshot of active connections using netstat.

```
C:\Windows\system32>netstat

Active Connections

  Proto  Local Address          Foreign Address        State
  TCP    10.0.102.23:49210      wds:microsoft-ds       ESTABLISHED
  TCP    10.0.102.23:49332      shu:8080               ESTABLISHED
  TCP    10.0.102.23:49763      shu:8080               CLOSE_WAIT
  TCP    10.0.102.23:49764      shu:8080               CLOSE_WAIT
  TCP    10.0.102.23:49765      shu:8080               CLOSE_WAIT
  TCP    10.0.102.23:49766      shu:8080               CLOSE_WAIT
  TCP    10.0.102.23:49767      shu:8080               CLOSE_WAIT
  TCP    10.0.102.23:49768      shu:8080               CLOSE_WAIT
  TCP    10.0.102.23:49769      shu:8080               CLOSE_WAIT
  TCP    10.0.102.23:49770      shu:8080               CLOSE_WAIT
  TCP    10.0.102.23:49781      shu:8080               CLOSE_WAIT
  TCP    10.0.102.23:49782      shu:8080               CLOSE_WAIT
  TCP    10.0.102.23:49926      shu:8080               CLOSE_WAIT
  TCP    10.0.102.23:49996      shu:8080               CLOSE_WAIT
  TCP    10.0.102.23:49997      shu:8080               CLOSE_WAIT
  TCP    10.0.102.23:49998      shu:8080               CLOSE_WAIT
  TCP    10.0.102.23:49999      shu:8080               CLOSE_WAIT
  TCP    10.0.102.23:50000      shu:8080               CLOSE_WAIT
  TCP    10.0.102.23:50001      shu:8080               CLOSE_WAIT
  TCP    10.0.102.23:50002      shu:8080               CLOSE_WAIT
  TCP    10.0.102.23:50003      shu:8080               CLOSE_WAIT
  TCP    10.0.102.23:50004      shu:8080               CLOSE_WAIT
  TCP    10.0.102.23:50005      shu:8080               CLOSE_WAIT
  TCP    10.0.102.23:50006      shu:8080               CLOSE_WAIT
  TCP    10.0.102.23:50007      shu:8080               CLOSE_WAIT
  TCP    10.0.102.23:50012      shu:8080               ESTABLISHED
  TCP    10.0.102.23:50013      shu:8080               ESTABLISHED
  TCP    10.0.102.23:50015      shu:8080               ESTABLISHED
  TCP    10.0.102.23:50016      shu:8080               ESTABLISHED
  TCP    [fe80::1170:d0a6:89b4:8d16%12]:2179   RM02ST00:49733    ESTABLISHED

  TCP    [fe80::1170:d0a6:89b4:8d16%12]:2179   RM02ST00:49742    ESTABLISHED

  TCP    [fe80::1170:d0a6:89b4:8d16%12]:49733  RM02ST00:2179     ESTABLISHED

  TCP    [fe80::1170:d0a6:89b4:8d16%12]:49742  RM02ST00:2179     ESTABLISHED
```

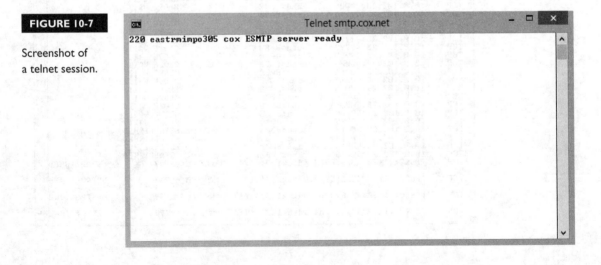

FIGURE 10-6

Screenshot of
ARP showing
both the Internet
address and the
physical address.

If a user wants to connect their computer to another computer or server running the telnet service over the network, they can enter commands via the telnet program, and the commands are executed as if they were being entered directly on the server console. Telnet enables the user to control a server and communicate with other servers over the network. A valid username and password are required to activate a telnet session; nonetheless, telnet has security risks when it is used over any network. Secure shell (SSHv2) has become a more popular option for providing a secure remote command-line interface. Figure 10-7 shows an example of a telnet session established with a remote server.

FIGURE 10-7

Screenshot of
a telnet session.

ex**a**m

ⓦ**atch** *Telnet and SSH both allow* *SSH offers security mechanisms to protect*
an administrator to remotely connect to *against malicious intent.*
a server, the primary difference being that

Documentation

Being able to use the proper tools is a good start when troubleshooting cloud computing issues. Properly creating and maintaining the correct documentation makes the troubleshooting process quicker and easier. It is important for the IT administrator to document every aspect of the cloud environment, including its setup and configuration and which applications are running on which host computer or virtual machine. In addition, the IT administrator should assign responsibility for each application and its server platform to a specific support person who can respond quickly if an issue should arise that impacts the application.

Documentation needs to be clear and easy to understand for anyone who may need to use it and should be regularly reviewed to ensure that it is up to date and accurate. Documenting the person responsible for creating and maintaining the application and where it is hosted is a good process that saves valuable time when troubleshooting any potential issues with the cloud environment.

In addition to documenting the person responsible for the application and hosting computer, an organization also needs to document device configurations. This provides a quick and easy way to recover a device in the case of failure. By utilizing a document to quickly swap a faulty device and mimic its configuration, the company can quickly replace the failed device. When documenting device configuration, it is imperative that the document be updated every time a change is made to that device. For example, let's say you are working on a firewall that has been in place and running for quite some time. You first check the documentation to make sure that the current configuration is documented so that if there are any issues you can revert the device back to its original configuration. After making the required changes, you then update or re-create the documentation so that there is a current document listing all the device settings and configurations for that firewall. This makes it easier to manage the device if there are problems later on, and it gives you a hard copy of the configurations that can be stored and used for future changes.

EXAM AT WORK

A Real-World Look at Documentation

We were recently tasked with creating documentation for an application that was going to be monitored in a distributed application diagram within Microsoft SharePoint. In order to have a successful diagram to display inside of Microsoft SharePoint for the entire organization to view, we needed to collect as much information as possible. The organization wanted to monitor the application from end to end, so we needed to know which server the application used for the web server, which server it used for the database server, which network devices and switches the servers connected to, the location of the end users who used the application, and so on. The information-gathering process took us from the developer who created the application to the database administrator who could explain the back-end infrastructure to the server

administrator and then the network administrator and so on. As you can see, to truly document and monitor an application, you need to talk to everyone that is involved in keeping that application operational. From our documentation the organization now has a clear picture of exactly what systems are involved with keeping that application operational and functioning at peak performance. It makes it easier to troubleshoot and monitor the application and set performance metrics. It also allows for a true diagram of the application with true alerting and reporting of any disruptions. As new administrators join the organization, they can use the documentation to better understand how the application and the environment work together and which systems support each other.

System Logs

Another option to using the command-line utilities is to use system logs. Most operating systems have some form of system log file that tracks certain events as they occur on the computer. System log files can store a variety of information, including device changes, device drivers, system changes, events, and much more. These log files allow for closer examination of events that have occurred on the system over a longer period of time. Some system logs keep information for months at a time, allowing an IT administrator to go back and see when an issue started and if any issues seem to coincide with a software installation or a hardware configuration change. There are a variety of software applications that can be used to gather the system logs from a group of machines and send those logs to a central administration console, making it possible for the administrator to view the logs of multiple servers from a single console.

If the standard system logs do not seem to provide enough information when troubleshooting an issue, verbose logging offers another option. Verbose logging records more detailed information than standard logging but is recommended only for troubleshooting a specific problem. Since verbose logging records more detailed information, it should be disabled after the issue is resolved so that it doesn't impact the performance of the application or the computer.

CERTIFICATION SUMMARY

The ability to test the availability of a cloud deployment model allows an organization to be proactive with the services and data that it stores in the cloud. Understanding which tools are best suited to troubleshoot different issues as they arise with a cloud deployment model saves an administrator time and helps maintain service level agreements set forth by the organization.

KEY TERMS

Use the list below to review the key terms that were discussed in this chapter. The definitions can be found within this chapter and in the glossary.

Separation of duties   Divides tasks and privileges among multiple individuals to help reduce potential damage caused by the actions of a single administrator

Ping   Command-line utility used to test the reachability of a destination host on an IP network

Internet control message protocol (ICMP)   A protocol that is part of the Internet protocol suite used primarily for diagnostic purposes

Traceroute   Utility to record the route and measure the delay of packets across an IP network

Tracert   Microsoft Windows command-line utility that tracks a packet from your computer to a destination host displaying how many hops the packet takes to reach the destination host

Time-to-live (TTL) The length of time that a router or caching name server stores a record

Ipconfig Command-line tool to display TCP/IP network configuration settings and troubleshoot dynamic host configuration protocol (DHCP) and domain name system (DNS) settings

Ifconfig Interface configuration utility to configure and query TCP/IP network interface settings from a Unix or Linux command line

Domain information groper (dig) Command-line tool for querying domain name system (DNS) servers operating in both interactive mode and batch query mode

Nslookup Command-line tool used to query DNS mappings for resource records

Netstat Command-line tool that displays network statistics, including current connections and routing tables

Address resolution protocol (ARP) Protocol used to resolve IP addresses to media access control (MAC) addresses

Telnet A terminal emulation program for TCP/IP networks that connects the user's computer to another computer on the network

System logs Files that store a variety of information about system events, including device changes, device drivers, and system changes

✓ TWO-MINUTE DRILL

Testing Techniques

❑ Configuration testing allows an administrator to test and verify that the cloud environment is running at optimal performance levels.

❑ Testing network latency measures the amount of time between a networked device's request for data and the network's response from the requester.

❑ Separation of duties is the process of segregating specific duties and dividing tasks and privileges required for a specific security process among multiple administrators.

Troubleshooting and Tools

❑ The ping command is used to troubleshoot the reachability of a host over a network.

❑ The traceroute (or tracert) command can be used to determine the path that an IP packet has to take to reach a destination.

❑ The route command can be used to view and modify routing tables.

❑ Ipconfig and ifconfig are command-line utilities that can be used to display the TCP/IP configuration settings of the network interface.

❑ In order to query a DNS server to obtain domain name or IP address mappings for a specific DNS record, either the nslookup or dig command-line tools can be used.

❑ The netstat command allows for the display of all active network connections, routing tables, and network protocol statistics.

❑ Telnet and SSH allow for execution of commands on a remote server.

❑ System logs can track events as they happen on a computer and store information such as device drivers, system changes, device changes, and events. To get more detailed information, verbose logging can be used.

SELF TEST

The following questions will help you measure your understanding of the material presented in this chapter.

Testing Techniques

1. Dividing tasks and privileges required to perform a specific IT process among a number of administrators instead of a single administrator would be defined as which of the following?
   A. Penetration testing
   B. Vulnerability assessment
   C. Separation of duties
   D. Virtualization

2. Which configuration test measures the amount of time between a networked device's request for data and the network's response?
   A. Network bandwidth
   B. Network latency
   C. Application availability
   D. Load balancing

Troubleshooting and Tools

3. Which of the following command-line tools allows for the display of all active network connections and network protocol statistics?
   A. Netstat
   B. Ping
   C. Traceroute
   D. Ifconfig

4. You need to verify the TCP/IP configuration settings of a network adapter on a virtual machine running Microsoft Windows. Which of the following tools should you use?
   A. Ping
   B. ARP
   C. Tracert
   D. Ipconfig

5. Which of the following tools can be used to verify if a host is available on the network?
  A. Ping
  B. ARP
  C. Ipconfig
  D. Ifconfig

6. Which tool allows you to query the domain name system to obtain domain name or IP address mappings for a specified DNS record?
  A. Ping
  B. Ipconfig
  C. Nslookup
  D. Route

7. Users are complaining that an application is taking longer than normal to load. You need to troubleshoot why the application is experiencing startup issues. You want to gather detailed information while the application is loading. What should you enable?
  A. System logs
  B. Verbose logging
  C. Telnet
  D. ARP

8. You need a way to remotely execute commands against a server that is located on the internal network. Which tool can be used to accomplish this objective?
  A. Ping
  B. Dig
  C. Traceroute
  D. Telnet

9. You need to modify a routing table and create a static route. Which command-line tool can you use to accomplish this task?
  A. Ping
  B. Traceroute
  C. Route
  D. Host

SELF TEST ANSWERS

Testing Techniques

1. Dividing tasks and privileges required to perform a specific IT process among a number of administrators instead of a single administrator would be defined as which of the following?
   A. Penetration testing
   B. Vulnerability assessment
   C. Separation of duties
   D. Virtualization

   ☑ **C.** Separation of duties is the process of segregating specific duties and dividing the tasks and privileges required for a specific security process among multiple administrators.
   ☒ **A, B,** and **D** are incorrect. A penetration test is the process of evaluating the security of the cloud environment by simulating an attack on that environment from external and internal threats. A vulnerability assessment looks at the potential impact of a successful attack as well as the vulnerability of the environment. Virtualization is the process of creating a virtual version of a device or component, such as a server, switch, or storage device.

2. Which configuration test measures the amount of time between a networked device's request for data and the network's response?
   A. Network bandwidth
   B. Network latency
   C. Application availability
   D. Load balancing

   ☑ **B.** Testing network latency measures the amount of time between a networked device's request for data and the network's response. Testing network latency helps an administrator determine when a network is not performing at an optimal level.
   ☒ **A, C,** and **D** are incorrect. Network bandwidth is the measure of throughput and is impacted by latency. Application availability is something that needs to be measured to determine the uptime for the application. Load balancing allows you to distribute HTTP requests across multiple servers.

Troubleshooting and Tools

3. Which of the following command-line tools allows for the display of all active network connections and network protocol statistics?

A. Netstat

B. Ping

C. Traceroute

D. Ifconfig

☑ **A.** The netstat command can be used to display protocol statistics and all of the currently active TCP/IP network connections, along with Ethernet statistics.

☒ **B, C,** and **D** are incorrect. The ping utility is used to troubleshoot the reachability of a host on an IP network. Traceroute is a network troubleshooting tool that is used to determine the path that an IP packet has to take to reach a destination. Ifconfig is used to configure the TCP/IP network interface from the command line.

4. You need to verify the TCP/IP configuration settings of a network adapter on a virtual machine running Microsoft Windows. Which of the following tools should you use?

A. Ping

B. ARP

C. Tracert

D. Ipconfig

☑ **D.** Ipconfig is a Microsoft Windows command that displays the current TCP/IP network configuration settings for a network interface.

☒ **A, B,** and **C** are incorrect. The ping utility is used to troubleshoot the reachability of a host on an IP network. ARP resolves an IP address to a physical address or MAC address. Tracert is a Microsoft Windows network troubleshooting tool that is used to determine the path that an IP packet has to take to reach a destination.

5. Which of the following tools can be used to verify if a host is available on the network?

A. Ping

B. ARP

C. Ipconfig

D. Ifconfig

☑ **A.** The ping utility is used to troubleshoot the reachability of a host on an IP network. Ping sends an Internet control message protocol (ICMP) echo request packet to a specified IP address or host and waits for an ICMP reply.

☒ **B, C,** and **D** are incorrect. ARP resolves an IP address to a physical address or MAC address. Ifconfig and ipconfig display the current TCP/IP network configuration settings for a network interface.

6. Which tool allows you to query the domain name system to obtain domain name or IP address mappings for a specified DNS record?

   A. Ping
   B. Ipconfig
   C. Nslookup
   D. Route

☑ **C.** Using the nslookup command, it is possible to query the domain name system to obtain domain name or IP address mappings for a specified DNS record.

☒ **A, B,** and **D** are incorrect. The ping utility is used to troubleshoot the reachability of a host on an IP network. The ipconfig command displays the current TCP/IP network configuration settings for a network interface. The route command can view and manipulate the TCP/IP routing tables of operating systems.

7. Users are complaining that an application is taking longer than normal to load. You need to troubleshoot why the application is experiencing startup issues. You want to gather detailed information while the application is loading. What should you enable?

   A. System logs
   B. Verbose logging
   C. Telnet
   D. ARP

☑ **B.** Verbose logging records more detailed information than standard logging and is recommended to troubleshoot a specific problem.

☒ **A, C,** and **D** are incorrect. System log files can store a variety of information, including device changes, device drivers, system changes, and events, but would not provide detailed information on a particular application. ARP resolves an IP address to a physical address or MAC address. Telnet allows a user to connect to another computer and enter commands and the commands are executed as if they were entered directly on the server console.

8. You need a way to remotely execute commands against a server that is located on the internal network. Which tool can be used to accomplish this objective?

A. Ping

B. Dig

C. Traceroute

D. Telnet

☑ **D.** Telnet allows you to connect to another computer and enter commands via the telnet program. The commands will be executed as if you were entering them directly on the server console.

☒ **A, B,** and **C** are incorrect. The ping utility is used to troubleshoot the reachability of a host on an IP network. The dig command can be used to query domain name servers and can operate in interactive command-line mode or batch query mode. Traceroute is a network troubleshooting tool that is used to determine the path that an IP packet has to take to reach a destination.

9. You need to modify a routing table and create a static route. Which command-line tool can you use to accomplish this task?

A. Ping

B. Traceroute

C. Route

D. Host

☑ **C.** You can use the route command to view and manipulate the TCP/IP routing tables and create static routes.

☒ **A, B,** and **D** are incorrect. The ping utility is used to troubleshoot the reachability of a host on an IP network. Traceroute is a network troubleshooting tool that is used to determine the path that an IP packet has to take to reach a destination. The host utility can be used to perform DNS lookups.

11

Security in the Cloud

T his chapter covers the concepts of security in the cloud as they apply to data both in motion across networks and at rest in storage, as well as the controlled access to data in both states. Our security coverage begins with some high-level best practices and then delves into the details of the mechanisms and technologies required to deliver against those practices.

CERTIFICATION OBJECTIVE 11.01

Network Security: Best Practices

Network security is the practice of protecting the usability, reliability, integrity, and safety of a network infrastructure and also the data traveling along it. As it does in many other areas, security in cloud computing has similarities to traditional computing models. If deployed without evaluating security, it may be able to deliver against its functional requirements, but will likely have many gaps that could lead to a compromised system. As part of any cloud deployment, attention needs to be paid to specific security requirements so that the resources that are supposed to have access to data and software in the cloud system are the only resources that can read, write, or change it.

Assess and Audit the Network

A network assessment is an objective review of an organization's network infrastructure in terms of current functionality and security capabilities. The environment is evaluated holistically against industry best practices and its ability to meet the organization's requirements. Once all the assessment information has been documented, it is stored as a baseline for future audits to be performed against.

Complete audits must be scheduled on a regular basis to make certain that the configurations of all network resources are not changed in such a way that increases risk to the environment or the organization. With technologies that enable administrators to move virtual machines between hosts with no downtime and very little administrative effort, IT environments have become extremely volatile. A side effect of that volatility is that the security posture of a guest on one host may not be retained when it has been migrated to a different host.

As covered in Chapter 9, a change management system can help identify changes to an environment, but initial baseline assessments and subsequent periodic audits are critical. Such evaluations make it possible for administrators to correlate performance logs on affected systems with change logs, so they can identify configuration errors that may be causing problems.

Leverage Established Industry Frameworks

The advent of the information age has spawned various frameworks for best practice deployments of computing infrastructures. These frameworks have been established both to improve the quality of IT organizations, like Information Technology Infrastructure Library (ITIL) and Microsoft Operations Framework (MOF), and to ensure regulatory compliance for specific industries or data types, like the payment card industry regulation (PCI), the Sarbanes-Oxley Act (SOX), and the Health Insurance Portability and Accountability Act (HIPAA). In addition to publishing best practices, there are many tools that can raise alerts when a deviation from these compliance frameworks is identified. While these regulations can help guide the design of some secure solutions, they come at a price. Regulatory compliance is expensive for IT organizations because not only do they need to build solutions according to those regulations, they must also demonstrate compliance to auditors. This can be costly both in terms of tools and labor required to generate the necessary proof.

Utilize Layered Security

In order to protect network resources from external threats, secure network design employs multiple networks in order to prevent unwanted access to protected resources. The most secure design possible blocks access to all network traffic between the Internet and the local area network (LAN), where all of an organization's protected resources reside. This secure design must be altered, however, to allow any services from those protected resources to access the Internet. Some examples of these services might be e-mail, web traffic, or FTP services. In order to expose these services securely, a demilitarized zone (DMZ) can be employed. A DMZ is a separate network that is layered in between two separate networks, and holds resources that need to be accessed by both. A DMZ enhances security through the concept of multiple layers, because if an intruder were to gain access to the DMZ, they would still not have access to the protected resources on the LAN since they are separated onto another network.

The most common architectural design for setting up a DMZ is to place a hardware firewall between the external network and the DMZ, and to both control access and protect against attacks using that device. The mechanisms that firewalls use to control access to specific network resources are called access lists. Access lists explicitly allow or deny network traffic to specific network addresses on specific network ports, and allow for very granular access. Access lists are a simple way to allow authorized traffic to network resources. In order for an administrator to be aware of any possible threats with just access lists in place, he or she must diligently review the audit logs to understand the successes and failures of all requests against the established access lists. In order to deter or actively prevent unauthorized access of internal network resources, there are several tools that can be implemented in addition to the ACLs. Intrusion detection systems can be layered on top of firewalls to detect malicious packets and send alerts to system administrators to take action. Intrusion prevention systems take security one step further, actively shutting down the malicious traffic without waiting for manual intervention from an administrator. Some of the attacks that these systems are meant to countermand are the following:

- Distributed Denial of Service (DDoS) attacks, which target a single system simultaneously from multiple compromised systems. The distributed nature of these attacks makes it difficult for administrators to block malicious traffic based on its origination point and to distinguish approved traffic from attacking traffic.

- Ping of Death (PoD) attacks, which send malformed ICMP packets with the intent of crashing systems that cannot process them and consequently shut down. Most modern firewall packages can actively detect these packets and discard them before they cause damage.

- Ping Flood attacks, which are similar to DDoS attacks in that they attempt to overwhelm a system with more traffic than it can handle. In this variety, the attack is usually attempted by a single system making it easier to identify and block.

The real strength in the mechanisms covered in this section is that they can all be used together, creating a layered security system for the greatest possible security.

Utilize a Third Party to Audit the Network

When assessing or auditing a network, it is best practice to utilize a third-party product or service provider. This is preferable to using internal resources, as they often have both preconceived biases and preexisting knowledge about the network and security configuration. That familiarity with the environment can produce unsuccessful audits because the internal resources already have an assumption about the systems they are evaluating, and those assumptions result in either incomplete or incorrect information. A set of eyes from an outside source not only eliminates the familiar as a potential hurdle but also allows for a different (and in many cases, greater) set of skills to be utilized in the evaluation. Additionally, by using an unbiased third party, the results of the audit are more likely to hold up under scrutiny. This is even required by many regulatory organizations.

"Harden" Host and Guest Computers

The hardening of computer systems and networks involves ensuring that the system is configured in such a way that reduces the risk of attack from either internal or external sources. While the specific configuration steps for hardening vary from one system to another, the basic concepts involved are largely similar regardless of the technologies that are being hardened. Some of these central hardening concepts are as follows:

- **Removing all software and services that are not needed on the system.** Most operating systems and all preloaded systems run applications and services that are not needed by all configurations as part of their default. These additional services and applications add to the attack surface of any given system.

- **Maintaining firmware and patch levels.** Security holes are discovered constantly in both software and firmware, and vendors release patches as quickly as they can to respond to those discoveries.

- **Controlling account access.** All unused accounts should be either disabled or removed entirely from the system. All necessary accounts should be audited to make sure they have only access to the resources they require. All default accounts should be disabled or renamed, because if hackers are looking to gain unauthorized access to a system and they can guess the username, then they already have half of the necessary information to log into that system. For the same reason, all default passwords associated with any secured system should be changed as well. In addition to security threats from malicious users who are attempting to access unauthorized systems or data, security administrators must also concern themselves with the threat from the well-meaning employee who unknowingly either opens up access to resources that shouldn't be made available, or worse yet, deletes data forever that he or she did not intend to delete. These potential insider threats require that privileged user management be implemented and that security policies follow the principle of least privilege (POLP). POLP, introduced in the preceding chapter, dictates that users are given the amount of access they need to carry out their duties and no additional privileges above that for anything else.

- **Disabling unnecessary network ports.** As with applications, only the necessary network ports should be enabled to be certain that no unauthorized traffic can compromise the system.

- **Deploying antivirus/antimalware.** All systems that are capable of deploying antivirus and antimalware should do so. The most secure approach to virus defense is one in which any malicious traffic must pass through multiple layers of detection before reaching its potential target.

- **Configuring log files.** Logging should be enabled on all systems so that if an intrusion is attempted, it can be identified and mitigated or, at the very least, investigated.

- **Limiting physical access.** If a malicious user has physical access to a network resource, they may have more options for gaining access to that resource. Because of this, any limitations that can be applied to physical access should be utilized. Some examples of physical access deterrents are locks on server room doors, network cabinets, and the network devices themselves. Additionally, servers need to be secured at the BIOS level with a password so that malicious users cannot boot to secondary drives and bypass operating system security.

- **Scanning for vulnerabilities.** Once all of the security configuration steps have been defined and implemented for a system, a vulnerability assessment should be performed using a third-party tool or service provider to make certain no security gaps were missed.

- **Deploy a host-based firewall.** As another part of a layered security strategy, software firewalls should be deployed to the hosts and guests that will support them. These software firewalls can be configured with access lists and protection tools in the same fashion as hardware firewalls.

Employ Penetration Testing

Penetration testing is the process of evaluating network security with a simulated attack on the network from both external and internal attackers. A penetration test involves an active analysis of the network by a testing firm that looks for potential vulnerabilities due to hardware and software flaws, improperly configured systems, or a combination of factors. The test is performed by a person who acts like a potential attacker, and it involves the exploitation of specific security vulnerabilities. Once the test is complete, any issues that have been identified by the test are presented to the organization. The testing firm might take the results from the test and combine them with an assessment that states the potential impacts to the organization and makes suggestions on how to reduce security risks.

Perform Vulnerability Assessments

A vulnerability assessment is the process used to identify and quantify any vulnerabilities in a network environment. It is a detailed evaluation of the network, indicating any weaknesses and providing appropriate mitigation procedures to help eliminate or reduce the level of the security risk.

<table>
<tr>
<td>

e x a m

ω a t c h
</td>
<td>

The difference between a penetration test and a vulnerability
</td>
<td>

assessment is that a penetration test simulates an attack on the environment.
</td>
</tr>
</table>

Secure Storage Resources

Data is the most valuable component of any cloud system. It is the reason that companies invest in these large, expensive infrastructures or services: to make certain that their users have access to the data they need to drive their business. Because it is such a critical resource to the users of our cloud models, special care must be taken with its security to make sure it is always available and accurate for only the resources that have been authorized to access it. In addition to the network system's hardening steps listed previously, some additional steps need to be taken for storage security. Here are some of these storage-specific practices.

Data Classification

Data classification is the practice of sorting data into discrete categories that help define the access levels and type of protection required for that set of data. These categories are then used to determine the disaster recovery mechanisms, cloud technologies required to store the data, and the placement of that data onto physically or logically separated storage resources.

Data Encryption

Data encryption is an algorithmic scheme that secures data by scrambling into a code that is not readable by unauthorized resources. The authorized recipient of encrypted data uses a key that triggers the algorithm mechanism to decrypt the coded message, transforming back into its original readable version. Without that key, even if an unauthorized resource were to secure a copy of the data, they could not use it.

Granular Storage Resource Controls

Based on the storage technology utilized in the cloud system, security mechanisms can be put in place to limit access to resources over the network. When using a storage area network (SAN), for example, resources can be limited to which storage logical unit numbers (LUNs) are accessible by the utilization of a LUN mask either at the host bus adapter or at the switch level. SANs can also utilize zoning, which is a practice of limiting access to LUNs that are attached to the storage controller. Much in the same way as we described antivirus configuration earlier, storage security is best implemented in layers, with data having to pass multiple checks before arriving at its intended target. All the possible security mechanisms, from software to operating system to storage system, should be implemented and configured in order to architect the most secure storage solution possible.

Protected Backups

Backups are copies of live data that are maintained in case something happens that makes the live dataset inaccessible. Because it is a copy of valuable data, it needs to have the same protections afforded it that the live data employs. It should be encrypted, password protected, and kept physically locked away from unauthorized access.

Keep Employees and Tools Up to Date

Rapid deployment is the ability to provision and release solutions with minimal management effort or service provider interaction. This new ability is known as rapid deployment, and it has been enabled by new and better virtualization technologies that allow IT organizations to roll out systems faster than ever before. One hazard of rapid deployment is the propensity to either ignore security or proceed with the idea that the organization will enable functionality for the system immediately, then circle back and improve the security once it is in place. Typically, however, the requests for new functionality continue to take precedence and security is rarely or inadequately revisited.

In addition to the risks of these fast-forward-type deployments, the rapidly evolving landscape of cloud technologies and virtualization presents dangers for IT departments that do not stay abreast of changes to both their tool sets and their training. Many networks were originally designed to utilize traditional network security devices that monitor traffic and devices on a physical network. If the intra-virtual-machine traffic that those tools are watching for never routes through a physical network, it cannot be monitored by that traditional tool set. The problem with limiting network traffic to guests within the host is that if the tools are not virtualization or cloud aware, they will not provide the proper information to make a diagnosis or even to suggest changes to the infrastructure. Therefore, it is critical that monitoring and management tool sets are updated as frequently as the technology that they are designed to control.

CERTIFICATION OBJECTIVE 11.02

Data Security

Data security encompasses data as it traverses a network as well as stored data, or data at rest. In its simplest form, data security is accomplished by authenticating and authorizing both users and hosts. Authentication means that an entity can prove that it is what it claims to be, and authorization means that an entity has access to all of the resources it is supposed to have access to, and no access to the resources it is not supposed to have access to. Beyond the two primary concepts of authentication and authorization, data confidentiality (encryption) ensures that only authorized parties can access data, whereas data integrity (digital signatures) ensures that data is tamper-free and comes from a trusted party. These control mechanisms can be used separately or together for the utmost in security, and this section will explore them in detail.

Public Key Infrastructure

A public key infrastructure (PKI) is a hierarchy of trusted security certificates, as seen in Figure 11-1. These security certificates (also called X.509 certificates, or PKI certificates) are issued to users or computing devices. PKI certificates are used to encrypt and decrypt data, as well as to digitally sign and verify the integrity of data. Each certificate contains a unique, mathematically related public and private key pair. When the certificate is issued, it has an expiration date; certificates must be renewed before the expiration date, otherwise they are not usable.

The certificate authority (CA) exists at the top of the PKI hierarchy, and it can issue, revoke, and renew all security certificates. Under it reside either user and device certificates or subordinate certificate authorities.

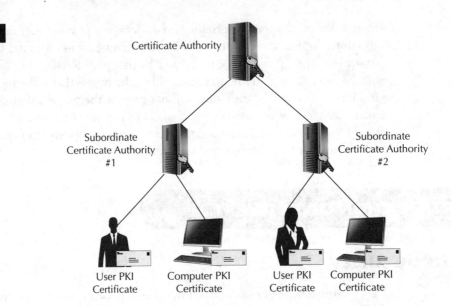

FIGURE 11-1

Illustration of
a public key
infrastructure
hierarchy.

Subordinate CAs can also issue, revoke, and renew certificates. A large enterprise, for example, Acme, might have a CA named Acme-CA. For the western region, Acme might create a subordinate CA named West and the same for East and Central. This allows the IT security personnel in each of the three regions to control their own user and device PKI certificates.

on the job *Instead of an organization creating their own PKI, they may want to consider acquiring PKI certificates from a trusted third party such as VeriSign or Entrust. Modern operating systems have a list of trusted certificate authorities, and if an organization uses their own PKI, they have to ensure that all of their devices trust their CA.*

Plaintext

Before data is encrypted, it is called plaintext. When an unencrypted e-mail message (i.e., an e-mail in plaintext form) is transmitted across a network, it is possible for a third party to intercept that message in its entirety.

Obfuscation

Obfuscation is a practice of using some defined pattern to mask sensitive data. This pattern can be a substitution pattern, a shuffling of characters, or a patterned removal of selected characters. Obfuscation is more secure than plaintext, but can be reverse engineered if a malicious entity were willing to spend the time to decode it.

Cipher Text

Ciphers are mathematical algorithms used to encrypt data. Applying an encryption algorithm (cipher) against plaintext results in what is called cipher text; it is the encrypted version of the originating plaintext.

Symmetric Encryption

Encrypting data requires a passphrase or key. Symmetric encryption, also called private key encryption, uses a single key that encrypts and decrypts data. Think of it as locking and unlocking a door using the same key. The key must be kept safe since anybody with it in their possession can unlock the door. Symmetric encryption is used to encrypt files, to secure some VPN solutions, and to encrypt Wi-Fi networks, just to name a few examples.

To see symmetric encryption in action, let's consider a situation where a user, Stacey, encrypts a file on a hard disk:

1. Stacey flags the file to be encrypted.

2. The file encryption software uses a configured symmetric key (or passphrase) to encrypt the file contents. The key might be stored in a file or on a smart-card, or the user might simply be prompted for the passphrase at the time. This same symmetric key (or passphrase) is used when the file is decrypted.

Encrypting files on a single computer is easy with symmetric encryption, but when other parties that need the symmetric key are involved (e.g., when connecting to a VPN using symmetric encryption), it becomes problematic: How do we securely get the symmetric key to all parties? We could transmit the key to the other parties via e-mail or text message, but we would already have to have a way to encrypt this transmission in the first place. For this reason, symmetric encryption does not scale well.

Asymmetric Encryption

Asymmetric encryption uses two different keys to secure data: a public key and a private key. This key pair is stored in a PKI certificate (which itself can be stored as a file), in a user account database, or on a smartcard. Using two mathematically related keys is what PKI is all about: a hierarchy of trusted certificates each with their own unique public and private key pairs.

The public key can be freely shared, but the private key must be accessible only by the certificate owner. Both the public and private keys can be exported to a certificate file or just the public key by itself. Keys are exported to exchange with others for secure communications or to use as a backup. If the private key is stored in a certificate file, the file must be password protected.

The recipient's public key is required to encrypt transmissions to them. Bear in mind that the recipient could be a user or a computer. The recipient then uses their mathematically related private key to decrypt the message.

Consider an example, shown in Figure 11-2, where user Roman sends user Trinity an encrypted e-mail message using a PKI, or asymmetric encryption:

1. Roman flags an e-mail message for encryption. His mail software needs Trinity's public key. PKI encryption uses the recipient's public key to encrypt. If Roman cannot get Trinity's public key, he cannot encrypt a message to her.

2. Roman's mail software encrypts and sends the message. Anybody intercepting the mail message will be unable to decipher the message content.

3. Trinity opens the mail message using her mail program. Because the message is encrypted with her public key, only her mathematically related private key can decrypt the message.

Unlike symmetric encryption, PKI scales well. There is no need to find a safe way to distribute secret keys because only the public keys need be accessible by others, and public keys do not have to be kept secret.

Digital Signatures

A PKI allows us to trust the integrity of data by way of digital signatures. When data is digitally signed, a mathematical hashing function is applied against the data in the message, which results in what is called a message digest, or hash. The PKI private key of the signer is then used to encrypt the hash: this is the digital signature.

FIGURE 11-2

Sending an encrypted e-mail message.

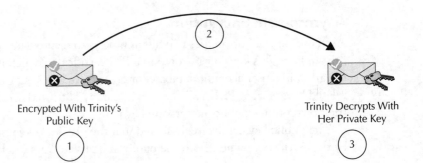

Encrypted With Trinity's Public Key

Trinity Decrypts With Her Private Key

Notice that the message content has not been secured; for that encryption is required. Other parties needing to trust the digitally signed data use the mathematically related public key of the signer to validate the hash. Remember that public keys can be freely distributed to anyone without compromising security.

As an example of the digital signature at work, consider user Ana, who is sending user Zoey a high-priority e-mail message that Zoey must trust really did come from Ana:

1. Ana creates the mail message and flags it to be digitally signed.
2. Ana's mail program uses her PKI private key to encrypt the generated message hash.
3. The mail message is sent to Zoey, but it is not encrypted in this example, only signed.
4. Zoey's mail program verifies Ana's digital signature by using Ana's mathematically related public key; if Zoey does not have Ana's public key, she cannot verify Ana's digital signatures.

Using a public key to verify a digital signature is valid because only the related private key could have created that unique signature, so the message had to have come from that party. This is referred to as nonrepudiation. If the message is tampered with along the way, the signature is invalidated. Again, unlike symmetric encryption, there is no need to safely transmit secret keys; public keys are designed to be publicly available.

For the utmost in security, data can be encrypted and digitally signed, whether it is transmitted data or data at rest (stored).

> **exam**
> **watch** **Data confidentiality is achieved with encryption. Data authentication and integrity are achieved with digital signatures.**

Ciphers

Recall that plaintext fed to an encryption algorithm results in cipher text. "Cipher" is synonymous with "encryption algorithm," whether the algorithm is symmetric (same key) or asymmetric (different keys). There are two categories of symmetric ciphers: block ciphers and stream ciphers. Table 11-1 lists some of the more common ones.

Block Ciphers

Designed to encrypt chunks or blocks of data, block ciphers convert plaintext to cipher text in bulk as opposed to one data bit at a time, either using a fixed secret key or by generating keys from each encrypted block. A 128-bit block cipher produces a 128-bit block of cipher text. This type of cipher is best applied to fixed-length segments of data, such as fixed-length network packets or files stored on a disk.

TABLE 11-1   Common Block and Stream Ciphers

Cipher Name	Cipher Type	Cipher Strength (in bits)	Usage
Advanced Encryption Standard (AES)	Symmetric, block	Up to 256	Replaced DES in 2001 as the U.S. federal standard
Digital Encryption Standard (DES, 3DES)	Symmetric, block	56 for DES, 168 for 3DES	U.S. federal standard until 2001
Digital Signature Algorithm (DSA)	Asymmetric, block	Up to 2048	U.S. federal standard for digital signatures
Rivest Cipher (RC4)	Symmetric, stream	128	Byte-oriented stream operation
Rivest Cipher (RC5)	Symmetric, block	Up to 2040	A simple and fast algorithm
Rivest, Shamir, Adleman (RSA)	Asymmetric, stream	Up to 4096	Some hardware and software may not support up to 4096 bits

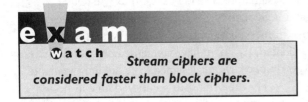

e x a m

ⓦ a t c h   *Stream ciphers are considered faster than block ciphers.*

Stream Ciphers

Unlike block ciphers, stream ciphers convert plaintext bits into cipher text and are considered much faster than block ciphers. Stream ciphers are best suited where there is an unknown variable amount of data to be encrypted, such as variable-length network transmissions.

Encryption Protocols

There are many methods that can be used to secure and verify the authenticity of data. These methods are called encryption protocols, and each is designed for specific purposes, such as encryption for confidentiality and digital signatures for data authenticity and verification (also known as nonrepudiation).

IPSec

Internet protocol security (IPSec) secures IP traffic using encryption and/or digital signatures. PKI certificates or symmetric keys can be used to implement this type of security. What makes IPSec interesting is that it is not application specific; so if IPSec secures the communication between hosts, it can encrypt and/or sign network traffic regardless of the application generating the traffic.

SSL/TLS

Unlike IPSec, secure sockets layer (SSL) and transport layer security (TLS) are used to secure the communication of specifically configured applications. Like IPSec, encryption and authentication (signatures) are used to accomplish this level of security. TLS is SSL's successor, although the improvements are minor.

Most computer people associate SSL with secured web servers, but SSL can be applied to any network software that supports it, such as simple mail transfer protocol (SMTP) mail servers and lightweight directory access protocol (LDAP) directory servers. SSL and TLS rely on PKI certificates to obtain the keys required for encryption, decryption, and authentication. Take note that some secured communication, such as connecting to a secured website using hypertext transfer protocol secure (HTTPS), uses public and private key pairs (asymmetric) to encrypt a session-specific key (symmetric).

CERTIFICATION OBJECTIVE 11.03

Access Control Methods

Controlling access to network resources such as files, folders, databases, and web applications starts with authenticating the requesting party. After successful authentication occurs, authorizing the use of network resources is achieved using various access control methods, as depicted in Table 11-2.

TABLE 11-2   Comparison of Access Control Methods

Role-Based Access Control (RBAC)	Mandatory Access Control (MAC)	Discretionary Access Control (DAC)
Permissions are granted to groups or roles	Operating system or application determines who has access to a resource	Permissions are granted to users
Suited for larger organizations	Resources are labeled for granular control	Suited for smaller organizations
Users are added to groups or roles to gain access to resources	User attributes can determine resource access	

Role-Based Access Controls

For many years IT administrators have found it easier to manage permissions to resources by using groups, or roles. This is the premise of role-based access control (RBAC). A group or role has one or more members, and that group or role is assigned permissions to a resource. Any user placed into that group or role inherits its permissions; this is known as implicit inheritance. Granting permissions to individual users is considered explicit permission assignment, and it does not scale as well in larger organizations as RBAC does. Sometimes the groups or roles in RBAC are defined at the operating system level, as in the case of a Microsoft Windows Active Directory group, and other times the group or role is defined within an application, as in the case of Microsoft SharePoint Server roles.

Mandatory Access Controls

The word mandatory is used to describe this access control model because permissions to resources are controlled, or mandated, by the operating system (OS) or application, which looks at the requesting party and their attributes to determine whether or not access should be granted. These decisions are based on configured policies that are enforced by the OS or app.

With mandatory access control (MAC), data is labeled, or classified, in such a way that only those parties with certain attributes can access it. For example, perhaps only full-time employees can access a specific portion of an Intranet web portal. Or perhaps only human resources employees can access files classified as confidential.

Discretionary Access Controls

With the discretionary access control (DAC) model, the power to grant or deny user permissions to resources lies not with the OS or an app but rather with the data owner. Protected resources might be files on a file server or items in a specific web application.

There are no security labels or classifications with DAC; instead, each protected resource has an access control list (ACL) that determines access. For example, we might add user RayLee with read and write permissions to the ACL of a specific folder on a file server so that she can access that data.

on the   *Most network environments use both DAC and RBAC; the data owner can give*
ⓘ**o b**   *permissions to the resource by adding a group to the access control list (ACL).*

Multifactor Authentication

Authentication means proving who (or what) you are. This can be done with the standard username and password combination or with a variety of other methods. These are the three categories of authentication:

1. Something you know

   Knowing your username and password is by far the most common. Knowing your first pet's name, or the PIN for your credit card, or your mother's maiden name all fall into this category.

2. Something you have

   Most of us have used a debit or credit card to make a purchase. We must physically have the card in our possession. For VPN authentication, possession of a hardware token with a changing numeric code synced with the VPN server is common.

3. Something you are

   This is where biometric authentication kicks in. Your fingerprints, your voice, your facial structure, the capillary pattern in your retinas—these are unique to you. Of course, voice impersonators could reproduce your voice, so some methods are more secure than others.

Some environments use a combination of the three authentication mechanisms; this is known as multifactor authentication. Possessing a debit card, along with knowledge of the PIN, comprises multifactor authentication. Combining these authentication methods is considered much more secure than single-factor authentication.

Single Sign-On

As individuals, we've all had to remember multiple usernames and passwords for various software at work, or even at home for multiple websites. Wouldn't it be great if we logged in only once and had access to everything without being prompted to log in again? This is what single sign-on (SSO) is all about!

SSO can take operating system, VPN, or web browser authentication credentials and present them to the relying party transparently so the user doesn't even know it is happening. Modern Windows operating systems use the credential vault to store varying types of credentials to facilitate SSO. Enterprise SSO solutions such as the open-source Shibboleth tool or Microsoft Active Directory Federation Services (ADFS) let IT personnel implement SSO on a large scale.

The problem with SSO is that different software and websites may use different authentication mechanisms. This makes implementing SSO in a large environment difficult.

Federation

Federation uses SSO to authorize users or devices to potentially many very different protected network resources, such as file servers, websites, and database applications. The protected resources could exist within a single organization or between multiple organizations.

For business-to-business (B2B) relationships, such as between a cloud customer and a cloud provider, federation allows the cloud customer to retain their own on-premises user accounts and passwords that can be used to access cloud services from the provider. This way the user does not have to remember a username and password for the cloud services as well as for the local network. Federation also allows cloud providers to rent, on demand, computing resources from other cloud providers to service their clients' needs.

Here is a typical B2B federation scenario (see Figure 11-3):

1. User Bob in company A attempts to access an application on web application server 1 in company B.
2. If Bob is not already authenticated, the web application server in company B redirects Bob to the federation server in company B for authentication.
3. Since Bob's user account does not exist in company B, the federation server in company B sends an authentication redirect to Bob.
4. Bob is redirected to the company A federation server and gets authenticated, since this is where his user account exists.
5. The company A federation server returns a digitally signed authentication token to Bob.
6. Bob presents the authentication token to the application on web application server 1 and is authorized to use the application.

FIGURE 11-3

An example of B2B federation at work.

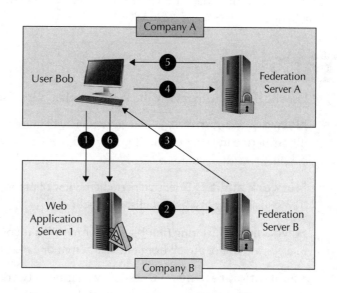

CERTIFICATION SUMMARY

This chapter focused on network security, data security, and access control models, all of which are of interest to IT personnel.

As a CompTIA Cloud+ candidate, you must understand the importance of applying best practices to your network. Assessing the network is only effective when comparing your results with an established baseline of normal configuration and activity. Auditing a network is best done by a third party, and you may be required to use only accredited auditors that conform to industry standards such as PCI or SOX. All computing equipment must be patched and hardened to minimize the potential for compromise.

An understanding of data security measures and access control methods is also important for the exam. Data security must be in place both for data as it traverses a network and for stored data. Encrypting data prevents unauthorized access of the data, while digital signatures verify the authenticity of the data. Various encryption protocols are used to accomplish these objectives. The various access control models discussed in this chapter include role-based access control, mandatory access control, and discretionary access control.

KEY TERMS

Use the list below to review the key terms that were discussed in this chapter.

Network assessment   Objective review of an organization's network infrastructure in terms of functionality and security capabilities, used to establish a baseline for future audits

Network audit   Objective periodic review of an organization's network infrastructure against an established baseline

Hardening   Ensuring that a system or network is configured in such a way that reduces the risk of attack from either internal or external sources

Penetration testing   Process of evaluating network security with a simulated attack on the network from both external and internal attackers

Vulnerability assessment   Process used to identify and quantify any vulnerabilities in a network environment

Data classification   Practice of sorting data into discrete categories that help define the access levels and type of protection required for that set of data

Data encryption   Algorithmic scheme that secures data by scrambling into a code that is not readable by unauthorized resources

Public key infrastructure (PKI)   Hierarchy of trusted security certificates issued to users or computing devices

Certificate authority (CA)   Entity that issues digital certificates and makes its public keys available to the intended audience to provide proof of its authenticity

Plaintext   Unencrypted data

Cipher text   Data that has been encrypted using a mathematical algorithm

Symmetric encryption   Encryption mechanism that uses a single key to both encrypt and decrypt data

Asymmetric encryption   Encryption mechanism that uses two different keys to encrypt and decrypt data

Public key   One-half of the keys used for asymmetric encryption, a public key is available to anyone and is used only for data encryption

Private key   One-half of the keys used for asymmetric encryption, a private key is available only to the intended data user and is used only for data decryption

Digital signature   Mathematical hash of a dataset that is encrypted by the private key and used to validate that dataset

Block cipher   A method of converting plaintext to cipher text in bulk as opposed to one data bit at a time, either using a fixed secret key or by generating keys from each encrypted block

Stream cipher   A method of converting plaintext to cipher text one bit at a time

Role-based access control (RBAC)   Security mechanism in which all access is granted through predefined collections of permissions, called roles, instead of implicitly assigning access to users or resources individually

Mandatory access control (MAC)   Security mechanism in which access is mandated by the operating system or application and not by data owners

Discretionary access control (DAC)   Security mechanism in which the power to grant or deny permissions to resources lies with the data owner

Multifactor authentication   Authentication of resources using proof from more than one of the three authentication categories: something you know, something you have, and something you are

Single sign-on (SSO)   Authentication process in which the resource requesting access can enter one set of credentials and use those credentials to access multiple applications or datasets, even if they have separate authorization mechanisms

Federation   Use of SSO to authorize users or devices to many different protected network resources, such as file servers, websites, and database applications

✓ TWO-MINUTE DRILL

Network Security: Best Practices

❑ Hardening is the process of ensuring that a system is not vulnerable to compromise. Logging must be enabled to track potential intrusions. Only the required software components should be installed on the system, software patches should be applied regularly, firewall and antimalware software should be functional and up to date, and any unused user accounts should be disabled or removed.

❑ A penetration test tests network and host security by simulating malicious attacks and then analyzing the results. Not to be confused with a vulnerability assessment, which only identifies weaknesses and can be determined without running a penetration test.

Data Security

❑ A public key infrastructure (PKI) is a hierarchy of trusted security certificates that each contain unique public and private key pairs; used for data encryption and verification of data integrity.

❑ Cipher text is the result of feeding plaintext into an encryption algorithm; this is the encrypted data. Block ciphers encrypt chunks of data at a time, whereas the faster stream ciphers encrypt data normally a binary bit at a time. Stream ciphers are best applied where there is an unknown variable amount of data to be encrypted.

❑ Symmetric encryption uses the same secret key for encryption and decryption. The challenge lies in safely distributing the key to all involved parties.

❑ Asymmetric encryption uses two mathematically related keys (public and private) to encrypt and decrypt. This implies a PKI. The public and private key pairs contained within a PKI certificate are unique to that subject. Normally data is encrypted with the recipient's public key, and the recipient decrypts that data with the related private key. It is safe to distribute public keys using any mechanism to the involved parties.

❑ A digital signature is a unique value created from the signer's private key and the data to which the signature is attached. The recipient validates the signature using the signer's public key. This assures the recipient that data came from who it says it came from and that the data has not been tampered with.

Access Control Methods

- ❑ Role-based access control (RBAC) is a method of using groups and roles to assign permissions to network resources. This scales well because once groups or roles are given the appropriate permissions to resources, users can simply be made members of the group or role to inherit those permissions.

- ❑ Mandatory access control (MAC) is a method of authorization whereby a computer system, based on configured policies, checks user or computer attributes along with data labels to grant access. Data labels might be applied to files or websites to determine who can access that data. The data owner cannot control resource permissions.

- ❑ Discretionary access control (DAC) allows the owner of the data to grant permissions, at their discretion, to users. This is what is normally done in smaller networks where there is a small user base. A larger user base necessitates the use of groups or roles to assign permissions.

- ❑ Multifactor authentication is any combination of two or more authentication methods stemming from what you know, what you have, and what you are. For example, you might have a smartcard and also know the PIN to use it. This is two-factor authentication.

- ❑ Single sign-on (SSO) requires users to authenticate only once. They are then authorized to use multiple IT systems without having to log in each time.

- ❑ Federation allows SSO across multiple IT systems using a single identity (username and password, for example), even across organizational boundaries.

SELF TEST

The following questions will help you measure your understanding of the material presented in this chapter.

Network Security: Best Practices

1. Which best practice configures host computers so that they are not vulnerable to attack?
  A. Vulnerability assessment
  B. Penetration test
  C. Hardening
  D. PKI

2. Which type of test simulates a network attack?
  A. Vulnerability assessment
  B. Establishing an attack baseline
  C. Hardening
  D. Penetration test

3. You have been asked to harden a crucial network router. What should you do? (Choose two.)
  A. Disable the routing of IPv6 packets
  B. Change the default administrative password
  C. Apply firmware patches
  D. Configure the router for SSO

Data Security

4. You are invited to join an IT meeting where the merits and pitfalls of cloud computing are being debated. Your manager conveys her concerns of data confidentiality for cloud storage. What can be done to secure data stored in the cloud?
  A. Encrypt the data
  B. Digitally sign the data
  C. Use a stream cipher
  D. Change default passwords

5. Which of the following works best to encrypt variable-length data?
   A. Block cipher
   B. Symmetric cipher
   C. Asymmetric cipher
   D. Stream cipher

6. With PKI, which key is used to validate a digital signature?
   A. Private key
   B. Public key
   C. Secret key
   D. Signing key

7. Which of the following is related to nonrepudiation?
   A. Block cipher
   B. PKI
   C. Symmetric encryption
   D. Stream cipher

Access Control Methods

8. Sean configures a web application to allow content managers to upload files to the website. What type of access control model is Sean using?
   A. DAC
   B. MAC
   C. RBAC

9. You are the administrator of a Windows network. When creating a new user account, you specify a security clearance level of top secret so that the user can access classified files. What type of access control method is being used?
   A. DAC
   B. MAC
   C. RBAC

10. True or False. DAC is suitable for large organizations.
   A. True
   B. False

SELF TEST ANSWERS

Network Security: Best Practices

1. Which best practice configures host computers so that they are not vulnerable to attack?
   A. Vulnerability assessment
   B. Penetration test
   C. Hardening
   D. PKI

   ☑ **C.** Hardening configures systems such that they are protected from compromise.
   ☒ **A, B,** and **D** are incorrect. While vulnerability assessments identify security problems, they do not correct them. Penetration tests simulate an attack, but do not configure machines to be protected from such attacks. PKI is a hierarchy of trusted security certificates; it does not address configuration issues.

2. Which type of test simulates a network attack?
   A. Vulnerability assessment
   B. Establishing an attack baseline
   C. Hardening
   D. Penetration test

   ☑ **D.** Penetration tests simulate a network attack.
   ☒ **A, B,** and **C** are incorrect. Vulnerability assessments identify weaknesses but do not perform simulated network attacks. While establishing a usage baseline is valid, establishing an attack baseline is not. Hardening is the process of configuring a system to make it less vulnerable to attack; it does not simulate such attacks.

3. You have been asked to harden a crucial network router. What should you do? (Choose two.)
   A. Disable the routing of IPv6 packets
   B. Change the default administrative password
   C. Apply firmware patches
   D. Configure the router for SSO

☑ **B, C.** Changing the default passwords and applying patches are important steps in hardening a device.

☒ **A and D** are incorrect. Without more information, disabling IPv6 packet routing does not harden a router, nor does configuring it for SSO.

Data Security

4. You are invited to join an IT meeting where the merits and pitfalls of cloud computing are being debated. Your manager conveys her concerns of data confidentiality for cloud storage. What can be done to secure data stored in the cloud?

A. Encrypt the data
B. Digitally sign the data
C. Use a stream cipher
D. Change default passwords

☑ **A.** Encrypting data at rest protects the data from those not in possession of a decryption key.

☒ **B, C, and D** are incorrect. Digital signatures verify data authenticity, but they don't deal with the question of confidentiality. Stream ciphers are best used for unpredictable variable-length network transmissions; a block cipher would be better suited for file encryption. While changing default passwords is always relevant, it does nothing to address the concern about data confidentiality.

5. Which of the following works best to encrypt variable-length data?

A. Block cipher
B. Symmetric cipher
C. Asymmetric cipher
D. Stream cipher

☑ **D.** Stream ciphers encrypt data, usually a bit at a time, so this works well for data that is not a fixed length.

☒ **A, B, and C** are incorrect. Symmetric and asymmetric ciphers do not apply in this context. Block ciphers are generally better suited for data blocks of fixed length.

6. With PKI, which key is used to validate a digital signature?

   A. Private key

   B. Public key

   C. Secret key

   D. Signing key

> ☑ **B.** The public key of the signer is used to validate a digital signature.
>
> ☒ **A, C,** and **D** are incorrect. Private keys create, and don't validate, digital signatures. A secret key is synonymous with an asymmetric key; PKI is implied when discussing signatures. Signing keys, as they are sometimes called, digitally sign data.

7. Which of the following is related to nonrepudiation?

   A. Block cipher

   B. PKI

   C. Symmetric encryption

   D. Stream cipher

> ☑ **B.** PKI is related to nonrepudiation, which means that a verified digital signature proves the message came from the listed party. This is true because only the private key of the signing party could have created the validated signature.
>
> ☒ **A, C,** and **D** are incorrect. Block ciphers and stream ciphers are not related to nonrepudiation; they are types of encryption methods. Symmetric encryption excludes the possibility of a PKI, and PKI relates to nonrepudiation.

Access Control Methods

8. Sean configures a web application to allow content managers to upload files to the website. What type of access control model is Sean using?

   A. DAC

   B. MAC

   C. RBAC

☑ **C.** Sean is using a role (content managers) to control who can upload files to the website. This is role-based access control (RBAC).

☒ **A** and **B** are incorrect. DAC allows data owners to grant permissions to users. MAC uses data classification and other attributes so that computer systems can determine who should have access to what.

9. You are the administrator of a Windows network. When creating a new user account, you specify a security clearance level of top secret so that the user can access classified files. What type of access control method is being used?

    A. DAC

    B. MAC

    C. RBAC

☑ **B.** Mandatory access control (MAC) uses attributes (such as "top secret") that enable computer systems to determine who should have access to what.

☒ **A** and **C** are incorrect. DAC allows data owners to grant permissions to users. RBAC uses groups and roles so that their members inherit permissions to resources.

10. True or False. DAC is suitable for large organizations.

    A. True

    B. False

☑ **B.** False. Discretionary access control (DAC) allows data owners, at their discretion, to grant permissions to users, but this is only viable with a small number of users.

☒ **A** is incorrect because DAC is not suitable for large organizations. RBAC, which uses groups and roles so that their members inherit permissions to resources, is better suited for large organizations.

12

Business Continuity and Disaster Recovery

A n organization's data must be backed up and key processes like payroll and billing need to be continually available even if the organization's data center is lost due to a disaster. Choosing a disaster recovery method is an important step in a reliable cloud implementation. A cloud computing model can be seen as an alternative to traditional disaster recovery. Cloud computing offers a more rapid recovery time and helps to reduce the costs of a disaster recovery model.

Disaster Recovery Methods

When an organization is choosing a disaster recovery method, they have to measure the level of service required. This means understanding how critical the application or server is and then determining the proper disaster recovery method for it. When implementing disaster recovery, it is important to form a disaster recovery plan (DRP) or business continuity plan (BCP) that will describe how the organization is going to deal with potential disasters. When creating a DRP, it is first necessary to focus on those applications or servers that are mission critical. A mission-critical system is any system whose failure results in the failure of business operations. If the failure of a system results in the organization's failure to operate and generate income, that system would be considered mission critical. These systems need to be identified and backed by a proper disaster recovery method to ensure there is no lost revenue for the organization. Another consideration when designing a DRP is where to place the disaster recovery center. Geographic diversity should be taken into account when planning for a disaster that may impact a particular geographic region. Disasters come in many forms, including natural disasters, so placing the disaster recovery center in a location that is 1000 miles away might prevent the same natural disaster from destroying both the primary data center and the disaster recovery center.

Another factor to consider when building a DRP is mean time between failures (MTBF) and mean time to repair (MTTR). MTBF is the average time a device will function before it fails. MTBF can be used to determine approximately how long a hard drive will last in a server. It can also be used to plan how long it might take for a particular hardware component to fail and thereby help with the creation of a DRP. MTTR, on the other hand, is the average time that it takes to repair a failed hardware component. MTTR needs to be a factor in the DRP, as it is often part of the maintenance contract for the virtualization host computers. An MTTR of 24 hours or less would be appropriate for a higher-priority server, whereas a lower-priority server might have an MTTR of seven days. All of these factors need to be considered in the DRP for the organization to have a successful disaster recovery environment.

Most organizations will have two recovery objectives. There is the recovery time objective (RTO), which is the amount of time between an outage and the restoration of the service, and then there is the recovery point objective (RPO), which is the maximum amount of time in which data can be lost for a service due to a major incident. For example, if you back up your system overnight, then the recovery point objective would be the end of the previous day.

One of the things that should be considered and that can help meet expected RTO and RPO is redundancy. A redundant system can be used to provide a backup to a primary system in the case of failure. Redundant components protect the system from failure and can include power supplies, switches, network interface cards, and hard disks. A good example of a redundant system is RAID (redundant array of independent disks), discussed in Chapter 2. A redundant component means you actually have more of that component than you need. For example, a virtualization host computer might have two power supplies to make it redundant, but it can actually function with a single power supply. Redundant does not mean that there is not an impact to performance if a component fails; it means that service can be restored to working condition (although the condition may be at a degraded state), without the need for external components. Redundancy differs from fault tolerance in that fault tolerance allows the system to tolerate a fault and continue running in spite of it. Fault tolerance is discussed in more detail later in the chapter.

Once an organization has established the DRP and created redundant systems, they have the ability to implement failover. Failover uses a constant communication mechanism between two systems called a heartbeat. As long as this heartbeat continues uninterrupted, failover to the redundant system will not initiate. If the heartbeat between the servers fails, the redundant system will take over processing for the primary system. If the primary system becomes operational again, the organization can initiate a failback. A failback is the process of restoring the processing back to the original state before the failure of the primary system.

Multisite Configuration

To help reduce downtime in case of a disaster, an organization can set up and configure a multisite environment. Using a multisite configuration is a more expensive solution to disaster recovery but helps provide a more advanced business continuity plan. In order to utilize a multisite configuration, the organization needs to establish a backup site where they can easily relocate their computer equipment if a disaster occurs at their primary location and data center. The backup site needs to be either another location that the company owns and has available to them to implement additional equipment or a space they purchase or rent from another provider for an annual or monthly fee. In either case the organization needs to have a secondary location that it can use to host the computer system in case of a disaster.

There are three types of backup sites an organization can use: a cold site, a warm site, and a hot site. The difference between each site is determined by the administrative effort to implement and maintain them and the costs involved with each type.

Of the three backup site options, the least expensive is the cold site. A cold site does not include any backup copies of data from the organization's original data center. When an organization implements a cold site, they do not have readily available hardware at the site; they only have the physical space and network connectivity for recovery operations, and it is their responsibility to provide the hardware. Because there is no hardware at the backup site, the cost for a cold site is lower; however, not having readily available hardware at the cold site is also one of its downfalls. Since there is no hardware set up and ready to use at the backup site, it takes longer to have the organization up and operating after a disaster.

A hot site, on the other hand, is a duplicate of the original site of the organization and has readily available hardware and a near-complete backup of the organization's data. A hot site can contain a real-time synchronization between the original site and the backup site and can be used to completely mirror the original data center.

If the original site is impacted by a disaster, the hot site is available for the organization to quickly relocate to, with minimal impact on the normal operations of the organization. This is the most expensive type of backup site and is popular with organizations that need this level of disaster recovery, including financial institutions and e-commerce providers.

The third available backup site type is a warm site. A warm site is in between a cold site and a hot site. It has readily available hardware but on a much smaller scale than the original site or a hot site. Warm sites will also have backups at the location, but they may not be complete backups or they might be a few days old.

Determining an acceptable RTO for an organization helps an IT administrator choose between the three types of backup sites. A hot site might have an RTO of a few hours, whereas a cold site might have an RTO of a day or more. It is important that the organization and the IT administrator completely understand the RTO of an application or service and the cost required to operate at that RTO. A hot site provides faster recovery time but is also at a much higher cost than a warm site. While a cold site is the least expensive to set up, it also takes the longest to implement in the event of a disaster. Understanding the benefits and costs of each of the three types of backup sites will help an organization determine which backup type best fits their needs and which backup strategy they should implement.

Backups and Recovery

Selecting the appropriate backup solution is a critical piece of a properly configured disaster recovery implementation. A backup is simply the process of copying and archiving data so that the data is available to be restored to either the original location or an alternate location should the original data be lost, modified, or corrupted. Creating backups of data serves two primary purposes. The first purpose of a backup is to restore data that is lost because either it was deleted or it became corrupt. The second purpose of a backup is to enable recovery of data from an earlier time frame. An organization should have a data retention policy that specifies how long data needs to be kept. For example, if an organization has a data retention policy that specifies all data must be kept for two weeks, an end user who needs to have a document restored from ten days ago could do so. When selecting a backup policy, several things need to be taken into consideration. First, the organization must determine how the backups will be stored, whether on tape or DVD-R media, to a dedicated hard disk, or to a cloud-based storage system. If they are storing data on tapes or DVD-R media, they need to determine if the backups should be stored at an off-site location. Storing backups at an off-site location or in the cloud allows for recovery of the data in the event of a disaster. After choosing a media type, the next step is to choose the style of backup. There are three backup styles that can be implemented: full, incremental, and differential. Each backup style has its own set of advantages and disadvantages.

A full system backup backs up the entire system, including everything on the hard drive. It makes a copy of all the data and files on the drive in a single process. A full backup takes up the most space on storage media because it does a full drive copy every time the backup is executed. So performing a full backup every day requires the same amount of space on the backup media as the drive being backed up. The benefit to a full backup is that an organization can take any of the backups from any day they were executed and restore data from a single backup media. Figure 12-1 shows an example of how a full system backup would look after four backups.

The differential style of backup backs up only those changes that were made since the last full backup was executed. In order to perform a differential backup, a full backup must first be performed. After the full backup is executed, every differential backup executed thereafter will contain only the changes made since the last full backup. One of the disadvantages to differential backups is that the time it takes to complete the backup will increase as files change between the last full backup. Another disadvantage is if the organization wants to restore an entire system to a particular point in time, they must first locate the last full backup taken prior to the point of failure and the last differential backup since the last full backup. Figure 12-2 shows an example of how a differential backup looks after three days.

An incremental backup also backs up only those files that have changed since the last backup was executed, but the last backup can be either a full backup or an incremental backup. This makes incremental backups faster and requires less space. However, the time it takes to perform a restoration is longer because both the last full backup and all the incremental backups must be restored. Figure 12-3 shows an example of how an incremental backup would look after three backups.

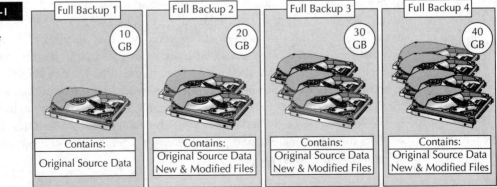

FIGURE 12-1

Illustration of a full system backup.

Full Backup 1 — 10 GB — Contains: Original Source Data

Full Backup 2 — 20 GB — Contains: Original Source Data / New & Modified Files

Full Backup 3 — 30 GB — Contains: Original Source Data / New & Modified Files

Full Backup 4 — 40 GB — Contains: Original Source Data / New & Modified Files

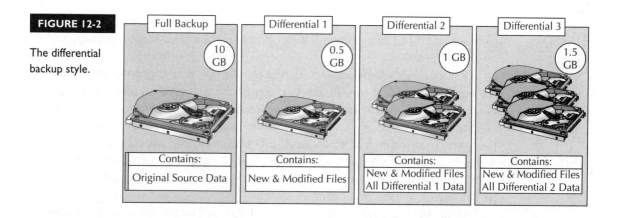

FIGURE 12-2

The differential backup style.

exam

ⓦatch   *Incremental backups require less space to store the backup and complete much more quickly but require more time to perform a restoration.*

Backups are a secondary copy of the organization's data and are used to replace the original data in the event of loss. The backup process needs to be monitored just like any other process that is running in the environment. Proper monitoring of the backup system helps to ensure that the data is available if there is a disaster. Remember, a backup is only as good as the restore strategy that is in place. Testing the restoration process of all the backups in an organization should be done on a scheduled and routine basis. Backups have the ability to be fully automated and scheduled so that they can run without interaction from an administrator. A proper disaster recovery and data retention plan should be established to ensure that no data is lost if a disaster occurs.

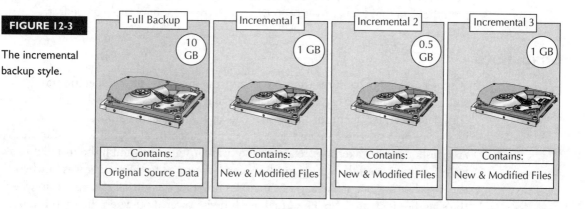

FIGURE 12-3

The incremental backup style.

The backup plan should include how the data is to be stored and, if the data is going to be stored off-site, how long it is kept off-site and how many copies are kept at the off-site facility.

In addition to backups, an organization has the option of capturing an image of the server. When capturing an image, the entire hard drive is captured block by block. Because the entire hard drive was captured, the image can be used to restore an entire server in the event of a disaster, allowing the image to be restored on new hardware. Creating an image of a server differs from the file-based backups discussed earlier in that the file-based backups only allow you to restore what was configured to be backed up, whereas an image allows for the entire restoration of the server, including files, folders, and operating system.

Backups are sometimes confused with replication. The two differ in that backups are created to store unchanged data for a predetermined amount of time, whereas replicas are used to create a mirrored copy of the data between two redundant hardware devices. Replicas help to improve reliability and fault tolerance. When replicating data, the data is stored on multiple storage devices preferably at different locations so that if one location suffers a disaster the other location is available with the exact same data. When replicating data there are two types of replication: synchronous and asynchronous. Synchronous replication copies the data over the network to another device, allowing for multiple copies of up-to-date data. Synchronous replication writes data to both the primary and secondary sites at the same time so both locations have the same data. Synchronous replication is more expensive than asynchronous replication and can impact the performance of the application that is being replicated. With asynchronous replication there is a delay before the data is written to the secondary site. New data can be accepted at the primary site without having to wait for the data to be written to the secondary site. If the primary site fails before the data can be replicated to the secondary site, then the data that had not yet been written to the secondary site may be lost.

Snapshots

A snapshot simply captures the state of a virtual machine at the specific time when the snapshot was taken. While similar to a backup, a snapshot should not be considered a replacement for traditional backups. A virtual machine snapshot can be used to preserve the state and data of a virtual machine at a specific point in time. A snapshot can be taken before a major software installation, and if the installation fails or causes issues, the virtual machine can be restored to the state it was in when the snapshot was taken. A snapshot includes the state the virtual machine is in when the snapshot is created. So if a virtual machine is powered off when the snapshot is created, the virtual machine will be powered off. The snapshot includes all the data and files that make up the virtual machine, including hard disks, memory, and virtual network interface cards. Snapshots and snapshot chains can be created and managed in a variety of different ways. It is possible to create snapshots, revert to any snapshot in the chain, and even delete snapshots. Although snapshots should not replace normal backup software, they are a good way to repeatedly revert a virtual machine to the same state without having to create multiple virtual machines.

Since snapshots are not a replacement for regular backups, they should only be kept for a short period of time, preferably a few days. A snapshot keeps a delta file of all the changes after the snapshot was taken. The delta file records the differences between the current state of the virtual disk and the state the virtual machine was in when the snapshot was taken. So if the snapshot is kept for long periods of time the file can grow and might become too large to remove. This can cause performance issues for the virtual machine. If there is a need to keep a snapshot longer than a few days, it is recommended to create a full system backup.

on the
Ĵob

A few weeks ago we were asked to deploy a new application to a development server. The application was a new application and was being deployed to the development environment because it had never been tested. Instead of taking a backup of the development server prior to installing the application, we simply created a snapshot of the virtual machine before the install in case the new application caused a failure of the server.

CERTIFICATION OBJECTIVE 12.02

High Availability

High availability is a system design approach that ensures a system or component is continuously available for a predefined length of time. Organizations need to have their applications and services available to end users at all times. If the end user cannot access the service or application, it then becomes unavailable, commonly referred to as downtime. Downtime comes in two different forms: scheduled downtime and unscheduled downtime. Scheduled downtime is downtime that has been predefined in a service contract that allows an administrator to perform routine maintenance on a system, like installing critical updates, firmware, or service packs. Unscheduled downtime usually involves interruption to a service or application due to a physical event, such as a power outage, hardware failure, or security breach. Most organizations exclude scheduled downtime from their availability calculation for an application or service as long as the scheduled maintenance does not impact the end users. Making sure that an IT department can meet availability requirements and that an application or service is always available to the end user is a critical component of the organization. In order to guarantee a certain level of availability for an application or service, fault tolerance can be employed.

Fault Tolerance

Fault tolerance allows a computer system to function as normal in the event of a failure in one or more of the system's components. Fault-tolerant systems are designed for high availability and reliability by installing multiple critical components. For example, a virtualization host computer would have multiple CPUs, power supplies, and hard disks in the same physical computer. If one of the components were to fail, the spare component would take over without bringing the system down. However, having a system that is truly fault tolerant does result in greater expense because the system requires additional components to achieve fault-tolerant status.

In addition to adding components to achieve fault tolerance, two or more computers can be connected together to act as a single computer. Connecting multiple computers to provide parallel processing and redundancy is known as clustering. The computers are connected over a fast local area network (LAN), and each node (i.e., each computer used as a server) constituting the cluster runs its own operating system. Clusters can thereby improve performance and availability as compared to using a single computer. In addition to local clustering, there is also the ability to use geoclustering. Geoclustering allows for the connection of multiple redundant computers while those computers are located in different geographical locations. So instead of having the nodes connected over a LAN, the nodes are connected over a wide area network (WAN) but still appear as a single highly available system. Geoclustering allows an organization to support enterprise-level continuity by providing a system that is location independent.

Having an infrastructure that is redundant and highly available helps an organization provide a consistent environment and a more productive workforce. Determining which systems require the investment to be highly available is up to each organization. There will be some systems or applications that do not need to be highly available and do not warrant the cost involved to make them so. One of the benefits of a public cloud model is that the cost of making the systems highly available falls on the cloud provider and allows the cloud consumer to take advantage of that highly available system. If a system is not highly available, it means that the system will fail if a single component fails. For example, if a system

---

e x a m

Ⓦ a t c h *Fault tolerance allows the system to tolerate a fault and to continue to run in spite of it.*

that is not highly available has a single power supply and that power supply fails, then the entire system is lost until the power supply can be replaced. Determining which systems and which applications require redundancy can help reduce costs and administrative overhead. A standard needs to be established to help determine the availability required for each application. An organization might use a scale of 0 to 4 to rate the availability requirements of an application. In that scenario an application that has a rating of 0 would need to be available 99.99% of the time, whereas an application with a rating of 4 might only have to be available 98% of the time. Creating a scale allows an organization to prioritize their applications and appropriately distribute costs so that they can maximize their compute resources.

on the *Recently we worked with an organization to help define their business*
Job *continuity plan (BCP). The organization had never done a BCP and had not envisioned how to start creating a highly available environment. We worked with them on creating the BCP by having them define the importance of all the applications they were currently using. After putting a priority on each of the applications, the organization was able to clearly identify the level of redundancy and availability required for each system to function in an efficient and cost-effective manner.*

Multipathing

Having a fault-tolerant system is a great start to achieving high availability, but it is not the only requirement. When planning for high availability, all aspects of the network must be considered. If the connection between the fault-tolerant systems is a single point of failure, then it is limiting the high availability of the system. Implementing multipathing allows for the configuration of multiple paths for connectivity to a storage device, providing redundancy for the system to connect to the storage device.

Load Balancing

Another form of high availability is load balancing. Load balancing allows you to distribute a workload across multiple computers, networks, and disk drives. Load balancing helps to optimize workloads and resources, allowing for maximum throughput, and helps minimize response times for the end user. Load balancing can also help to create reliability with the use of multiple computers instead of a single computer and is delivered either with dedicated software or hardware. Load balancing uses the resources of multiple systems to provide a single, specific Internet service; it can be used with a website or a file transfer protocol (FTP) site, for example. Load balancing can distribute incoming HTTP requests across multiple web servers in a server farm, which can help distribute the load across multiple servers to prevent overloading any single server. If one of the servers in the server farm starts to become overwhelmed, load balancing begins to distribute HTTP requests to another node in the server farm so that no one node becomes overloaded.

on the
job

Recently we were tasked with creating a solution for a website that was being overwhelmed with incoming requests. The solution was to deploy a hardware load balancer and to add two additional web servers to a server farm. By adding load balancing we were able to distribute the incoming requests across three servers, thus improving performance and reliability for the organization and the website.

In addition to using load balancing, some organizations may want to implement a mirror site. A mirror site is either a hosted website or set of files that reside as exact copies of one another on multiple computers. This mirror copy ensures that the website or files are accessible from multiple locations to increase availability and reduce network traffic on the original site and is updated on a regular basis to reflect any changes in content from the original site. A mirror site can be set up to reflect geographic discrepancies, making it faster to download from various places throughout the world. A site that is heavily used in the United States might have multiple mirror sites throughout the country or even a mirror site in Germany so that the end user who is trying to download the files can access a site that is in closer proximity to their location. Sites that offer a large array of software downloads and have a large amount of network traffic can use mirror sites to meet the demand of the downloads and improve response time for the end user. For example, Microsoft might have multiple mirror sites available for users to download software; or downloads.com might have mirror sites so that end users can retrieve files from a location that is closer to them.

CERTIFICATION SUMMARY

A proper disaster recovery plan (DRP) can help an organization plan for and respond to a disaster by preparing the environment for a variety of disasters with redundancy and failover. An organization can set up a multisite configuration to have a hot site, warm site, or cold site so that in the event something happens to the primary data center the organization can migrate to a secondary data center and continue to operate.

Achieving a highly available computer environment is something that takes careful planning and consideration. There are multiple devices that need to be considered and multiple components in each device that need to be redundant and fault tolerant to truly achieve a highly available environment. High availability helps to prevent unplanned downtime and maintain service level agreements.

KEY TERMS

Use the list below to review the key terms that were discussed in this chapter. The definitions can be found within this chapter and in the glossary.

Disaster recovery plan (DRP)   Documented set of procedures that defines how an organization can recover and protect the IT infrastructure in the event of a disaster

Business continuity plan (BCP)   Documented set of procedures and information about the organization that is collected and maintained so that the organization can continue operations in the event of a disaster

Mean time between failures (MTBF)   The average time a hardware component will function before failing, usually measured in hours

Mean time to repair (MTTR)   The average time it takes to repair a hardware component

Recovery time objective (RTO)   The maximum amount of time a system can be down after a failure or disaster

Recovery point objective (RPO)   The maximum amount of time that data might be lost due to a disaster

Redundant system   A system that is used as a backup to the primary system in case of failure

Failover   The process of switching to a redundant system upon failure of the primary system

Failback   The process of restoring operations to the primary system after a failover

Cold site   A backup site used in the event of a failure, which includes only network connectivity and does not include any backups of the original site or hardware

Warm site   A backup site used in the event of a failure that is somewhere between a cold site and a hot site; it includes some hardware and some backups although the backups could be a few days old

Hot site   A backup site used in the event of a failure that is a duplicate of the original site with complete hardware and backups

Full backup   Starting point for incremental and differential backups that can be restored independently and contains all information on the hard disk

Incremental backup   A backup system that backs up the files that have changed since the last full or incremental backup and requires all incremental backups to perform a restore

Differential backup   A backup system that backs up all files that have changed since the last full backup and requires the last differential and the last full backup to perform a restore

Replica   A mirrored copy of data created between two redundant hardware devices

Synchronous replication   A process of replicating information over a network to a secondary device where the system must wait for the replication to copy the data to the secondary device before proceeding

Asynchronous replication   A process of replicating information over a network to a secondary device where the system is not required to wait for the replication to copy the data to the secondary device before proceeding

Snapshot   A method of capturing the state of a virtual machine at a specific point in time

Fault tolerance   A feature of computer system design that increases reliability by adding multiple hardware components so that the system can continue to function in the event of a single component failure

Load balancing   A means of distributing workloads across multiple computers to optimize resources and throughput and to prevent a single device from being overwhelmed

Mirror site   A duplicate website used to provide improved performance and to reduce network traffic

✓ # TWO-MINUTE DRILL

Disaster Recovery Methods

❑ Organizations should build a disaster recovery plan (DRP) to ensure that they have implemented the proper disaster recovery strategy for their organization.

❑ Mean time between failures (MTBF) is used to determine approximately how long it takes a device to fail.

❑ Mean time to repair (MTTR) defines the amount of time it takes to repair a failed component.

❑ An organization can use recovery time objective (RTO) and recovery point objective (RPO) to help define a DRP.

❑ A redundant system can be used to provide a backup to the primary system in case the primary system fails.

❑ Failover allows a system to automatically switch to a redundant system in the event the primary system fails.

❑ Organizations can implement a multisite configuration to create a backup site at an alternate location that allows the environment to be quickly relocated.

❑ A cold site does not include any backups or hardware. It is a physical location that has network connectivity where an organization can move their equipment in case of a failure.

❑ A hot site is a duplicate of the original site and has readily available hardware and a near-complete backup of the organization's data.

❑ A warm site is a combination of a hot and cold site and has readily available hardware but at a much smaller scale than a hot site.

❑ A backup is the process of copying and archiving data so that it is available to be restored in case the original data is lost or corrupted.

❑ Full system backups back up the entire system, including everything on the hard drive.

❑ Incremental backups back up only the files that have changed since the last backup and require the last full backup plus all the incremental backups to perform a restore.

❑ Differential backups only back up the changes since the last full backup and require the last full backup and the last differential to perform a restore.

❏ Backups are different from replication in that backups are created to store unchanged data for a predetermined amount of time and replicas are used to create a mirrored copy of data between two redundant hardware devices.

❏ Snapshots are used to preserve the state of a virtual machine at a specific point in time. While similar to a backup, snapshots should not be considered a replacement for traditional backups.

High Availability

❏ High availability is a system design approach that ensures a system or component is continuously available for a predefined amount of time.

❏ Fault tolerance allows a computer system to function as normal in the event of a failure in one or more of the system's components.

❏ Geoclustering allows an organization to support enterprise-level continuity by providing a system that is location independent.

❏ A system that is not highly available will fail if a single component fails.

❏ Multipathing allows the configuration of multiple paths of connectivity to a storage device, providing redundancy for the connection to the storage device.

❏ Load balancing is achieved through either software or a dedicated hardware device and distributes incoming HTTP requests across multiple web servers in a server farm to provide redundancy and maximize throughput.

❏ A mirror site can be used to create an exact copy of the original site to offset connection requests and improve performance for end users.

SELF TEST

The following questions will help you measure your understanding of the material presented in this chapter.

Disaster Recovery Methods

1. Which of the following would be considered a cold site?
   A. A site with no heating system
   B. A site that has a replication enabled
   C. A site that is fully functional and staffed
   D. A site that provides only network connectivity and a physical location

2. You are designing a disaster recovery plan that includes a multisite configuration. The backup site must include all necessary hardware and current backups of the original site. Which type of site do you need to design?
   A. Cold site
   B. Warm site
   C. Hot site
   D. Virtual site

3. Which of the following is a documented set of procedures that defines how an organization recovers and protects their IT infrastructure in the event of a disaster?
   A. MTBF
   B. MTTR
   C. RPO
   D. DRP

4. Which term is used to describe the maximum amount of time that a system can be down after a failure or a disaster occurs?
   A. RPO
   B. RTO
   C. BCP
   D. MTBF

5. An organization recently had a disaster and the data center failed over to the backup site. The original data center has been restored and the administrator needs to migrate the organization back to the primary data center. What process is the administrator performing?

   A. Failover

   B. Failback

   C. DRP

   D. RTO

6. Which of the following backup processes needs the last backup and all additional backups since that backup to perform a restore?

   A. Incremental

   B. Differential

   C. Full

   D. Image

7. Which of the following backups could be restored without any additional backups?

   A. Incremental

   B. Differential

   C. Full

   D. Image

8. What is the easiest method for an administrator to capture the state of a virtual machine at a specific point in time?

   A. Backup

   B. Snapshot

   C. Image

   D. Clone

9. Which of the following processes allows a system to automatically switch to a redundant system in the event of a disaster at the primary site?

   A. Failback

   B. DRP

   C. Failover

   D. Redundancy

High Availability

10. You have been tasked with distributing incoming HTTP requests to multiple servers in a server farm. Which of the following is the easiest way to achieve that goal?
   - **A.** Mirror site
   - **B.** Fault tolerance
   - **C.** Redundancy
   - **D.** Load balancing

11. When replicating data in a multisite configuration from the primary site to a backup site, which form of synchronization requires the system to wait before proceeding with the next data write?
   - **A.** Asynchronous replication
   - **B.** Synchronous replication
   - **C.** Failover
   - **D.** Mirror site

12. Which of the following terms can be used to describe a system that is location independent and provides failover?
   - **A.** Clustering
   - **B.** Load balancing
   - **C.** Geoclustering
   - **D.** Failover

SELF TEST ANSWERS

Disaster Recovery Methods

1. Which of the following would be considered a cold site?
   A. A site with no heating system
   B. A site that has a replication enabled
   C. A site that is fully functional and staffed
   D. A site that provides only network connectivity and a physical location

   ☑ **D.** A cold site does not include any backup copies of data from the organization's original data center. When an organization implements a cold site, they do not have readily available hardware at the site; it only includes the physical space and network connectivity for recovery operations and it is the organization's responsibility to provide the hardware.
   ☒ **A, B,** and **C** are incorrect. A site that has replication enabled would not be considered a cold site. Also, a cold site would not be fully functional and staffed.

2. You are designing a disaster recovery plan that includes a multisite configuration. The backup site must include all necessary hardware and current backups of the original site. Which type of site do you need to design?
   A. Cold site
   B. Warm site
   C. Hot site
   D. Virtual site

   ☑ **C.** A hot site is a duplicate of the original site of the organization and has readily available hardware and a near-complete backup of the organization's data. A hot site can contain a real-time synchronization between the original site and the backup site and can be used to completely mirror the organization's original data center.
   ☒ **A, B,** and **D** are incorrect. A cold site does not include any backup copies of data from the organization's original data center. A warm site is a combination of a cold site and a hot site and would not include a current backup of the original site.

3. Which of the following is a documented set of procedures that defines how an organization recovers and protects their IT infrastructure in the event of a disaster?
   A. MTBF
   B. MTTR

C. RPO

D. DRP

☑ **D.** A DRP (disaster recovery plan) describes how an organization is going to deal with recovery in the event of a disaster.

☒ **A, B,** and **C** are incorrect. MTBF is the average time a hardware component will function before failing, usually measured in hours. MTTR is the average time it takes to repair a hardware component. RPO is the maximum amount of time that data might be lost due to a disaster.

4. Which term is used to describe the maximum amount of time that a system can be down after a failure or a disaster occurs?

A. RPO

B. RTO

C. BCP

D. MTBF

☑ **B.** RTO (recovery time objective) is the maximum amount of time a system can be down after a failure or disaster.

☒ **A, C,** and **D** are incorrect. RPO is the maximum amount of time that data might be lost due to a disaster. A BCP is a documented set of procedures and information about the organization that is collected and maintained so that the organization can continue operations in the event of a disaster. MTBF is the average time a hardware component will function before failing, usually measured in hours.

5. An organization recently had a disaster and the data center failed over to the backup site. The original data center has been restored and the administrator needs to migrate the organization back to the primary data center. What process is the administrator performing?

A. Failover

B. Failback

C. DRP

D. RTO

☑ **B.** Failback is the process of switching back to the primary site after the environment has been shifted to the backup site.

☒ **A, C,** and **D** are incorrect. Failover is the process of switching to a redundant system upon failure of the primary system. A DRP is a documented set of procedures that defines how an organization can recover and protect their IT infrastructure in the event of a disaster. RTO is the maximum amount of time a system can be down after a failure or disaster.

6. Which of the following backup processes needs the last backup and all additional backups since that backup to perform a restore?

   A. Incremental
   B. Differential
   C. Full
   D. Image

   ☑ **A.** An incremental backup backs up the files that have changed since the last full or incremental backup and requires all incremental backups to perform a restore.
   ☒ **B, C,** and **D** are incorrect. A differential backup backs up all files that have changed since the last full backup and requires the latest differential and the last full backup to perform a restore. A full backup is a starting point for incremental and differential backups that can be restored independently and contains all the information on the hard disk. An image is an exact copy of a system at the time the image was taken.

7. Which of the following backups could be restored without any additional backups?

   A. Incremental
   B. Differential
   C. Full
   D. Image

   ☑ **C.** A full backup backs up the entire system, including everything on the hard drive. It does not require any additional backups to perform a restore.
   ☒ **A, B,** and **D** are incorrect. An incremental backup backs up the files that have changed since the last full or incremental backup and requires all incremental backups to perform a restore. A differential backup backs up all files that have changed since the last full backup and requires the last differential and the last full backup to perform a restore. An image is just an exact copy of a system at the time the image was taken.

8. What is the easiest method for an administrator to capture the state of a virtual machine at a specific point in time?

   A. Backup
   B. Snapshot
   C. Image
   D. Clone

☑ **B.** Snapshots can be used capture the state of a virtual machine at a specific point in time. They can contain a copy of current disk state as well as memory state.

☒ **A, C,** and **D** are incorrect. A backup could be used to capture the state of a virtual machine if the administrator used a full backup, but the process takes considerably more time to complete than a snapshot and would not be the easiest method. An image is an exact copy of a system at the time the image was taken and would take a considerable amount of time. A clone would copy the entire contents of a disk to another disk but again would take a considerable amount of time, whereas a snapshot takes only a few seconds or minutes to complete.

9. Which of the following processes allows a system to automatically switch to a redundant system in the event of a disaster at the primary site?

   A. Failback
   B. DRP
   C. Failover
   D. Redundancy

☑ **C.** Failover is the process of switching to a redundant system upon failure of the primary system.

☒ **A, B,** and **D** are incorrect. Failback is the process of switching back to the primary site after the environment has been shifted to the backup site. A DRP is a documented set of procedures that defines how an organization can recover and protect their IT infrastructure in the event of a disaster. Redundancy is used to protect a primary system from failure by performing the operations of a backup system.

High Availability

10. You have been tasked with distributing incoming HTTP requests to multiple servers in a server farm. Which of the following is the easiest way to achieve that goal?

    A. Mirror site
    B. Fault tolerance
    C. Redundancy
    D. Load balancing

☑ **D.** Load balancing distributes workloads across multiple computers to optimize resources and throughput and to prevent a single device from being overwhelmed.

☒ **A, B,** and **C** are incorrect. A mirror site is a duplicate website used to provide improved performance and reduce network traffic. Fault tolerance involves adding multiple hardware components to the system so it can continue to function in the event of a single component failure. Redundancy is used to protect a primary system from failure by performing the operations of a backup system. None of these options deals with balanced distribution of workloads.

11. When replicating data in a multisite configuration from the primary site to a backup site, which form of synchronization requires the system to wait before proceeding with the next data write?

A. Asynchronous replication

B. Synchronous replication

C. Failover

D. Mirror site

☑ **B.** Synchronous replication replicates information over a network to a secondary device where the system must wait for the replication to copy the data to the secondary device before proceeding.

☒ **A, C,** and **D** are incorrect. Asynchronous replication replicates information over a network to secondary devices where the system is not required to wait for the replication to copy the data to the secondary device before proceeding. Failover is the process of switching to a redundant system upon failure of the primary system. A mirror site is a duplicate website used to provide improved performance and reduce network traffic.

12. Which of the following terms can be used to describe a system that is location independent and provides failover?

A. Clustering

B. Load balancing

C. Geoclustering

D. Failover

☑ **C.** Geoclustering uses multiple redundant systems that are located in different geographical locations to provide failover and yet appear as a single highly available system.

☒ **A, B,** and **D** are incorrect. Clustering connects computers together over a LAN, whereas geoclustering enables connections over a WAN. Load balancing distributes workloads across multiple computers to optimize resources and throughput and to prevent a single device from being overwhelmed. Failover is the process of switching to a redundant system upon failure of the primary system.

A

About the CD

T he CD-ROM included with this book comes complete with two MasterExam practice exams and the electronic book in PDF format.

System Requirements

The MasterExam software requires Windows XP Pro, Service Pack 2 or later and Internet Explorer 8.0 or later, and 200 MB of hard disk space for full installation. The electronic book requires Adobe Acrobat Reader.

Installing and Running MasterExam

If your computer CD-ROM drive is configured to auto run, the CD-ROM will automatically start up upon inserting the disk. From the opening screen, you may install MasterExam by clicking the MasterExam link. This will begin the installation process and create a program group named LearnKey.

To run MasterExam, select Start | All Programs | LearnKey | MasterExam. If the auto run feature does not launch your CD-ROM, browse to the CD-ROM and click the LaunchTraining.exe icon.

MasterExam

MasterExam provides a simulation of the actual exam. The number of questions, the type of questions, and the time allowed are intended to be an accurate representation of the exam environment. You have the option to take an open book exam (including answers), a closed book exam, or the timed MasterExam simulation.

When you launch MasterExam, a digital clock display will appear in the bottom right-hand corner of your screen. The clock will continue to count down to zero (unless you choose to end the exam before the time expires).

Help

You can access the help file by clicking the Help button on the main page (in the lower left corner). An individual help feature is also available through MasterExam.

Removing Installation(s)

MasterExam is installed to your hard drive. For best results removing the program, use the Start | All Programs | LearnKey | Uninstall option.

Electronic Book

The entire contents of the book are provided in PDF format on the CD-ROM. This file is viewable on your computer and many portable devices. Adobe's Acrobat Reader is required to view the file on your PC and has been included on the CD-ROM. You may also use Adobe Digital Editions to access your electronic book.

For more information on Adobe Reader, and to check for the most recent version of the software, visit Adobe's website at www.adobe.com and search for the free Adobe Reader or look for Adobe Reader on the product page. Adobe Digital Editions can also be downloaded from the Adobe website.

To view the electronic book on a portable device, copy the PDF file to your computer from the CD-ROM and then copy the file to your portable device using a USB or other connection. Adobe does offer a mobile version of Adobe Reader, the Adobe Reader mobile app, which currently supports iOS and Android. For customers using Adobe Digital Editions and the iPad, you may have to download and install a separate reader program on your device. The Adobe website has a list of recommended applications. McGraw-Hill Education recommends the Bluefire Reader.

Technical Support

Technical support information is provided in the following sections by feature.

LearnKey Technical Support

For technical problems with the software (installation, operation, removing installations), please visit www.learnkey.com, e-mail techsupport@learnkey.com, or call toll free at 1-800-482-8244.

McGraw-Hill Content Support

For questions regarding the electronic book, videos, or additional resources, e-mail techsolutions@mhedu.com or visit http://mhp.softwareassist.com.

For questions regarding book content, please e-mail customer.service @mheducation.com. For customers outside the United States, e-mail international .cs@mheducation.com.

Glossary

Address resolution protocol (ARP) Protocol used to resolve IP addresses to media access control (MAC) addresses

Advanced technology attachment (ATA) Disk drive implementation that integrates the drive and the controller

Anything as a Service (XaaS) Cloud model that delivers IT as a service through hybrid cloud computing and works with a combination of SaaS, IaaS, PaaS, CaaS, DBaaS, or BPaaS

Approval process Set of activities that presents all relevant information to stakeholders and allows an informed decision to be made about a request for change

Asset accountability The documented assignment of a CI to a human resource

Asymmetric encryption Encryption mechanism that uses two different keys to encrypt and decrypt data

Asynchronous replication A process of replicating information over a network to a secondary device where the system is not required to wait for the replication to copy the data to the secondary device before proceeding

Automated event responses Automation of minute tasks that continuously generate alerts on a computer system

Backout plan Action plan that allows a change to be reverted to its previous baseline state

Bandwidth The amount of data that can be transferred from one network location to another in a specific amount of time

Basic input/output system (BIOS) Built-in software that allows the computer to boot without an operating system and controls the code required to manage the keyboard, display, disk drives, and a number of other functions

Block cipher A method of converting plaintext to cipher text in bulk as opposed to one data bit at a time, either using a fixed secret key or by generating keys from each encrypted block

Bus Communication system used to transfer data between the components inside of a computer motherboard, processor, or network device. It gets its name from the concept of a bus line where it stops and allows people to get off and board. It is a communication system that is attached at many points along the bus line.

Business continuity plan (BCP) Documented set of procedures and information about the organization that is collected and maintained so that the organization can continue operations in the event of a disaster

Business Process as a Service (BPaaS) Any business process that is delivered as a service by utilizing a cloud solution

Caching Process of transparently storing data at a quicker response location so that any future requests for that data can be accessed faster than through the slower medium

Capacity management A process to ensure that the capacity of IT services and the IT infrastructure is able to meet agreed capacity- and performance-related requirements in a cost-effective and timely manner

Central processing unit (CPU) Hardware device responsible for executing all of the instructions from the operating system and software

Certificate authority (CA) Entity that issues digital certificates and makes its public keys available to the intended audience to provide proof of its authenticity

Change management The process of making changes to the IT environment from its design phase to its operations phase in the least impactful way possible

Chargeback An accounting strategy that attempts to decentralize the costs of IT services and apply them directly to the teams or divisions that utilize those services

Cipher text Data that has been encrypted using a mathematical algorithm

Cloud bursting Allows an application running in a private cloud to burst into a public cloud on an on-demand basis

Cold site A backup site used in the event of a failure, which includes only network connectivity and does not include any backups of the original site or hardware

Communication as a Service (CaaS) Allows a cloud consumer to utilize enterprise-level voice over IP (VoIP), virtual private networks (VPNs), private branch exchange (PBX), and unified communications using a cloud model

Community cloud Cloud model where the infrastructure is shared between several organizations from a specific group with common computing needs and objectives

Compression Reduction in the size of data being traversed across the network

Compute resources   The resources that are required for the delivery of virtual machines: disk, processor, memory, and networking

Configuration control   The ability to maintain updated, accurate documentation of all configuration items (CIs)

Configuration management   The process that ensures all assets required to deliver IT services are controlled, and that accurate and reliable information about them is available when and where it is needed, including details of how the assets have been configured and the relationships between assets

Configuration management database (CMDB)   Database used to store configuration records throughout their life cycle. The configuration management system maintains one or more CMDBs, and each database stores attributes of configuration items and relationships with other configuration items.

Configuration standardization   Documented baseline configuration for similar configuration items

Console port   Allows an administrator to use a cable to directly connect to a hypervisor host computer or virtual machine

CPU wait time   The delay that results when the CPU can't perform computations because it is waiting on I/O operations

Data BLOB   Collection of binary data stored as a single entity

Data classification   Practice of sorting data into discrete categories that help define the access levels and type of protection required for that set of data

Data encryption   Algorithmic scheme that secures data by scrambling into a code that is not readable by unauthorized resources

Database as a Service (DBaaS)   Cloud model that delivers database operations as a service to multiple cloud consumers over the Internet

Differential backup   A backup system that backs up all files that have changed since the last full backup and requires the last differential and the last full backup to perform a restore

Digital signature   Mathematical hash of a dataset that is encrypted by the private key and used to validate that dataset

Direct attached storage (DAS)   Storage system that is directly attached to a server or workstation and cannot be used as shared storage

Disaster recovery plan (DRP)   Documented set of procedures that defines how an organization can recover and protect the IT infrastructure in the event of a disaster

Discretionary access control (DAC)   Security mechanism in which the power to grant or deny permissions to resources lies with the data owner

Documentation   Written copy of a procedure, policy, or configuration

Domain information groper (dig)   Command-line tool for querying domain name system (DNS) servers operating in both interactive mode and batch query mode

Domain name system (DNS)   Translates Internet domain or host names into IP addresses

Dynamic host configuration protocol (DHCP)   Network protocol that automatically assigns IP addresses from a predefined range of numbers called a scope to computers on a network

Elasticity   Allows an organization to dynamically provision and de-provision processing, memory, and storage resources to meet the demands of the network

Encrypted File System (EFS)   A feature of the NTFS file system that provides file-level encryption

Extended file system (EXT)   First file system created specifically for Linux where the metadata and file structure is based on the Unix file system

Extranet   Extension of an Intranet with the difference being an Extranet allows access to the network from outside the organization

Failback   The process of restoring operations to the primary system after a failover

Failover   The process of switching to a redundant system upon failure of the primary system

Fault tolerance   A feature of computer system design that increases reliability by adding multiple hardware components so that the system can continue to function in the event of a single component failure

Federation   Use of SSO to authorize users or devices to many different protected network resources, such as file servers, websites, and database applications

Fibre Channel (FC)   Technology used to transmit data between computers at data rates of up to 10 Gbps

Fibre Channel over Ethernet (FCoE)   Enables the transport of Fibre Channel traffic over Ethernet networks by encapsulating Fibre Channel frames over Ethernet networks

Fibre Channel protocol (FCP)   Transport protocol that transports SCSI commands over a Fibre Channel network

File allocation table (FAT)   Legacy file system used in Microsoft operating systems and is still used today by a variety of removable media

File transfer protocol (FTP)   Network protocol that allows for access to and the transfer of files over the Internet using either the command-line or graphical-based FTP client

File transfer protocol secure (FTPS)   Uses secure sockets layer (SSL) or transport layer security (TLS) to secure the transfer of files over FTP

Firmware   Set of instructions that are programmed for a specific hardware device that instructs the hardware device how to communicate with the computer system

Full backup   Starting point for incremental and differential backups that can be restored independently and contains all information on the hard disk

Guest tools   Software additions that are added to a virtual machine after the operating system has been installed to improve the interaction between the virtual machine and the virtualization host

Hard disk drive (HDD)   Uses rapidly rotating aluminum or non-magnetic disks called platters coated with a magnetic material known as ferrous oxide to store and retrieve digital information in any order rather than only being accessible sequentially, as in the case of data on a tape

Hardening   Ensuring that a system or network is configured in such a way that reduces the risk of attack from either internal or external sources

Hardware-assisted virtualization   Enables efficient full virtualization used to simulate a complete hardware environment or a virtual machine

Hierarchical Storage Management (HSM) Allows for automatically moving data among four different tiers of storage

Hop count The total number of devices a packet passes through in order to reach its intended network target

Host bus adapter (HBA) A network card that allows a device to communicate directly with a storage area network (SAN) or a SAN switch

Hot site A backup site used in the event of a failure that is a duplicate of the original site with complete hardware and backups

Hybrid cloud Cloud model that utilizes both private and public clouds to perform distinct functions within the same organization

Hypertext transfer protocol (HTTP) Protocol used to distribute HTML files, text, images, sound, videos, multimedia files, and other information over the Internet

Hypertext transfer protocol secure (HTTPS) An extension of the HTTP protocol that provides secure communication over the Internet using secure sockets layer (SSL) or transport layer security (TLS)

Hypervisor Piece of software or hardware that creates and runs a virtual machine and allows multiple operating systems to run on a single physical computer

I/O throttling Defined limits utilized specifically for disk resources assigned to virtual machines to ensure they are not performance or availability constrained when working in an environment that has more demand than availability of disk resources

Ifconfig Interface configuration utility to configure and query TCP/IP network interface settings from a Unix or Linux command line

Incremental backup A backup system that backs up the files that have changed since the last full or incremental backup and requires all incremental backups to perform a restore

Infrastructure as a Service (IaaS) Cloud model where the cloud consumer outsources responsibility for their infrastructure to an external cloud provider that owns the equipment, such as storage, servers, and connectivity domains

Integrated drive electronics (IDE) Integrates the controller and the hard drive, allowing the manufacturer to use proprietary communication and storage methods without any compatibility risks for connecting directly to the motherboard

Intelligent platform management interface (IPMI) Used for out-of-band management of a computer allowing an administrator to manage a system remotely without an operating system

Internet Global system of interconnected computer networks that is not controlled by a single organization or country.

Internet control message protocol (ICMP) A protocol that is part of the Internet protocol suite used primarily for diagnostic purposes

Internet small computer system interface (iSCSI) The communication protocol that leverages standard IP packets to transmit typical SCSI commands across an IP network; it then translates them back to standard SCSI commands, which enables servers to access remote disks as if they were locally attached

Intranet Private network that is configured and controlled by a single organization and is only accessible to users that are internal to that organization

IOPS Input/output operations per second

Ipconfig Command-line tool to display TCP/IP network configuration settings and troubleshoot dynamic host configuration protocol (DHCP) and domain name system (DNS) settings

Jumbo frames Large frames that are used with large data transfers to lessen the burden on processors

Latency The delay in time calculated from the time a service request is made until that request is fulfilled. Typically used to describe network and hard drive speeds.

Limit A floor or ceiling on the amount of resources that can be utilized for a given entity

Load balancing Distributes workloads across multiple computers to optimize resources and throughput for preventing a single device from being overwhelmed

Local area network (LAN) Network topology that spans relatively small areas like an office building and allows people to share files, devices, printers, and applications

Logical unit numbers (LUNs)   Unique identifier used to identify a logical unit or collection of hard disks in a storage device

LUN masking   Makes a LUN available to some hosts and unavailable to others

Maintenance windows   An agreed upon, predefined time period during which service interruptions are least impactful to the business. This could fall at any time, and depends on the patterns of business activity for that particular entity.

Mandatory access control (MAC)   Security mechanism in which access is mandated by the operating system or application and not by data owners

Mean time between failures (MTBF)   The average time a hardware component will function before failing, usually measured in hours

Mean time to repair (MTTR)   The average time it takes to repair a hardware component

Memory ballooning   A device driver loaded inside a guest operating system that identifies underutilized memory and allows the host to reclaim memory for redistribution

Mesh   Network topology where every node is interconnected to every other node in the network

Metadata   Data about data, used to describe particular attributes of data including how the data is formatted

Metadata performance   A measure of how quickly files and directories can be created, removed, or checked on a disk resource

Metering   The ability of a cloud platform to track the use of its IT resources; this is focused primarily on measuring usage by cloud consumers

Metropolitan area network (MAN)   Network topology connecting multiple LANs together to span a large area like a city or a large campus

Mirror site   A duplicate website used to provide improved performance and to reduce network traffic

Monitoring for changes   Process of watching the production environment for any unplanned configuration changes

Multifactor authentication   Authentication of resources using proof from more than one of the three authentication categories: something you know, something you have, and something you are

Multipathing   Creates multiple paths for a computer to reach a storage resource

Multitenancy   Architecture providing a single instance of an application to serve multiple clients or tenants

N_Port ID Virtualization (NPIV)   Allows multiple host computers to share a single physical Fibre Channel port identification or N_Port

Netstat   Command-line tool that displays network statistics, including current connections and routing tables

Network address translation (NAT)   Allows a router to modify packets so that multiple devices can share a single public IP address

Network assessment   Objective review of an organization's network infrastructure in terms of functionality and security capabilities, used to establish a baseline for future audits

Network attached storage (NAS)   Provides file-level data storage to a network over TCP/IP

Network audit   Objective periodic review of an organization's network infrastructure against an established baseline

Network interface card (NIC)   Computer component that is used to connect a computer to a computer network

Network isolation   Allows for a section of the network to be isolated from another section so that multiple identical copies of the environment are executed at the same time

Network latency   Any delays typically incurred during the processing of any network data

Network shares   Storage resources that are made available across a network and appear as if they are a resource on the local machine

New technology file system (NTFS)   Proprietary file system developed by Microsoft to support the Windows operating systems; it was originally derived from a joint effort with IBM to provide a common OS called OS2, which used the HPFS or High Performance File

Nslookup   Command-line tool used to query DNS mappings for resource records

Object ID   Unique identifier used to name an object

Offline migration   Migrates a physical server to a virtual machine by taking the source computer offline so that it is not available during the migration process

On-demand self-service/just-in-time service   Gives cloud consumers access to cloud services through an online portal allowing them to acquire computing resources automatically and on demand without human interaction from the cloud provider

Online migration   Migrates a physical server to a virtual machine while the source computer remains available during the migration process

Open source   Hypervisor software provided at no cost and delivers the same ability to run multiple guest virtual machines on a single host

Orchestration   Process of automating tasks based upon specific thresholds or events

Out-of-band management   Allows for remote management and monitoring of a computer system without the need for an operating system

Pay as you grow   A concept in cloud computing where you pay for cloud resources as an organization needs those resources

Penetration testing   Process of evaluating network security with a simulated attack on the network from both external and internal attackers

Performance baselines   Performance chart displaying current performance of the environment

Physical to virtual (P2V)   Process of migrating a physical server's operating system, applications, and data from the physical server to a newly created guest virtual machine on a virtualization host

Ping   Command-line utility used to test the reachability of a destination host on an IP network

Plaintext   Unencrypted data

Platform as a Service (PaaS) Cloud model that provides the infrastructure to create applications and host them with a cloud provider

Policies Rule sets by which users and administrators must abide

Port address translation (PAT) Mapping of both ports and IP addresses from a private to a public system

Ports Application-specific endpoint to a logical connection

Private cloud Cloud delivery model that is owned and maintained by a single organization; it is implemented behind the corporate firewall that enables an organization to centrally access IT resources

Private key One-half of the keys used for asymmetric encryption, a private key is available only to the intended data user and is used only for data decryption

Procedures Prescribed methodologies by which activities are carried out in the IT environment according to defined policies

Proprietary Software that is developed and licensed under an exclusive legal right of the copyright holder

Public cloud A pool of computing resources and services delivered over the Internet by a cloud provider

Public key One-half of the keys used for asymmetric encryption, a public key is available to anyone and is used only for data encryption

Public key infrastructure (PKI) Hierarchy of trusted security certificates issued to users or computing devices

Quality of Service (QoS) A set of technologies that provide the ability to manage network traffic and prioritize workloads in order to accommodate defined service levels as part of a cost-effective solution

Quota The total amount of resources that can be utilized for a system

RAID Storage technology that combines multiple hard disk drives into a single logical unit so that the data can be distributed across the hard disk drives for both improved performance and increased security according to their various RAID levels

Read operations Operations in which a resource requests data from a disk resource

Recovery point objective (RPO)   The maximum amount of time that data might be lost due to a disaster

Recovery time objective (RTO)   The maximum amount of time a system can be down after a failure or disaster

Redundant system   A system that is used as a backup to the primary system in case of failure

Remote desktop protocol (RDP)   Provides remote display and input capabilities over a computer network

Remote hypervisor access   The ability to manage a hypervisor from another computer across a network

Remote shell (RSH)   Command-line program that executes shell commands across a network in an unsecured manner

Replicas   Used to create a mirrored copy of data between two redundant hardware devices

Reservation   A mechanism that ensures a lower limit is enforced for the amount of resources guaranteed to an entity

Resource pooling   Allows compute resources to be pooled to serve multiple consumers by using a multitenant model

Resource pools   Partitions of compute resources from a single host or a cluster of hosts

Ring   Network topology where each node is connected to another forming a circle or a ring

Role-based access control (RBAC)   Security mechanism in which all access is granted through predefined collections of permissions, called roles, instead of implicitly assigning access to users or resources individually

Router   Device that connects multiple networks together and allows a network to communicate with the outside world

Routing tables   Data table stored on a router used by the router to determine the destination of network packets it is responsible for routing

Scalability   Ability of a system or network to manage a growing workload in a proficient manner or its ability to be expanded to accommodate the workload growth

Secure file transfer protocol (SFTP)   Provides secure access to files, file transfers, file editing, and file management over the Internet using secure shell (SSH)

Secure shell (SSH)   Used to secure logins, file transfers, and port forwarding

Secure shell file transfer protocol (SSH)   Used to secure logins, file transfers, and port forwarding

Separation of duties   Divides tasks and privileges among multiple individuals to help reduce potential damage caused by the actions of a single administrator

Serial ATA (SATA)   Used to connect host bus adapters to mass storage devices

Serial attached SCSI (SAS)   Data transfer technology that was designed to replace SCSI and to transfer data to and from storage devices

Server message block (SMB)   Network protocol used to provide shared access to files and printers

Server upgrades and patches   Updates to the software running on servers that can either provide fixes for known errors or add functionality

Shared resources   Allows a cloud provider to provide compute resources as a centralized resource and distribute those resources on an as-needed basis to the cloud consumer

Short message service (SMS)   Text messaging service that allows an alert to be sent to a mobile device

Simple mail transfer protocol (SMTP)   Protocol used to send electronic messages (e-mail) over the Internet

Simple network management protocol (SNMP)   Commonly supported protocol on devices such as routers, switches, printers, and servers and can be used to monitor those devices for any issues

Single sign-on (SSO)   Authentication process in which the resource requesting access can enter one set of credentials and use those credentials to access multiple applications or datasets, even if they have separate authorization mechanisms

Small computer system interface (SCSI)   Set of standard electronic interfaces accredited by the American National Standards Institute (ANSI) for connecting and transferring data between computers and storage devices

Snapshot   A method of capturing the state of a virtual machine at a specific point in time

Software as a Service (SaaS)   Cloud model that allows a cloud consumer the ability to use on-demand software applications delivered by the cloud provider via the Internet

Solid state drive (SSD)   High-performance storage device that contains no moving parts

Star   Network topology where each node is connected to a central hub or switch and the nodes communicate by sending data through the central hub

Storage area network (SAN)   Storage device that resides on its own network and provides block-level access to computers that are attached to it

Storage migration   Process of transferring data between storage devices allowing data from a virtual machine to be migrated to a new location and across storage arrays while maintaining continuous availability and service to the virtual machine

Storage virtualization   Groups multiple network storage devices into a single storage unit that can be managed from a central console and presented to a virtual machine or host computer as a single storage unit

Stream cipher   A method of converting plaintext to cipher text one bit at a time

Subnetting   Creates subnetworks through the logical subdivision of IP networks

Supernetting   Combines multiple networks into one larger network

Switch   Network device that connects multiple devices together on the same network or LAN

Symmetric encryption   Encryption mechanism that uses a single key to both encrypt and decrypt data

Synchronous replication   A process of replicating information over a network to a secondary device where the system must wait for the replication to copy the data to the secondary device before proceeding

Syslog   Provides a mechanism for a network device to send event messages to a logging server or a syslog server

Syslog server   Computer used as a centralized repository for syslog messages

System logs   Files that store a variety of information about system events, including device changes, device drivers, and system changes

Systems life cycle management   The process or processes put in place by an organization to assist in the management, coordination, control, delivery, and support of their configuration items from requirement to retirement

Tape   Storage device for saving data by using digital recordings on magnetic tape

Telnet   A terminal emulation program for TCP/IP networks that connects the user's computer to another computer on the network

Thick provisioning   Allocates the amount of disk space required when the virtual disk is created

Thin provisioning   Allows a virtual disk to allocate and commit storage space on demand and use only the space it currently requires

Thresholds   Used to set the amount of resources that can be consumed before an alert is generated

Throughput   The amount of data that can be realized between two network resources

Time-to-live (TTL)   The length of time that a router or caching name server stores a record

Traceroute   Utility to record the route and measure the delay of packets across an IP network

Tracert   Microsoft Windows command-line utility that tracks a packet from your computer to a destination host displaying how many hops the packet takes to reach the destination host

Tree   Network topology containing multiple star networks that are connected through a linear bus backbone

Trending   The pattern of measurements over the course of multiple time periods

Type 1 hypervisor   Hypervisor that is created and deployed on a bare metal installation

Type 2 hypervisor   Hypervisor loaded on top of an already existing operating system installation

Ubiquitous access   Allows a cloud service to be widely accessible via a web browser from anywhere, allowing for the same level of access either from home or work

Unix file system (UFS)   Primary file system for Unix and Unix-based operating systems that uses a hierarchical file system structure where the highest level of the directory is called the root (/, pronounced "slash") and all other directories span from that root

USB drive   External plug-and-play storage device that is plugged into a computer's USB port and recognized by the computer as a removable drive and assigned a drive letter

Virtual CPU (vCPU)   Used on a guest virtual machine and is similar to a physical CPU

Virtual data center   Provides compute resources, network infrastructure, external storage, backups, and security similar to a physical data center

Virtual disk   Emulates a physical disk drive to a virtual machine

Virtual local area network (VLAN)   Partitions a physical network to create separate, independent broadcast domains that are part of the same physical network

Virtual machine cloning   Allows a virtual machine to be copied either once or multiple times for testing

Virtual machine file system (VMFS)   VMware's cluster file system used with VMware ESX server and vSphere and created to store virtual machine disk images, including virtual machine snapshots

Virtual machine templates   Provides a standardized group of hardware and software settings that can be reused multiple times to create a new virtual machine that is configured with those specified settings

Virtual machine/guest   Emulates a physical computer where the virtualization host translates requests for compute resources to the underlying physical hardware

Virtual NIC (vNIC)   Similar to a physical NIC and has the ability to connect to a virtual switch and be assigned an IP address, default gateway, and subnet mask

Virtual switch   Similar to a physical switch, it allows network devices to be connected and is used to control how the network traffic flows between the virtual machines and the virtualization host

Virtual to physical (V2P)   Migrates a virtual machine to a physical computer

Virtual to virtual (V2V)   Migrates an operating system, applications, and data from one virtual machine to another virtual machine

Virtualization host   System that hosts or contains guest virtual machines

Vulnerability assessment   Process used to identify and quantify any vulnerabilities in a network environment

Warm site   A backup site used in the event of a failure that is somewhere between a cold site and a hot site; it includes some hardware and some backups although the backups could be a few days old

Web-Based Enterprise Management (WBEM)   Standardized way of accessing management information in an enterprise environment

Wide area network (WAN)   Network that covers a large geographic area and can contain multiple LANs or MANs

Windows Management Instrumentation (WMI)   Protocol used to gather information about installed hardware, software, and operating system of a computer

World Wide Name (WWN)   Unique identifier used in storage technologies similar to Ethernet MAC addresses on a network card

Write operations   Operations in which a resource requests that new data be recorded on a disk resource

Z file system (ZFS)   Combined file system and logical volume manager designed by Sun Microsystems that provides protection against data corruption and support for high-storage capacities

Zoning   Controls access from one node to another in a storage network and enables isolation of a single server to a group of storage devices or a single storage device

INDEX

S